T5-AFF-854

Information Technology
for Knowledge Management

Springer

Berlin
Heidelberg
New York
Barcelona
Budapest
Hong Kong
London
Milan
Paris
Santa Clara
Singapore
Tokyo

Uwe M. Borghoff   Remo Pareschi (Eds.)

Information Technology
for Knowledge Management

Foreword by Dan K. Holtshouse
With 59 Figures

 Springer

Editors

Dr. Uwe M. Borghoff
Xerox Research Centre Europe
Grenoble Laboratory
6, chemin de Maupertius
F-38240 Meylan, France

Dr. Remo Pareschi
Xerox Professional Document Services
Strada Padana Superiore 28
I-20063 Cernusco S/N, Italy

Library of Congress Cataloging–in–Publication Data

Information technology for knowledge management/Uwe Borghoff, Remo
  Pareschi, eds.; foreword by D.K. Holtshouse.
     p.   cm.
  Includes bibliographical references and index.
  ISBN 3-540-63764-8
  1. Information techonolgy.   2. Information resources management.
  I. Borghoff, Uwe, 1959–   . II. Pareschi, Remo.
  T58.5.I5377   1998
  658.4'038–dc21   98-5676
                                                                       CIP

ISBN 3-540-63764-8 Springer-Verlag Berlin Heidelberg New York

© Springer-Verlag Berlin Heidelberg 1998
Printed in Germany

The use of general descriptive names, trademarks, etc. in this publication does not imply,
even in the absence of a specific statement, that such names are exempt from the relevant
protective laws and regulations and therefore free for general use.

Cover Design: Künkel + Lopka, Werbeagentur, Heidelberg
Typesetting: Camera ready by the editors
SPIN 10648591   45/3142 – 5 4 3 2 1 0 – Printed on acid-free paper

JK

Foreword

As we approach the beginning of the 21st century, we are beginning to see the emergence of knowledge management as a natural evolution of the focus and importance of quality in the 1980s and reengineering in the 1990s. Quality placed a huge emphasis on getting all employees to use their brainpower better. Reengineering emphasized the use of technology to streamline business processes and take out costs. With the lessons of quality and reengineering firmly embedded in our everyday operations (continual cost containment and higher quality is a way of life), businesses are now turning their attention to growth.

Growth is a common pursuit. Customers are calling for it. Financial markets are calling for it. Employees are asking for it because they want an exciting and stimulating environment in which to work. If a business doesn't grow, it will eventually die because knowledge workers of the 21st century won't want to work with or for a business that's not growing. Skilled workers have plenty of options to choose from as demand for knowledge workers escalates around the world.

The primary key to growth is innovation. Innovation, enabled through knowledge, is what fuels the growth side of this business equation. The need to create and deliver innovative new products and services at an ever increasing rate is requiring organizations today to take a more deliberate and systematic approach to managing the drivers of innovation. The main drivers are 1) productivity improvements of the knowledge worker, and 2) the rapid building and utilization of the collective knowledge of the organization.

One of the biggest barriers to a successful knowledge initiative is in seeing and internalizing the distinction between knowledge and information. Information consists largely of data organized, grouped, and categorized into patterns to create meaning; knowledge is information put to productive use, enabling correct action. Knowledge is quite different from information, and managing knowledge is therefore decisively and qualitatively different from managing information.

Information is converted into knowledge through a social, human process of shared understanding and sense-making at both the personal level and the organizational level. Managing knowledge starts with stressing the importance of people, their work practices, and their work culture, before deciding whether or how technology should be brought into the picture. Information management, on the other hand, often starts with a technological solution first—with consideration of people's work practices and work culture usually a distant second.

This can be a source of low worker morale, turnover, and lower-than-expected improvement from investments in information technology. In our own experience at Xerox, technology is the easier piece of the problem to solve. It's far more challenging to change people's behavior and to create a learning environment that fosters the expansion of individual's personal knowledge. It's perhaps even more difficult for organizations to continually expand and leverage the collective knowledge of the work communities. Managing knowledge does require a very different perspective than the one we have traditionally applied to information management. At Xerox, we like to say that "managing for knowledge" is about creating a thriving work and learning environment that fosters the continuous *creation, aggregation, and use/re-use* of both organizational and personal knowledge in the pursuit of new business value. The ideas in this book, in many regards, are *about how to think about structuring for knowledge* in the pursuit of growth and *how to build superior work environments* that support these three distinct, but related, knowledge processes.

The overall vision for how knowledge environments will be structured in the future is contained within and expressed through the knowledge based framework described throughout this book. The architectural framework consists of social and technological capabilities for digital libraries/repositories, communities of knowledge workers, navigation systems and tools, and knowledge flow enablers. It has evolved over the last year through much discussion and research, as well as through lengthy conversation with customers and a variety of industry experts who have been willing to share their ideas.

The importance of a high-level architectural framework is that it sharpens the vision, and makes more concrete what the knowledge work environment is trying to become. We also find that the framework helps bring alive the concept of a "place for knowledge to thrive and expand." Lastly, the value of an architecture is that it creates pull, or creates a vacuum that draws creative ideas from others to help build and develop the components needed to manifest the environment.

So as you read this book, I suggest you keep the overall architectural framework in mind, because it not only shaped the organization and content of this book, but more importantly, it is continually shaping our thinking and our concept of the ideal knowledge environment that will be required for the 21st century knowledge worker.

Stamford, CT   *Dan K. Holtshouse*
January 1998

Table of Contents

Part III. Knowledge Cartography

5.   A Technology for Supporting Knowledge Work: The RepTool

Part IV. Communities of Knowledge Workers

6.   An Environment for Cooperative Knowledge Processing

Part I

Introduction

1. Introduction

Uwe M. Borghoff [†] and Remo Pareschi [‡]
[†] Xerox Research Centre Europe, Grenoble Laboratory, France
[‡] Xerox Professional Document Services, Cernusco S/N, Italy

On the verge of a new millennium, the knowledge movement in organizational think-ing has impulsively come of age. This movement is essentially about knowing about knowledge—becoming aware that knowledge is the foremost, most valuable organi-zational asset by mapping out where it resides and by identifying the conditions that foster its re-use and generation.

1.1 Why Knowledge?

Knowledge has become increasingly relevant for organizations since the shift from an industrial economy based on assembly lines and hierarchical control to a global, decentralized, information-driven economy. Due to the global economy, organiza-tions now work, compete, and co-operate on a worldwide scale. As a consequence, they must be able to maintain and reproduce their core competencies and corpo-rate identity regardless of geographical distance and linguistic and cultural differ-ences of the markets in which they operate. At the same time, they must be capable of creatively enriching such competencies with knowledge coming from the local communities that participate in their global workforce. Furthermore, they must be able to keep up with the fast pace of worldwide competition by optimizing time-to-market and by being highly innovative in their products and services. Ultimately, they must put maximal effort into preserving, re-using, and generating intangible assets, in the form of competencies, image, and reputation. Tangibles, such as land and labor, can be bought at competitive prices in the global marketplace. Intangibles cannot, because their value is tightly bound to the specific and unique organizational context in which they originate.

The global economy is itself related to an epochal evolution. The industrial age that has ruled human life since the late 18th century is quickly fading away. The evolution of technology, through such developments as cheap networks for data transmission like the Internet, is shifting the focus of economic activities from the production and consumption of material things (starting from the basic material units given by *atoms*) to the production and consumption of information (starting from the basic information units given by *bits*). Indeed, it is the existence of a global information infrastructure that makes the global economy possible in the first place.

Thus, information is now a commodity that can bridge people directly with one another, irrespective of geographic and physical barriers. This contrasts sharply with the way information was spread during the industrial age. At that time, there was a need for resorting to hierarchical, centralized distribution processes that were a direct consequence of geographical barriers and physical constraints. The typical media for this type of distribution of information were local central authorities such as national governments and management pyramids.

The information age is replacing this institutional apparatus with a transnational global village based on participatory decision making from the bottom-up. It is also reversing the patterns of "intellectual work." During the industrial age this type of work was essentially viewed as the continuation in the office of the assembly line on the shop floor. Thus, "white collar" workers were not different from "blue collar" workers in their re-use of pre-defined content (i.e., the application of fixed procedures) and compliance with standardized information schemes. By contrast, what is now emerging is "knowledge work"—a new type of intellectual work that is all about *making sense*, namely, about turning information into knowledge through the interpretation of incoming highly non-standardized information for the purposes of problem solving and decision making. It is also about content creation: the generation of new knowledge to propel the innovation process of organizations.

Recent studies in knowledge work demographics show the prevalence of knowledge workers in sectors directly related to content creation, such as research, design, consulting, computer software, advertizing, and media. They also show an evolution towards knowledge work, under the pressure of higher productivity in the context of global competition, in traditional white collar organizations, as can be found in sales, insurance and financial services.

The diversified, ad-hocratic behavior and highly variable organizational networks of knowledge workers clearly do not fit the organizational mould of white collar work, which hinges on consistency of method and output and on stable, well-defined roles and responsibilities. As a consequence, understanding and supporting knowledge work requires a paradigm shift in organizational thinking with respect to industrial age approaches, such as Taylorism and business process re-engineering. Quoting Peter Drucker, "to make knowledge work productive is the great management task of this century, just as to make manual work productive was the great management task of the last century."

1.2 Structure and Content of the Book

This book shows how information technology (IT) can support the management of organizational knowledge through a number of technological components. Each chapter describes a type of technology that fits within a general framework for IT for the support of knowledge management that we shall refer to as the Knowledge Management (KM) Architecture.[1]

---

[1] Source Xerox.

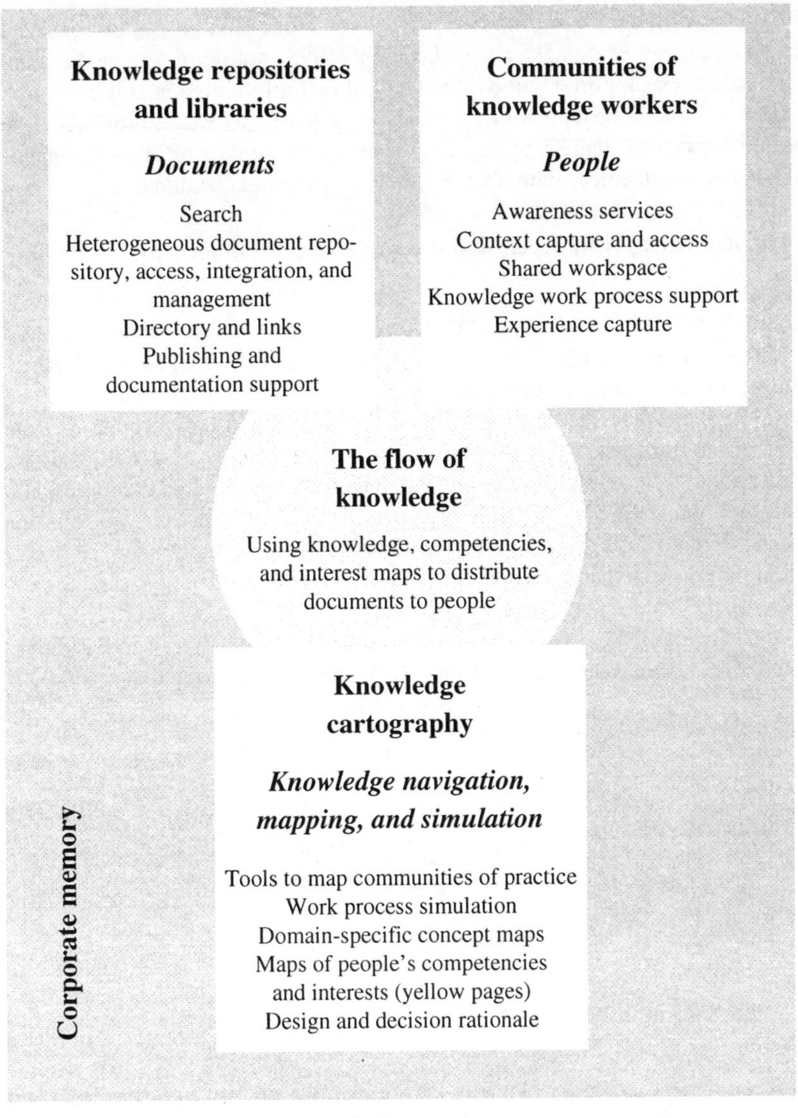

**Knowledge repositories
and libraries**

Documents

Search
Heterogeneous document repository, access, integration, and
management
Directory and links
Publishing and
documentation support

**Communities of
knowledge workers**

People

Awareness services
Context capture and access
Shared workspace
Knowledge work process support
Experience capture

**The flow of
knowledge**

Using knowledge, competencies,
and interest maps to distribute
documents to people

**Knowledge
cartography**

*Knowledge navigation,
mapping, and simulation*

Tools to map communities of practice
Work process simulation
Domain-specific concept maps
Maps of people's competencies
and interests (yellow pages)
Design and decision rationale

Corporate memory

Fig. 1.1. Knowledge management architecture

As depicted in Fig. 1.1, the KM Architecture is composed of four components:

1. The flow of knowledge
2. Knowledge cartography: knowledge navigation, mapping, and simulation
3. Communities of knowledge workers
4. Knowledge repositories and libraries

The "Flow of Knowledge" component glues the other three together.

This framework can be seen in two ways. On the one hand, it can be seen as a theoretical extension of Nonaka and Takeuchi's (1995) notion of knowledge conversion to cover IT support. On the other hand, it is firmly rooted in empirical soil. It has been validated through Xerox internal experiences as well as through case studies and interviews that Xerox has conducted on the subject of IT requirements for knowledge management with a wide variety of user organizations.

1.2.1 The Knowledge Life-Cycle and the Knowledge Management Architecture

We can think of Nonaka and Takeuchi's four phases of knowledge conversion as a kind of life-cycle of organizational knowledge (see Fig. 1.2). This knowledge life-cycle hinges on the distinction between "tacit knowledge" and "explicit knowledge." Explicit knowledge is formal knowledge that can be packaged as information. It can be found in the documents of an organization: reports, articles, manuals, patents, pictures, images, video, sound, software, etc. It can also be found in the representations that an organization has of itself: organizational charts, process maps, mission statements, domains of expertise, etc. Tacit knowledge is personal knowledge embedded in individual experience and is shared and exchanged through direct, face-to-face contact. Tacit knowledge can be communicated in a direct and effective way. By contrast, acquisition of explicit knowledge is indirect: it must be decoded and re-coded into one's mental models, where it is then internalized as tacit knowledge.

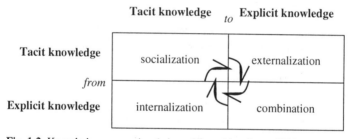

Fig. 1.2. Knowledge conversion (adapted from Nonaka and Takeuchi 1995)

In reality, these two types of knowledge are like two sides of the same coin, and bear equal weight in the overall knowledge of an organization. Tacit knowledge is practical knowledge that is key to getting things done, but has been sadly neglected in the past, very often falling victim to the latest management fad. For instance, the recent spate of business process re-engineering initiatives, where cost reduction was generally identified with the laying off of people—the real and only repositories of tacit knowledge—has damaged the tacit knowledge of many organizations. Explicit knowledge defines the identity, the competencies, and the intellectual assets of an organization independently of its employees; thus, it is organizational knowledge par excellence, but it can grow and sustain itself only through a rich background of tacit knowledge.

The crux of the knowledge life-cycle lies in the following simple observation, corroborated by the empirical evidence coming from a bulk of case studies. Knowledge that doesn't flow doesn't grow and eventually ages and becomes obsolete and useless—similarly, money saved without being invested eventually loses value until it becomes worthless. By contrast, knowledge that flows, by being shared, acquired, and exchanged, generates new knowledge. Existing tacit knowledge can be expanded through its socialization in communities of interest and of practice, and new tacit knowledge can be generated through the internalization of explicit knowledge by learning and training. New explicit knowledge can be generated through the externalization of tacit knowledge, as happens, for instance, when new best practices are selected among the informal work practices of an organization. Existing explicit knowledge can be combined to support problem-solving and decision-making, for instance by matching intellectual capital in the form of patents with marketing data showing customers' preferences for new products. Under this view, "knowledge management" can be explained as the management of the environment that makes knowledge flow through all the different phases of its life-cycle.

The KM Architecture goes beyond the purely social characterization of the environment given by Nonaka and Takeuchi, and tackles issues directly related to the management of the IT infrastructure. Indeed, in today's information-driven society, much of the environment of an organization is given by its IT infrastructure. Thus we have asked ourselves: How can such an infrastructure effectively contribute to an environment that makes knowledge flow? Then, to answer meaningfully this high-level question, we have broken it into smaller, more specific pieces, namely:

- What kind of information technology can contribute to make knowledge flow, supporting its conversion from explicit to tacit and from tacit to explicit?
- What kind of information technology can best support the explicit knowledge that an organization has about itself?
- What kind of software is needed to support the exchange of tacit knowledge in organizations of knowledge workers?
- How can we manage through IT the bulk of explicit knowledge contained in the collections of documents of an organization?

The four components of the KM Architecture try to answer these questions, and the overall way they interact as in Fig. 1.1 is an attempt to give a full answer to the high-level question from which the more specific questions originate.

Indeed, this book can be thought not just as an externalization to the larger world of our approach, but also as a further step toward its validation. In fact, we have scoped our search for contributions describing information technologies that answer the questions above within the whole community of IT practitioners of knowledge management, inside and outside Xerox. We are happy to present the results of our quest here, showing that our architecture can harmoniously accommodate a number of independently developed modules.

1.2.2 The Flow of Knowledge

We have characterized the flow of knowledge as the fundamental goal of knowledge management. That's why the "Flow of Knowledge" component is central in our knowledge management framework, and brings together the other three components. In particular, it supports the interaction between the tacit knowledge that is exchanged and generated within communities of knowledge workers, with the explicit knowledge that is contained in knowledge repositories in the form of libraries and document archives, and the explicit meta-knowledge through which an organization maps its own territory.

Chapter 2, by van Heijst et al., the first chapter in the section *The Flow of Knowledge*, illustrates a taxonomy of mechanisms for supporting the flow of knowledge, from the simplest case given by the Knowledge Attic, where knowledge is provided and is accessed without any mechanism to facilitate and automate the match between requested knowledge and produced knowledge, to the most advanced case, given by the Knowledge Pump, where the technology tries proactively to match seekers and providers of knowledge.

Knowledge attics are fairly simple and easy to implement, and will be appropriate in many cases. However, they require a community of users strongly motivated toward finding and providing the relevant knowledge all by themselves, as the system is completely passive as far as the distribution of knowledge is concerned. A good example of community-based solving the "knowledge attic" problem is given by the Eureka project, which was launched at Xerox to help field technicians for customer service of reprographic equipment capture and share the knowledge they amass through the million customer visits they make every month. Based on a community sharing model, which was first started in France, Eureka provides a social/technical infrastructure for technicians to share and build their service repair knowledge. This infrastructure is given by a knowledge attic in the form of a Web-accessible online database of tips and hints with references to technical repair documentation. Here, incentives based on personal recognition—as a motive for knowledge sharing—helped overcome the technological limitations of the knowledge attic approach. Technicians have begun to use the system at the rate of more than 5,000 tips/month, and generate more than 1,000 new suggestions a month.

When the knowledge to be shared is more complex, and simple community models for knowledge sharing do not apply, there is a need for more powerful and sophisticated mechanisms. The most advanced of such mechanisms, the Knowledge Pump, was recently given a simple but powerful illustration by Paul Allaire, the Xerox Chief Executive Officer, at the conference on *Knowledge in International Corporations* held in Rome during November 1997. Quoting from his speech, its purpose is "to help make the vital connections between the providers of knowledge and the seekers of knowledge. The knowledge provider may not know who is seeking knowledge and must organize the knowledge ahead of time by attempting to second guess the seeker's questions. The knowledge seeker, on the other hand, understands the question but has insufficient perspective to know where to find the answer. This leads to *"information overload"* and *"knowledge underload."* The primary idea behind supporting knowledge flow is to provide a system that learns and observes the usage and communication patterns of the seekers and providers, and then develops interest and work practice profiles for both individuals and communities of workers."

In practical terms, the Knowledge Pump is conceived as a knowledge management tool that provides online support for existing intranet- and extranet-based communities. This takes the form of a technology that channels the flow and use of knowledge in an organization, connecting document repositories, people, and processes, and leveraging formal and informal organizational charts and structure. In particular, the main objective of the Knowledge Pump is to help communities, defined by their common interests and practices, more effectively and more efficiently share knowledge, be it in the form of must-read documents or new ways to get work done. In an organization, knowledge can flow in many different ways and there are many different ways in which knowledge can be created and leveraged. The Knowledge Pump takes a document-centric view of the knowledge generation, by relating the knowledge life-cycle directly to the reading and writing of documents, namely with the consumption and with the production of explicit knowledge. On the individual level, what a person writes reveals his/her competencies; what a person reads reveals his/her interests; who a person interacts with reveals the communities to which s/he belongs. On the aggregate level, individual actions sum to reveal communities of practice: members, interests, patterns of communication. The Knowledge Pump is intended to support the many paths along which knowledge already flows as well as to help forge new ones. Furthermore, the Knowledge Pump is intended to support interaction between the tacit knowledge generated from communities of practice with the explicit knowledge contained in documents, and with the representation of knowledge flow in organizations.

Chapter 3, by Glance et al., the second contribution of this section, goes into the technical details of an architecture for a Knowledge Pump-enabled organization that connects together repositories, people, and processes via enhancements of software technology already in place. The chapter has two main contributions. The first is a technique called community-centered collaborative filtering for distributing information to people likely to find it relevant and useful and setting it within the context of a working community of their peers. This technique uses statistical methods and social network maps to predict user preferences from the set of peer recommendations. The second main contribution is the analysis of the user and organizational incentive issues to be addressed: the cold-start problem, the critical mass barrier, and the need for top-down support.

1.2.3 Knowledge Cartography: Knowledge Navigation, Mapping, and Simulation

To be usable by technologies like the Knowledge Pump, organizational knowledge needs to be described in a large number of ways tailored to serve a variety of user interests. This implies the development of a number of tools for the Cartography of Knowledge that map and categorize the knowledge of organizations in all of its different aspects, from core competencies to individual expertise, from communities of practice and of interest to customer databases and competitive intelligence. To some extent, these representations have always existed, in the form of organizational charts, process maps, official domains of expertise, etc. But what is crucially needed now is a way of capturing this variety of representations as they dynamically come into existence and then adapt themselves to the highly unstable "geography" of organizations of knowledge workers.

The two contributions to the section *Knowledge Cartography* show how IT can be used to identify maps of relationships in organizations of knowledge workers as they evolve, respectively, through time and through space.

Chapter 4, by Buckingham Shum, illustrates the recording of relevant team activities in organizations of knowledge workers through the use of representations in the form of hypertexts that link the different steps of the activities, highlight the different options considered at each step, and associate actions and decisions with the roles and competencies of the people involved. Such hypertexts are created and negotiated by the workers while executing the activities themselves; they record process knowledge related to knowledge-intensive problem-solving and decision-making activities, that can then be easily identified for further re-use. The negotiation aspect is very relevant, because activity maps of this type often come dressed with a deceptive appearance of "objectivity" which in reality hides a specific point of view. Acknowledging the existence of this point of view and allowing for its negotiation is an important step toward getting organizations to know themselves and to fully empower their workers. In this way, the negotiated point of view will effectively reflect the commitments of all involved stakeholders, and not just of single groups and individuals holding "power" roles and positions in the organization.

Chapter 5, by Jordan et al., introduces the RepTool, a software environment in which people may learn how to think together, not just by analyzing a shared problem, but also by occupying a space of collective sensibility where the thoughts, emotions, and resulting actions belong not to one individual but to all of them together. The authors characterize knowledge work activities as multi-person activities located in "workscapes" or work ecologies. These work ecologies can be described in terms of space physically occupied by the knowledge workers, social relationships, work practices, etc. The RepTool can map out and relate several views of the same ecology, such as physical space, social space, technology space, and cognitive space. The chapter provides a number of technical details, such as database support and the graphical user interface of the system. Its use is illustrated through two examples in the work context of an advertizing agency. The first example is about planning a client-focused campaign, the other is about supporting the agency's daily operations.

1.2.4 Communities of Knowledge Workers

The previous section illustrates the relevance of work practices in communities of knowledge workers. Evidence from sociological studies shows that it is here that a great deal of knowledge generation takes place, through the informal exchange of tacit knowledge among fellows and colleagues. In global organizations characterized by geographically dispersed communities, it becomes very relevant to make use of information technology that can re-create even in the situation of physical distance the conditions of face-to-face interaction.

A very effective way to support these communities of practice and of interest is precisely by acknowledging their status as communities, that is as emergent forms of social aggregation that can be neither planned nor installed but that can only be detected. The AmberWeb experiment inside Xerox worked just that way. It started as a virtual workspace on the Xerox corporate intranet to help scientists share files electronically. An important feature of the system is that it was specifically designed in such a way that it could be communally owned, without the need to make use of a central administration. In AmberWeb,[2] any user can create a workspace and open an account for all kinds of files with other users. This notion of community ownership worked very effectively because the use of the system quickly spread from an initial pool of 500 people at the Xerox Wilson Center in Rochester to a virtual community of more that 10,000 people throughout the corporation, spanning a large set of distributed communities.

There are however cases where there is need to support the interaction between communities and more formal types of social aggregation such as teams and workgroups. This is particularly true when this interaction is associated with a process with goals and deliverables that needs to be performed. An interesting case of IT support of the interaction between teams and communities is given by the Future Watch process for knowledge creation at Nokia Corporation.

Nokia Future Watch leverages an existing Lotus Notes deployment with a community of 18,000 Nokia users but makes use also of specialized software for the support of knowledge-intensive team work. This software, called TeamRoom and developed at the Lotus Institute, runs on top of Lotus Notes. It provides the capabilities of a virtual team room where information about deliverables, assignments, deadlines, etc. can be shared among the team members. Future Watch is essentially about sharing novel ideas and collaboratively making them into more than just ideas. It works as follows. There is a repository, called Future Watch (FW) Forum, where contributions are sent in by all members of the Nokia *community*. These ideas are reviewed by *teams* of experts in the FW Team Room. The experts write reports that are either sent back to the FW Forum, as part of the process of feedback and of refinement of ideas, or are sent to the Horizon Team Room, if the idea is judged mature enough to justify the development of a new product, or even of a new business division. The people in the Horizon Team Room are strategy teams and corporate planners who collaborate in the definition of business plans, marketing strategies, etc.

The two contributions in the *Communities* section are specifically devoted to this situation of interplay between teams and communities, and informal work practices and formal processes, in organizations of knowledge workers.

---

[2] Now available as DocuShare.

Chapter 6, by Prinz and Syri, shows how existing process knowledge can be enriched by letting workers externalize their understanding of new types of tasks through dynamic extensions of the workflow. Furthermore, it shows the benefit of coupling formalized ways of doing things with informal work practices obtained through direct interactions among people. These informal practices create the conditions for sharing tacit knowledge about processes. The chapter describes a workgroup system where both approaches co-exist and communicate, and shows its use in the context of a ministerial environment. Finally, the authors show how the system was easily accepted by ministerial workers because it fits, and extends, the way they already work.

Chapter 7, by Simone and Divitini, starts from the complementary aspect of internalizing process knowledge. It is argued that workflow management systems can be "knowledge-enabled" by moving them to a higher level in the value chain: from systems for executing processes to systems for learning about processes while they are executed. This means essentially that the workflow management system must come with different levels of sophistication in the definition of a given process, just as a search engine may provide basic search features for casual users and more sophisticated features for advanced users. As workers get more acquainted and confident with the process, they will choose and experiment with more sophisticated ways of doing things. This in turn may lead to the creation of new process knowledge, as workers may decide to design new definitions themselves for certain parts of the process, or to add new sub-processes. The authors describe an experimental workflow management system that supports this free interplay between learning and creation of process knowledge, and present a case study of its application in a typical organization of knowledge workers, namely a funding agency for R&D projects.

1.2.5 Knowledge Repositories and Libraries

Digital libraries are becoming just as relevant in corporate life as they are in academic and scientific life. Corporations have realized that documents, either in electronic or paper form, contain a lot of valuable explicit knowledge that can be efficiently organized through electronic media for intelligent access and reuse.

For instance, hi-tech vendor Sequent has implemented a corporate digital library to support the operations of its sales force. This repository contains everything, from PowerPoint presentations to marketing white papers and sales plans, used in the course of sales activity. The availability of this material optimizes the preparation of new material through the reuse of what already exists and speeds up learning by new sales people who have to absorb the culture and the way of working of the new organization. This library has quickly become one of the main assets of Sequent, and is now directly associated with the external image of the company.

Chapter 8, by Rösner et al., the first chapter in this section, describes a full-fledged knowledge engineering approach suitable for building a knowledge repository containing the corporate memory of the *product knowledge* of large manufacturing organizations such as automotive companies. Starting from collections of documents about the products of these organizations (such as service documents, product specifications, instruction manuals, trouble shooting guides, etc.), the authors show how to extract the knowledge from these documents and integrate it with further knowledge obtained by making explicit the context of use of the documents. The knowledge thus acquired is represented in the form of conceptual graphs that relate the different parts of the products, associate parts with properties and connect single actions for operating the products into complex plans corresponding to full operating instructions. The chapter then shows how the initial investment needed for building this type of knowledge repository pays off in a number of ways. First, it provides capabilities for automatic multilingual document generation. Furthermore, it defines a knowledge space of existing product knowledge to support the fast design of new products. Finally, it provides a language-independent semantic representation of product knowledge that could be used to enforce enterprise coherence for companies operating in multilingual and multicultural environments.

Chapter 9, by Kühn and Abecker, complements the previous chapter by defining the software engineering requirements for supporting knowledge repositories of this type. Three case studies in different manufacturing organizations are used to characterize the need for strong integration of corporate memories with existing IT infrastructures, with particular regard to existing capabilities for database management, document management, and business process support. The chapter ends with a description of a corporate memory architecture that meets these requirements.

Acknowledgements

First of all, we would like to thank the contributing authors.

Although most of the invited contributions evolved from other, already refereed publications, we decided to have another round of reviews to ensure consistency of the contributions with regard to the targeted audience and the overall structure of the book. We would like to thank our reviewers Alessandra Agostini, Boris Chidlovskii, Antonietta Grasso, Laurence Hubert, Allan MacLean, Johann Schlichter, and Giuseppe Valetto.

The Knowledge Management Architecture that provides the structure of the book, and motivated our selection of contributions, originates from the Xerox Knowledge Initiative directed by Dan Holtshouse. We owe a lot to Dan for a number of reasons. Our understanding of knowledge in organizations has been greatly advanced by the KM case studies that he has made available to us through the collaboration with the American Productivity & Quality Center and the European Foundation for Quality Management. Indeed, Xerox has conducted research on knowledge work both through internal and sponsored case studies of knowledge initiatives in other organizations. Even more relevant, Dan has given great support to the expanding Xerox community of interest in knowledge, both by fostering a general climate of enthusiasm and by organizing workshops and other events for direct, face-to-face exchange of ideas. Our understanding of knowledge has grown and matured also through the participation in this community.

The Knowledge Management Architecture has itself received a fundamental early contribution from our former colleague Daniele Pagani.

Last but not least, we would like to acknowledge Hans Wössner from Springer-Verlag, who gave us his support from the very beginning and thus made this book possible.

Grenoble, France   *Uwe M. Borghoff*
Milan, Italy   *Remo Pareschi*
January 1998

Part II

The Flow of Knowledge

2. The Lessons Learned Cycle

Gertjan van Heijst, Rob van der Spek, and Eelco Kruizinga
Kenniscentrum CIBIT, Utrecht, The Netherlands

This chapter presents some preliminary thoughts on how corporate memories should be organized in such a way that they maximally contribute to the competitiveness of an organization. We argue that a corporate memory should support three types of organizational learning, which are described. Then we formulate functional requirements and present an architecture for corporate memories that would satisfy these requirements. The chapter ends with pointers to related work and future research issues.

2.1 Introduction

In the first wave of business computerization, companies mainly focused on automating existing tasks in organizations, usually with the use of special purpose software. In particular, clerical activities such as the registration of stocks, transactions, addresses of business relations and the like were automated. Because automation was often initiated at the level of individual divisions, it was not uncommon that the different databases in an organization contained partially overlapping information. This was an unfortunate situation because duplication and separate maintenance of data may lead to inconsistencies and, as a result of this, uncoordinated and erroneous actions. To make things worse, the databases were often based on idiosyncratic data models, which made it hard to check for such inconsistencies. This state of affairs led to a situation where administration with computers was almost as tedious and error-prone as administration without computers.

To overcome these problems, a lot of effort has since been directed to the integration of the various computer systems that are being used in organizations. For example, a number of data exchange standards have been developed and for some types of organizations there are now integrated software packages on the market which support cooperative work (groupware) and which streamline the flow of information in the organization (workflow management tools). As a result of these developments many companies nowadays have an integrated network of computers through which they share documents and data.

More recently, an increasing number of people have begun to realize not only that computer networks enable large scale data sharing but also that it is possible to exploit them for *knowledge sharing*, thus enhancing the learning capacity of the organization. With knowledge sharing we mean that insights developed at one place in an organization are made available to other parts of the organization by storing them in an organizational knowledge repository, the *corporate memory* (see also Chapter 9). A number of organizations have begun to implement such corporate memories, usually using either Lotus Notes or Intranet[1] technology. However, what is still missing at the moment is a methodology for setting up such a corporate memory in such a way that it truly contributes to the effectiveness of the organization.

In this chapter we present some initial ideas about how such a corporate memory could be organized. These ideas are based on the assumption that the main function of a corporate memory is that it should enhance the learning capacity of an organization. Section 2.3 therefore presents an analysis of organizational learning processes. From this analysis we derive some functional requirements that a corporate memory implementation should satisfy. Section 2.4 reviews a number of implemented corporate memories and investigates to what extent the requirements are satisfied. Section 2.5 presents some principles for organizing a corporate memory in such a way that the requirements can be satisfied. It should be emphasized that this chapter only presents a conceptual outline of corporate memories, and it raises more questions than it provides answers. In Sect. 2.6 these questions are summarized and related to other research efforts in this direction.

2.2 Corporate Memories

The notion of corporate—or organizational—memory has been around for more than a quarter of a century (see Stein (1995) for a review of related concepts), and many definitions have been proposed. Most often, these definitions focus on the persistence of knowledge in an organization, independently of how this persistence is achieved. Therefore the knowledge in the minds of the individual workers is also considered as part of the corporate memory. Because our ultimate goal is to investigate how computer systems can be used to realize corporate memories, we have chosen a narrower interpretation of the concept: "a corporate memory is an explicit, disembodied, persistent representation of the knowledge and information in an organization". Note that definition restricts the form of the corporate memory, but not the contents. Any piece of knowledge or information that contributes to the performance of an organization could (and perhaps should) be stored in the corporate memory. This includes knowledge about products, production processes, customers, marketing strategies, financial results, strategic plans and goals, etc.

What is the most suitable organization of a corporate memory, depends on how that corporate memory will be used. As mentioned above, the main function of a corporate memory is to improve the competitiveness of the organization by improving the way in which it manages its knowledge. In this context, the notion of learning organizations as first formulated by Argyris and Schon (1978) is worth mentioning. These authors, and also Prahalad and Hamel (1990) view the knowledge assets and

---

[1] Intranet = Internet technology used for in-house purposes.

the learning capacity of an organization as the main source of competitive advantage.

In the literature on knowledge management, four basic knowledge processes are distinguished, which we will now briefly describe (Wiig 1993b, Nonaka and Takeuchi 1995, van der Spek and Spijkervet 1996).

Developing new knowledge. Companies survive by the continuous development of new knowledge based on creative ideas, the analysis of failures, daily experiences and work in R&D departments. Corporate memories can support these processes by, for instance, recording failures and successes.

Securing new and existing knowledge. Individual knowledge must be made accessible to others in the organization who need that knowledge. This knowledge must be available at the right time and place. Knowledge stored in corporate memories becomes persistent over time and—if properly indexed—it can be retrieved easily.

Distributing knowledge. Knowledge must be actively distributed to those who can make use of it. The turn-around speed of knowledge is increasingly crucial for the competitiveness of companies. To support this process, corporate memories need a facility for deciding who should be informed about a particular new piece of knowledge.

Combining available knowledge. A company can only perform at its best if all available knowledge areas are combined in its new products. Products and services are increasingly being developed by multi-disciplinary teams. Corporate memories may facilitate this by making it easier to access knowledge developed in other parts of the organization.

It is argued that good knowledge management involves the continuous streamlining of these processes to improve the learning capacity of the organization. Therefore, a corporate memory must be organized in such a way that it maximally supports each of them. However, it is not enough to have a corporate memory that supports each of these processes individually. In real organizations the processes interact in complex ways and the nature of these interactions should be taken into account as well. For example, it will be clear that the ability to combine different types of knowledge depends on the way knowledge is distributed throughout the organization.

Further, we believe that the basic knowledge processes do not provide the right level of abstraction for formulating the requirements that a corporate memory implementation should satisfy, because they are not directly related to the goals of organizations (Stein and Zwass 1995). The ultimate goal of organizations is not to maximize knowledge development, storage, distribution and combination per se, but to improve their competitive power by continuously adapting the organization to the external environment (market, social and political climate, customer preferences, etc.). The requirements of a corporate memory implementation should therefore be formulated in terms of these adaptation (= learning) processes. The next section presents an analysis of how the learning takes place in organizations and how these learning processes relate to the abovementioned basic knowledge processes.

2.3 Lessons Learned Processes

On a global level, two forms of learning in organizations can be distinguished: top-down learning and bottom-up learning. With top-down learning, or strategic learning, we mean that (at some management level) a particular knowledge area is recognized as promising, and that deliberate action is undertaken to acquire that knowledge. Bottom-up learning refers to the process where a worker (either on the management level or on the "work floor") learns something which might be useful and that this "lesson learned" is then distributed through the organization. With the term lesson learned we refer to any positive or negative experience or insight that can be used to improve the performance of the organization in the future. This can be a revolutionary idea that completely changes the ways in which business processes are realized, but more often it will be a relatively down-to-earth idea about how some task could be performed more efficiently with minor changes.

In this chapter, we restrict our analysis to bottom-up learning. Because bottom-up learning is centered around the lesson learned concept, we will in the sequel call this type of learning the lessons learned process. It is hypothesized that a full understanding of lessons learned processes requires insight into three forms of learning which occur in parallel: (i) individual learning, (ii) learning through communication, and (iii) learning through the development of a knowledge repository. We will first describe these forms of learning individually, together with their organizational requirements and and their relations to the basic knowledge processes (development, storage, distribution and combination).Then it is described how the three learning processes interact.

2.3.1 Individual Learning

A basic assumption of our model of the lessons learned process is that organizational learning is based on individual learning: workers gain experience with the way they do their jobs and use these experiences to improve the work processes. This form of learning is depicted in Fig. 2.1.

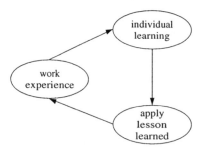

Fig. 2.1. Individual learning in organizations

In the learning sciences, a large number of different types of individual learning have been distinguished. To name a few: incidental learning, learning by reflection, simulation based learning, case-based learning, learning by exploring, goal directed learning, etc. (Reimann and Spada 1996). Each of these types of learning may occur in the workplace and may lead to useful lessons learned. Therefore, corporate memory implementations should create environments that stimulate these types of learning. For example, case based learning could be supported by maintaining a repository of case descriptions in the corporate memory. Which kinds of individual learning should actually be supported in an organization depends on a plethora of situational factors.

Organizational requirements. Despite its obvious nature, some organizational requirements have to be satisfied before this type of learning can take place. Firstly, workers need to get feedback about their performance. They need to know the effects of the way they do their job on the processes that they are involved in. Secondly, workers need to have a certain freedom in deciding how they do their job. If this is not the case, workers will not be able to experiment.

Individual learning and the knowledge processes. In this type of learning, new knowledge is *developed* and to some extent integrated in the organizational processes and applied. Knowledge is not *distributed* and it is not *secured* for reuse. For these three processes it is not directly clear how they could be supported by a corporate memory. However, the new knowledge could be the result of *combining* an insight with insights from other parts in the organization. This could be supported by a corporate memory, since this would make it easier to access knowledge from other parts in the organization.

2.3.2 Learning Through Communication

A second aspect of organizational learning is centered around the concept of communication. This learning process is summarized in Fig. 2.2. Learning through communication begins with individual learning, but then the individual experiences are shared among co-workers. This may lead to a kind of group learning. Compared with individual learning, learning through communication will be more efficient since lessons learned by one individual can now also be applied by others.

We can make a distinction between two forms of learning through communication: supply driven learning and demand driven learning. In supply driven learning, an individual worker has found a way to improve the work process and communicates this to his/her fellow workers. In demand driven learning, a worker has recognized a problem in the current process and asks fellow workers whether they have a solution for this problem.

As shown in Fig. 2.2, learning through communication requires five steps. We will focus on the communication step because this is the step that distinguishes this type of learning from individual learning.

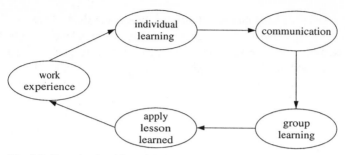

Fig. 2.2. Organizational learning through communication

Communication. There are two types of learning through communication: demand driven learning and supply driven learning. In both cases, the individual has to decide on the recipients of the message and on the medium to use. Two factors should be taken into account when taking this decision: (i) overhead, the number of useless messages that are acceptable for recipients, and (ii) hit rate, the amount of people that get the message compared to the amount of people that should have received the message. There are three options:

Personal casting (Only send the message to people directly involved). This is the most efficient way of communication. Only people who can directly help or can take direct advantage of the new knowledge are informed. This way the communication overhead is kept to a minimum, which is important for keeping the communication channel alive.

Broadcasting (Send the message to everybody in the department or organization). This way, the hit rate is maximized at the cost of a large communication overhead. Usually this is not a good strategy but in cases of direct needs with high associated costs it could be considered. An advantage of sending the message to a large audience is that it creates redundancy in the knowledge assets of the organization, which facilitates knowledge development through combination.

Narrow casting (Send the message to everybody who is interested). This option combines the advantages of the first two options, but it requires that workers decide beforehand which kinds of messages they are interested in (e.g. by means of a user profile). This in turn requires that there is a predefined set of possible topics or, otherwise, that there are guidelines for creating new topics. An example of a mechanism for creating such topic-specific discussion groups are Usenet newsgroups.

Organizational requirements. Because learning through communication is based on individual learning, it has the same prerequisites, plus two additional ones. Firstly, there must be possibilities to communicate experiences between co-workers on a regular basis. This suggests that a corporate memory should provide a mechanism to discuss work related issues, and to archive these discussions. In the sequel we will call this mechanism a discussion forum. Secondly, the organization should have an atmosphere in which it is rewarding to communicate lessons learned (including failures) to others.

Communication and the knowledge processes. In learning through communication, knowledge is *developed, distributed* and possibly *combined* with knowledge from other parts of the organization. However, the knowledge is not *secured*.

2.3.3 Developing a Knowledge Repository

A third aspect of learning in organizations focuses on storing lessons learned in some information repository so that they can be retrieved and used when needed. This form of learning is summarized in Fig. 2.3. The process is similar to learning through communication, but now communication is replaced by collection, storage and retrieval. We will briefly describe each of these steps.

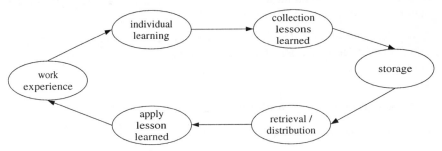

Fig. 2.3. Organizational learning through maintaining an corporate memory

Collecting knowledge. The knowledge for the corporate memory may be collected actively or passively (from the viewpoint of the corporate memory). Active collection means that some people in the organization are scanning communication processes in order to detect lessons learned. Passive collection means that workers recognize themselves that a piece of knowledge has sufficient value to be stored in the corporate memory. Both forms of knowledge collection require well-defined criteria for deciding if something is a lesson learned.

Storing knowledge. The storage step involves two activities: evaluating the submitted lessons learned (and possibly editing them) and indexing the lessons learned. Both steps may be no-ops but this will make retrieval more difficult. Evaluation might include getting answers to questions such as:

1. Is the lesson learned really new?
2. Is the lesson learned consistent with the information already stored in the corporate memory?
3. Is the lessons learned stand alone or should it be integrated with documents already stored in the corporate memory?
4. Is the lesson learned sufficiently general to be useful?

Depending on the result of the evaluation, the submitted lessons learned, may be accepted with or without editing, or rejected.

Retrieving and distributing knowledge. As was the case for collection, the knowledge in the corporate memory may be distributed actively or passively (from the viewpoint of the corporate memory). We will call the former distribution and the latter retrieval. In the case of retrieval, a worker recognizes that s/he needs a piece of information and consults the corporate knowledge base. In the case of distribution, it is somehow decided that a piece of information stored in the corporate memory should be distributed to a number of workers in the organization (thereby entering the learning through communication cycle).

Organizational requirements. The obvious organizational requirement for this form of acquiring knowledge is that the organizations maintains some kind of knowledge repository. Further, workers should be motivated to take time to write down their lessons learned and submit them to the knowledge repository. Especially this latter requirement is often difficult to achieve.

Knowledge repositories and the basic knowledge processes. With knowledge repositories, knowledge is *developed*, *secured*, and *distributed*. The newly developed knowledge is possibly the result of knowledge *combination*.

2.3.4 Dependencies Between the Learning Processes

It should be emphasized that the three types of learning are complementary and occur in parallel. The three learning cycles may interact in complicated ways. Typically, workers will first test a lesson learned by applying the new knowledge themselves, then they will communicate the results to their fellow workers and finally, if the lesson learned is truly effective, it will find its way into the rule books and manuals that are part of the knowledge repository of the organization. When implementing a corporate memory, also these interactions should be taken into account. Otherwise, the corporate memory will not improve the learning capacity of the organization. Figure 2.4 shows how the types of learning are related to the knowledge processes, and how they interact.

Individual learning and communication. As already shown in Fig. 2.2, individual learning is a prerequisite for learning through communication. This is particularly true for supply driven learning through communication. Further, individual learning can be the result of combining knowledge acquired through communication with knowledge already available to the individual worker. Thus, the interaction works in both directions.

Individual learning and knowledge repositories. Again, individual learning is a prerequisite for the development of a knowledge repository (see Fig. 2.3). Individual learning can also be the result of combining available knowledge with knowledge retrieved from the knowledge repository, or even of combining two pieces of retrieved knowledge.

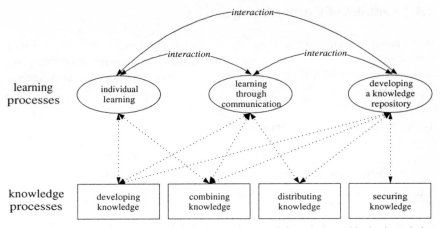

Fig. 2.4. The types of learning and their interactions and the relation with the knowledge processes

Communication and knowledge repositories. The interaction between communication and the development is also bidirectional. On the one hand, the discussions of communication processes may be archived in the knowledge repository, thus facilitating the learning through communication. On the other hand, the distribution process in the corporate memory cycle is basically a communication process.

2.3.5 Summary

In this section we have discussed three aspects of bottom-up learning in organization. During this discussion a number of requirements were put forward that a corporate memory should satisfy, which we repeat here.

1. It should be easy for individual workers to access the knowledge in the corporate memory, to facilitate individual learning by combination.
2. It should be easy for workers to decide which of the co-workers could have the knowledge needed for a particular activity.
3. It should be easy for workers to decide which of the co-workers would be interested in a lesson learned.
4. It should be easy (and rewarding) for a worker to submit a lesson learned to the corporate memory.
5. There should be well-defined criteria for deciding if something is a lesson learned, how it should be formulated and where it should be stored.
6. There should be mechanisms for keeping the corporate memory consistent.
7. The corporate memory should have a facility to distribute a newly asserted piece of knowledge to the workers who need that knowledge.

2.4 Examples of Corporate Memories

In the previous section it was observed that both the collection and the retrieval of knowledge from the corporate memory can be active and passive. Based on these dimensions, we can therefore distinguish between four types of corporate memories (Table 2.1).

Table 2.1. Types of corporate memories

	Passive collection	Active collection
Passive distribution	The knowledge attic	The knowledge sponge
Active distribution	The knowledge publisher	The knowledge pump

We will know briefly describe each of these types of corporate memories, illustrate three of them with a case study, and discuss to what extent they support the three forms of learning described in the previous section. It should be emphasized that we have collected the cases by means of a WWW scan, and our discussion is based on the information published on the web. For none of the cases have we verified our conclusions with the developers.

2.4.1 The Knowledge Attic

This is the simplest form of corporate memory management. The corporate memory is used as an archive which can be consulted when needed. In practice this type of corporate memory will often be the most feasible one. The advantage of this type of corporate memory is that is not intrusive. It emphasizes the bottom-up nature of organizational learning. However, in order to function well it requires a high discipline of the workers in the company.

The NASA Space Engineering Lessons Learned Programme. The Space Engineering Lessons Learned (SELL) programme[2] is an initiative of the System Engineering Group of Goddard Space Flight Center. The mission of this group is to ensure that the flight system undergoing design, development, integration, test and evaluation will meet the requirements. To facilitate this, the group has created a lessons learned database which can be accessed through electronic forms.

Collecting the knowledge. The initial contents of the lessons learned database were retrieved from a survey conducted in 1989. The survey distinguished between three types of lessons learned: most often repeated mistakes, worst practices, and recommendations. These lessons learned were further classified according to their domains (general, materials, optics, electrical, mechanical, etc.). New lessons learned can be submitted by filling out an electronic form which includes fields for the name, address, e-mail address and organization of the

---

[2] http://www710.gsfc.nasa.gov/704/lesslrnd/lesslrnd.html

submitter, the subject of the lesson learned, the category of the subject and a description of the lesson learned.

Storing the knowledge. From the documentation on the Web it is not entirely clear how the lessons learned database is organized. It is evident, however, that submitted lessons learned are reviewed and edited before they are asserted, since there is no direct correspondence between the attributes that must be filled in on submission forms and the attributes that can be specified on retrieval forms.

Retrieving and distributing the knowledge. To retrieve lessons learned from the corporate memory of SELL, a query form must be filled out. This form includes fields for the development phase, the discipline (general, optics, mechanical, etc.), a project name and a number of keywords. However there is no predefined set of keywords to choose from.

The SELL corporate memory and organizational learning. Of the requirements specified in Sect. 2.3.5 only requirement 1 and to some extent 4 are satisfied by the SELL architecture. Assuming that the submitted lessons learned are indeed edited, it is likely that requirements 5 and 6 are realized by the editors.

2.4.2 The Knowledge Sponge

In knowledge sponge corporate memories, the organization is actively trying to develop a more or less complete corporate memory. Whether the memory is actually used to improve the quality of the organizational processes is left to the individual workers. We have not yet found real life examples of implemented knowledge sponge corporate memories.

2.4.3 The Knowledge Publisher

In this type of corporate memory, asserting lessons learned is left to the individual workers. The role of the corporate memory maintainers is to analyze the incoming lessons learned, combine these with knowledge in the corporate memory and forward them to the workers for which the lesson learned might be relevant. This can be done in the form of briefings, newsletters courses, etc.

The Department of Energy Lessons Learned Programme. The US Department of Energy (DoE) has developed a standard for lessons learned programmes based on Internet technology.[3] The purpose of this standard is promote consistency and compatibility across the different lessons learned programmes that currently are in place within DoE, thus enabling a DoE-wide sharing of lessons learned. The DoE lessons learned standard includes directives for how the responsibilities for the lessons learned program should be distributed, how lessons learned documents should be structured, how they should be reviewed and how they should be stored and distributed.

---

[3] http://www.tis.eh.doe.gov/others/ll/ll.html

Collecting the knowledge. According to the DoE lessons learned standard, lessons learned may come from any reliable source. There is no unit which has as mission to actively search for lessons learned. Thus, lessons learned collection is a passive process. Lessons learned should be submitted using a standardized (non-electronic) form. Forms have fields for the title of the lesson learned, the originator and the contact person for the lesson learned, the priority and the functional category of the lesson learned, a number of keywords, references, a description of the lesson learned. a discussion of the activities which resulted in the lesson learned, an analysis of the lesson learned and a list of recommended actions.

Storing the knowledge. Before the lesson learned is stored and disseminated, it is first reviewed by a technical expert and an authorized derivative classifier (someone with the authority to decide whether information is classified). DoE lessons learned are stored in the DoE Lessons Learned Information System (DOELLIS) which is based on Internet technology.

Retrieving and distributing the knowledge. In the DoE programme, lessons learned are actively disseminated with an assigned priority description. The lessons learned are distributed to the DoE institutes, where local managers decide who in the institute could benefit from such information. The DoE programme does not include protocols for local lessons learned dissemination. Further, the DoE programme also maintains a mailing list to which individual workers can subscribe.

The DoE lessons learned architecture and organizational learning. Of the requirements summarized in Sect. 2.3.5, the DoE architecture supports 1, 5 and 7. Requirement 6 (consistency) is implicitly supported by having the lessons learned edited before they are stored.

2.4.4 The Knowledge Pump

The knowledge pump is the most complex type of corporate memory. In theory, this model ensures that the knowledge developed in the organization is fully exploited to improve the performance of the organization. The management of the organization enforces an efficient functioning of the lessons learned cycle.[4]

The center for army lessons learned (CALL). The Center of Army Lessons Learned[5], which was founded in 1985, collects and distributes lessons learned in combat missions of the US army. One way in which CALL collects lessons learned is by electronic observation forms, which are then evaluated, analyzed and organized.

---

[4] Note, however, that it is still a case of bottom-up learning, although it is enforced in a top-down manner! In top-down learning, the top of the organization decides which knowledge should be learned. Here, the top only enforces that knowledge developed in a bottom-up manner is exploited to the fullest in the organization.

[5] http://call.army.mil:1100/call.html

Collecting the knowledge. The starting point for the lessons learned architecture of CALL is that all CALL products originate with input in the form of an *observation* by an individual. Therefore it stimulates army members, and in particular soldiers, to report observation regarding tactics, techniques, or procedures that their unit used to work around unfavorable situations or circumstances. To facilitate reporting, CALL maintains a WWW site that includes an electronic observation form.

However, besides this passive form of collection, CALL also has a collection division which performs missions to collect lessons learned with respect to particular subjects. The personnel of this division are trained collectors of information and observations. The collection operations are derived from a Contingency Collection Plan, which is maintained by CALL. Collection operations are guided by a collection plan which states which kinds of observation should be made. The procedures for collection missions are described in a handbook which is also published on the WWW.

Storing the knowledge. Storage in CALL involves both editing and indexing. Editing is performed by CALL's analysis division. In the case of a collection mission as described above, the analysis team is in continuous interaction with the collection teams. A well defined procedure exists for analyzing incoming lessons learned. The collected and edited lessons learned are organized and published in a number of products: newsletters, bulletins and handbooks. To some extent, these products are also published on the WWW.

Retrieving and distributing the knowledge. The corporate memory consists of a number of publications which are distributed to the soldiers. It is not clear in which ways the soldiers are stimulated to actually read the CALL products. In the case of retrieval, the soldier looking for information can make use of an electronic search form on the WWW.

The CALL corporate memory and organizational learning. The CALL corporate memory supports requirements 1, 4, 5, 6 and 7. However, many of these requirements are not directly supported through the way the CALL corporate memory is implemented, but through the functioning of CALL as a whole. For example, the decision which employees should be informed of a new lesson learned is taken by CALL workers. Nowhere in the corporate memory is made explicit which employees should be informed about which subjects.

2.5 Structuring Corporate Memories

Whereas the previous sections concentrated on the requirements that a corporate memory should satisfy, this section will focus on the internal organization. We will first discuss with which types of elements the corporate memory should be populated. Then, Section 2.5.2 describes possible indexing schemes that can be used to navigate in the corporate memory. In Sect. 2.5.3 we will discuss the types of knowledge required for realizing these indexing schemes.

2.5.1 Elements of the Corporate Memory

As the corporate memory is intended as a mechanism for securing corporate knowledge, it is evident that it should be populated with "knowledge objects". However, knowledge objects can be specified at different levels of details. For example, Wiig (1993b) distinguishes between seven levels of detail (see Table 2.2).

Table 2.2. Knowledge objects at different levels of detail (Wiig 1993b)

Knowledge object	Example
Knowledge domain	Internal medicine
Knowledge region	Urology
Knowledge section	Kidney diseases
Knowledge segment	Diagnosis of kidney diseases
Knowledge element	Diagnostic strategies (e.g. "first collect all symptoms, then try to explain as many of them as possible with one disease candidate")
Knowledge fragment	"If the symptom is excruciating pain, then consider kidney stone"
Knowledge atom	"Excruciating pain is a symptom"

Even without agreeing that these seven values on the detail dimension are the appropriate landmarks, it is clear that we have a wide range of options. It is clear that the top-most level is too coarse grained. For many organizations this would mean that there would be only one or two objects in the corporate memory. On the other hand, the knowledge atom level is too fine grained. On this level, the objects are propositions. If the objects of the corporate memory are to be propositions, this would require the formalization of all the knowledge in the organization, which is obviously not feasible. Thus the right level of detail is somewhere in the middle.

We propose to use *knowledge items*, as used in the CommonKADS organization model (de Hoog et al. 1994) and also described by van der Spek and de Hoog (1995) as the basic objects to populate the corporate memory. Knowledge items are modeled as objects with a number of attributes. These attributes are classified in three groups (see Table 2.3).

In terms of Wiig's classification, knowledge items correspond to knowledge segments, as they are specific for a particular activity in the organization. The particular choice of attributes for knowledge items is heavily influenced by their function within the CommonKADS framework: the identification of promising areas for knowledge based systems application in the organization. For the present purpose, organizing a corporate memory, some of these attributes are less important, whilst others should be added. In particular, we think that the attributes role description, generic task type, functions and nature can be dropped whereas an attribute "type" should be added. The attribute activity should be changed in activities, to emphasize

Table 2.3. Knowledge items as used in the CommonKADS organization model (de Hoog et al. 1994)

General	Name:	
	Role description:	The role the knowledge is associated with
	Activity:	The related organizational task
	Domain(s):	Reference to organizational areas/objects/processes
Content	Generic task type:	From the CommonKADS library tree
	Nature:	Heuristic, formal, uncertain ...
	Products/services:	Marketable products of the organization
	Functions:	Organizational functions involved
Availability	Time:	When available
	Location:	Where available
	Form:	Paper, electronic, mind, collective

that a knowledge item might be related to multiple activities. After having discussed how the knowledge items could be indexed, we will discuss in more detail the possible values of each of the attributes.

2.5.2 Indexing the Corporate Memory

Two of the requirements listed in Sect. 2.3.5 concern the ease of navigating in the corporate memory, which is directly related to the issue of indexing. We can distinguish between three types of navigation, which we will briefly describe.

Hierarchical searching. Here the knowledge items are organized in a fixed hierarchical structure. The corporate memory is searched by traversing this structure. Following hyperlinks on WWW documents is an example of this type of searching.

Attribute searching. Here, the corporate memory is searched by specifying values for attributes. The search mechanism returns the knowledge items that have the specified values on the attributes. Database engines typically use this type of searching.

Content searching. Here the user enters arbitrary search terms related to the topic of interest. The search mechanism simply returns all the knowledge items in which the terms occur, possibly with a relevance score. The relevance score expresses how relevant the document is for the goals of the user. This is based on simple heuristics like the frequency of the occurrence of the search terms in the document and the distance between the search terms in the document. This technology is applied by the crawlers of most search engines on the World Wide Web (Alta Vista, Lycos, etc.).

Each of the search methods has its own requirements and its own advantages and disadvantages. For example, whereas attribute searching is more flexible than hierarchical searching, it requires a pre-defined set of attributes. Similarly, while content search is the most flexible method, its ability to find the appropriate documents depends heavily on the capacity of the user to formulate appropriate search terms. Further, this method only works for textual knowledge items. The suitability of each of the methods depends on the types of knowledge items, the amount of structure in the corporate memory, and the number of possibly relevant knowledge items. Therefore, corporate memory implementations should probably be able to support each of the methods.

In the sequel, we will mainly focus on indexing based on attributes. Indexing by means of a hierarchical structure can be viewed as a compiled form of attribute indexing, where the order in which the attributes are specified is predefined. Although the availability of such predefined search paths facilitates navigation, and thus should be supported, the paths can easily be derived from attribute-based indexes. Indexing based on work frequencies is conceptually a simple well-understood technique (although the technical realization of search engines that implement it is quite complicated).

2.5.3 Attributes of Knowledge Items

We will now discuss the modified set of attributes that we propose for knowledge items. Because the ability to find knowledge items in the corporate memory depends to a large extent on string matching, it is important that there is a standard set of possible values for every attribute. For some of the attributes, this set can be standardized over many organizations, but for others every organization must define its own set of standard terms.

Activities. The activities attribute refers to the organizational activities to which the knowledge item is related. Since different organizations have different business processes, the possible values of this attribute must be specified for every organization individually. Thus, the organization must have an explicit model of the activities that are performed as part of the business processes. The names of these activities can then be used as values on this attribute.

Domains. The domains attribute concerns the subject of the knowledge item. In order to use this attribute, organizations must have an inventory of relevant knowledge domains. This inventory is a meta-description of the types of knowledge that exist in the organization. It is our experience that organizations usually don't have such an inventory, and that developing one is a difficult issue for which guidelines are needed. Unfortunately, research on knowledge modeling as thus far mainly focused on the development of guidelines for modeling knowledge on the micro level (e.g. concepts and relations). What is needed here are modeling principles and primitives on a more aggregate level. The hierarchy of medical domains which was used to structure an ontology library described by van Heijst et al. (1995) is an example of such an inventory. However this hierarchy was more the result of a trial and error modeling process than of a systematic application of guidelines.

Form. The form attribute refers to the physical representation of a particular piece of knowledge. De Hoog et al. (1994) identify four possible values for this attribute: paper, electronic, mind and collective. We think the latter should be dropped because it does not concern the form of the knowledge but the availability. Further, the value set is specified on a too coarse grained level, considering the currently available possibilities with multimedia technology. For example, the value electronic could refer to an electronic text document, an instruction video, or a recorded speech. Still, the number of possibilities is limited, and it should not be too difficult for an organization to specify the different forms in which knowledge is available in the organization.

Type. This attribute specifies the kind of "document" of the knowledge item. Possible values include concepts such as procedure, guideline, handbook, manual, best (or worst) practice, progress report, failure report, comment, etc. The values for this attribute are assumed to be reusable across a wide range of organizations, although a particular organization may choose to use only a limited subset. A methodology for corporate memory development could therefore provide a standard set of definitions for this dimension, which can then be adapted and refined for specific classes of organizations. For example, the "protocol" knowledge type could be added as a refinement of "procedure" for hospital organizations.

Products/services. Sometimes knowledge items are directly related to the products and services of an organization. By recording these relations, the corporate memory can be used to improve communication with the customer, which may lead to better consumer satisfaction. The possible values for this dimension are of course organization-specific, but they are easy to acquire since most organizations will have no difficulties in producing a list of their products and services.

Time and location. These attributes are mainly relevant for knowledge items which have "mind" as value on the form attribute. In cases where the knowledge is only available in a personal form, the corporate memory should support accessing this knowledge by making it easy to find out how this particular person can be contacted.

2.5.4 Knowledge Profiles of Employees

Three of the requirements listed in Sect. 2.3.5 have to do with deciding which co-workers would be interested in a particular lesson learned. To facilitate this, the corporate memory should contain knowledge profiles of all the workers in the organization. To facilitate the process of comparing knowledge items with these worker profiles, these should be formulated using the same attributes and attribute values as used for the knowledge items. However, not all attributes are relevant: it is for example unlikely that a worker will only be interested in lessons learned of the type "comment" on the type attribute. Of the attributes listed in the previous section, activity, domain and products/services seem to be the most relevant to be used in knowledge profiles.

As a default, the profiles of the workers should specify that they are interested in knowledge items that are about the activities, domains, and products and services that are directly related to their jobs. However, in order to facilitate learning through combination, it is important that workers have control over their own knowledge profile. This way they can tune the amount and type of information that they receive to their own interests, needs and information processing capacities.

2.6 Discussion and Future Work

This chapter presents some initial ideas about how corporate memories could be organized in such a way that they contribute to the competitiveness of organizations. In our view, the main function of corporate memories is that they contribute to the learning capacity of organizations. Therefore we have presented an analysis of learning processes in organizations and identified ways in which a corporate memory could facilitate these processes. Based on this analysis, we then identified a number of requirements that a corporate memory implementation should satisfy and verified to what extent this was the case for a number of actually implemented corporate memories. Then in Sect. 2.5 we have presented a framework for organizing corporate memories in such a way that all requirements could be satisfied.

The work presented here only forms an initial step to a complete methodology for corporate memory development, and the major contribution is probably that it has identified a number of issues that need to be resolved. Probably the most difficult issue is the need for a method for structuring knowledge at the "macro level" (the level of knowledge items). In order to identify relevant knowledge items in a corporate memory, it must be possible to characterize them on a global level. Thus far, the AI community has mainly focused on characterizing knowledge on the micro level. At this level ontologies have been identified as a powerful tool for specifying knowledge pieces without enumerating them. A similar mechanism is needed for the macro level.

Another interesting issue is how the work presented here relates to the work on enterprise modeling (e.g. Fraser 1994) and enterprise ontologies (Gruninger and Fox 1994). We expect that the standard vocabulary for describing several aspects of organizations developed in those projects can be used standardize the allowed values for some of the attributes of knowledge items. For example, the enterprise ontology described in (Uschold et al. 1995) contains definitions of activities and how they relate to other aspects of the enterprise. Such models could be used to refine the attribute structure of knowledge items as proposed in Sect. 2.5. However, we don't expect that enterprise ontologies can be used to resolve the issue of characterizing knowledge at the macro level. Enterprise ontologies can be used for modeling the organization, but what is needed here is a vocabulary and guidelines for modeling the *knowledge* in the organization.

3. Knowledge Pump: Supporting the Flow and Use of Knowledge

Natalie Glance, Damián Arregui, and Manfred Dardenne
Xerox Research Centre Europe, Grenoble Laboratory, France

This chapter proposes an information technology system we call the Knowledge Pump for connecting and supporting electronic repositories and networked communities. Our objectives are two-fold. The first is to facilitate getting the right information to the right people in a timely fashion. The second is to map community networks and repository content. These goals are complementary because the community and repository maps help channel the flow of information while the patterns inferred from information flow help refine the maps. By supporting these two elements of distribution and mapping, the Knowledge Pump can foster an environment that encourages the flow, use, and creation of knowledge.

3.1 Introduction

Sources of information technology for supporting knowledge management come from a number of well-established research domains, among them, computer-supported cooperative work (CSCW), groupware, information retrieval, and work-flow. What can we learn from these communities and how can we apply their research results to creating an IT framework for knowledge management support? In the next section, we start with a summary of relevant work from several of these fields projected along our particular dimensions of focus, the flow and use of information in organizations.

In the rest of this chapter, we report on a specification and first implementation of the central piece of our envisioned knowledge management framework. This piece is conceived as the engine that channels the flow and use of knowledge in an organization, connecting document repositories, people, and processes, and leveraging formal and informal organizational maps. Applying the taxonomy proposed in Chapter 2, we call our engine the Knowledge Pump, because it should manage facilities for collection, publication, distribution, and retrieval of information. In addition, the Knowledge Pump should track its own usage and use statistics to infer patterns from collected data. Inferences drawn from the flow of use can be used both to improve the operation of the Pump and to provide users with partial mappings of social networks, communities of practice, competencies, and repository contents.

Figure 3.1 shows schematically some of the different ways in which knowledge can flow and the different ways in which it can be created and leveraged. On the individual level, for example, what a person recommends reveals his/her competencies;

what a person reads reveals his/her interests; who a person interacts with reveals the communities to which s/he belongs. On the aggregate level, individual actions sum to reveal communities of practice: members, interests, patterns of communication, trails through repositories.

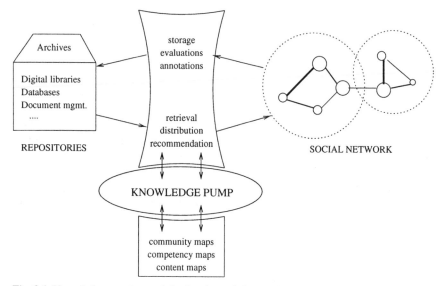

Fig. 3.1. Knowledge creation and sharing through flow and use (see also the knowledge management architecture in Fig. 1.1)

The Knowledge Pump is intended to be a general-purpose set of technologies that can be applied across multiple platforms, not a tool adapted to a particular application. Thus, the Pump is not a piece of software to be installed; instead, document management systems, digital libraries, groupware become systems that can be Knowledge Pump enabled. Once KP-enabled, the documents in a digital library, the participants of a collaborative virtual environment (Benford et al. 1995), the members of BSCW workspace (Bentley et al. 1997), can all feed into and from the flow.

The aspect of Knowledge Pump on which we focus primarily here is its distribution capability. In particular, our first goal is to help communities, defined by their common interests and practices, more effectively and more efficiently share knowledge, be it in the form of must-read documents or new ways to get work done. We introduce a technique we call community-centered collaborative filtering. This technique combines statistical algorithms and heuristic rules with a community bias to guide the distribution of information based on explicit and implicit recommendations.

In the next section, we give an overview of related work. Then, in Sect. 3.3, we state our initial objectives and elaborate three perspectives on the Knowledge

Pump technology—the individual, the community and the organizational—and discuss some requirements imposed by each of these. In Sect. 3.4, we describe our first implementation of the Pump. Finally, in Sect. 3.5 we conclude with a summary and outlook.

3.2 Related Work

3.2.1 Document Management and Digital Libraries

Work on both document management systems and digital library research has recently been re-aligning its focus towards aspects of knowledge management. On the one hand, there has been a rush to redefine existing technology as knowledge management, for example, sophisticated techniques for information retrieval and information filtering. More significantly, however, there have been a number of concerted efforts to bring people into the loop to improve the processes of managing documents, in particular search and distribution.

For example, grapeVINE (Brookes 1996), proposes a multi-tiered system for information distribution on top of Lotus Notes, the tiers being tailored to different levels of users' technological maturity. The most interesting aspect of grapeVINE is the concept of assigning gatekeepers to domains, individuals who agree to filter new documents according to timeliness and relevance. grapeVINE then "pushes" filtered documents to other users, in accordance with their interest profiles.

New Web-based document-management systems like BSCW and Xerox's DocuShare provide bottom-up suport for workgroups via collaborative workspaces. DocuShare's "What's new in the past X days" automated feature is a simple but effective mechanism to passively share new relevant documents. BSCW uses icons and color to indicate changes in the workspace. MetaWeb (Trevor et al. 1997), on top of BSCW, provides active event notification: a user logging in, the availibility of a new version of a document, etc.

Usage data provides a rich set of information that can be mined for implicit recommendations and associations (or match-making), as Nichols et al. (1997) explain in the context of digital libraries. Privacy questions aside, patterns mined from usage data promise to yield digital analogues of physical wear and tear, a metaphor that is explored further in Hill and Hollan (1994).

Usage data has also been studied in the context of Web-based repositories, see for example, Pirolli and Card (1995) and Pitkow and Pirolli (1997). This body of work examines how patterns of usage can be used to inform the subsequent Web navigations of other users and deduce properties of documents (faddish versus sustaining interest, for example).

3.2.2 Information Filtering

Malone et al.'s seminal paper (1987b) on information filtering describes three types of information filtering activities: cognitive, economic, and social. Cognitive activities filter based on content. In this section, we describe briefly current work on personalized content filtering which focuses on automating and personalizing this kind of activity.

Economic activities filter based on perceived information costs and benefits (an area beyond the scope of this chapter).

Social activities filter information based on individual quality judgments communicated through personal relationships. We describe two approaches influenced by the concept of social filtering: active and automated collaborative filtering. Finally, we introduce a new approach we call community-centered collaborative filtering which brings the social network back to automated collaborative filtering.

However, while we have tried to classify information filtering systems into distinct categories, many of the cited systems in fact use a combination of two or more techniques. We have taken care to point this out when this is the case.

Personalized content filtering. Content filtering involves categorization of items via content: text, images, sound, etc. Perhaps one of the most difficult outstanding research problems of vanilla content filtering is matching automatically generated categorizations (via such techniques as cluster analysis) to the individual user's classification scheme (not to mention merging those of many people). Another outstanding problem is executing complex queries over many databases with different content and different structure, addressed in Borghoff and Schlichter (1996) and Borghoff et al. (1996), for example.

Content filtering meets the user through the concept of "user profile," information obtained from the user either through a registration procedure or from his/her bookmarks, for instance. The user profile can be constructed using one or both of two distinct methods: (1) manual generation and update; and/or (2) automatic derivation and refinement from usage data via statistical learning algorithms.

With the addition of user profiles, we get personalized content filtering. Commercial services now offer everything from news clips—Individual (URL)—to book recommendations—Amazon.com (URL)—to Web sites—SiteSeer by Rucker and Polanco (1997).

Some of the more interesting services which offer personalized content filtering blur the distinction between information push to the desktop and pull by the user even further. Over the past year, companies like PointCast (URL), Netscape (URL), BackWeb (URL), and Marimba (URL) have populated this new playing field, offering a combination of technology and content that techs down the computer screen to a television with customizable information channels.

Collaborative filtering. The sharing of knowledge through recommendations, a facility known in the technical community as collaborative filtering, is more and more recognized as an important vehicle for distributing information. There are two distinct types of collaborative filtering mechanisms:

– those which enable "active" collaborative filtering by making it easier for people to share pointers to interesting documents; active means manual pointers or user-defined filters.

- those which automate collaborative filtering by using statistical algorithms to make recommendations based on correlations between personal preferences; recommendations usually consist of numerical ratings, but could alternatively be deduced from implicit measures, such as time spent reading a text (Morita and Shinoda 1994).

As pointed out in Hill et al. (1995), automated collaborative filtering systems are based on the premise that personal relationships are not necessary to social filtering, and that, in fact, social filtering and personal relationships can be teased apart (and put back together again in interesting ways).

Systems for active collaborative filtering have been around for a number of years. The first of these, Tapestry (Goldberg et al. 1992) from Xerox PARC, was built as a recommendations filter on top of electronic mail and newsgroups. Users could specify filters of the form, "Show me all articles recommended by A. Brown." A later system called Pointers (Maltz and Ehrlich 1995), from Lotus, is built around the same model and, in fact, was in part created by one member of the original implementation team for Tapestry. It has the additional ability to create digests of recommendations. grapeVINE provides similar functionality on top of Lotus Notes but adds the idea of gatekeepers, linking reputation and incentive to the work of filtering. Also from Xerox PARC, a proof-of-principle system called Beehive (Huberman and Kaminsky 1996) allows people to forward e-mail messages to communities whose composition is dynamically updated depending on personal historic patterns of interaction among its members.

Systems for automated collaborative filtering are showing up everywhere on the Web these days, although they have been around in different forms for a while (apparently, one of the earliest was a matchmaking system that worked via a touch-tone telephone interface). The latest WWW mantra seems to be "personalized," and there are two ways to achieve personalization of information in an impersonal world: by personalized content filtering, matching items to stated or inferred domains of interest, and by automated collaborative filtering, matching items to people by first using statistics to match people to each other. Many of these systems, in fact, implement collaborative filtering on top of (generic) content filtering, first sorting by domain or genre and then predicting the user's level of interest for items in a given domain.

Among the earliest and best known automated collaborative systems are two that started as university research projects. Firefly (Shardanand and Maes 1995) is a movie and music recommendation system from MIT; GroupLens (Resnick et al. 1994) is another newsgroup recommendation system (inspired by Tapestry) from the University of Minnesota. A third system from Bellcore (Hill et al. 1995) is also a movie recommendation system, but with a twist—it lets you know who has similar tastes to you and offers joint recommendations for more than one person. A relative newcomer is Fab (Balabanovic and Shohan 1997), a content-based, collaborative recommendation system for WWW pages, which is a project under the umbrella of the Stanford Digital Library Project. In fact, most automated collaborative filtering systems are moving towards filtering both on content and on automated recommendations, which greatly improves their performance.

Commercial applications are proliferating almost more rapidly than search engines can index them. (In fact, search engines are joining the foray; witness MyYahoo!, a personalized search engine from the makers of Yahoo (URL) which uses Firefly technology.) Firefly has gone commercial; other new enterprises offer similar services such as Each-to-each (URL) from DEC and Gustos (URL). Each-to-Each offers a customizable API to its "patent-pending" collaborative filtering engine and Gustos gives away for free a set of Java applets to allow anyone to plug ratings from their Web pages into any one of a number of collaborative filters (for books, movies, etc.) in return for the rights to sell aggregate data. These systems are differentiated from each other through additional services alongside collaborative filtering and through their domain of application.

Community-centered collaborative filtering. Our main critique of automated collaborative filtering systems is that the separation of filtering and personal relationships in fact limits their usefulness to a greater degree than perhaps expected by their designers. The network of existing social relationships is extremely valuable information that can be used to improve the performance of collaborative filtering. In turn, the person-person correlations calculated as part of a collaborative filtering algorithm can be used to refine the system's model of the network of social relationships. Thus, the existing social network can be used to seed the system, vital for overcoming the cold-start problem, and its usage can help track the social network's evolution over time.

The identification of social networks has long been a field of study in organizational theory (Scott 1992, Knipscheer and Antonucci 1990). More recently, Kautz et al. (1997a, 1997b) have developed methods for reconstructing social networks from the text of Web pages and hyperlinks between Web pages. They describe how the reconstructed social network can be used either to construct a referral chain or to refine a search; it could also be used to improve the performance of an automated collaborative filtering system.

In addition, the automated collaborative systems described above for the most part hide the identity of the recommenders. However, while anonymous evaluations have their place (peer reviews, for example), recommendations without signatures tend to be much less useful than signed ones, especially in communities where people know each other by name and reputation.

In our work, we propose to bring the focus of collaborative filtering back to the social network, and in particular, to the community and its network of interrelationships. We call this approach *community*-centered collaborative filtering. This approach focuses on communities and their special characteristics (as opposed to collections of people) and aims to leverage community currency in the form of reputation, trust, and reciprocity. In Sect. 3.3, we discuss further what we mean by a community and how the Knowledge Pump can leverage community currency both to create incentives for contributing and to deliver better recommendations.

3.3 Design Objectives and Requirements

Our first phase of design involved formulating collaborative technology for collective filtering of large collections of electronically available information, reducing the individual burden by distributing it among many. Knowledge Pump, in this first incarnation, helps people move information, carving channels out of the electronic pathways most often visited by people during their day-to-day interactions.

The operation of the Knowledge Pump can be seen from three perspectives, those of the individual, the community, and the organization. From the perspective of each level, the Pump both provides benefits and creates costs. Below we examine the operation of the Pump from the three viewpoints. We also discuss how benefits and costs lead to potential barriers to use and how these barriers influence design choices. While it is never possible to completely separate the use of the technology from the environment in which it is used, a number of general principles for groupware design (Grudin 1988) still apply.

3.3.1 Designing for the User

First, a description of Pump operation from the user perspective. From any KP-enabled repository (e.g., Web browser, document management system), the user can review any repository item (e.g., Web page, document, news article) or make a more general recommendation (e.g., recommend—or not—a procedure, a movie, a potential customer). A recommendation consists of a rating and comments. The Pump collects these reviews and distributes them to those it judges will find them relevant and useful. Each user's window to the Pump is periodically updated with these new recommendations. The added value to the user comes both from the Pump's filtering mechanisms and from the (optionally) signed comments from peers.

The provision of recommendations is a common good problem (Hardin 1968): pretty much everyone is happy to receive relevant recommendations, but few may be motivated to submit them. The incremental benefit to a person for submitting a recommendation is much less than the summed benefit to all those who receive it. Thus, as with any common good problem, recommendations are likely to be under-provided. The common good problem is a manifestation of Grudin's (1994) question vis-a-vis CSCW systems: "Who does the work and who gets the benefit?"

There are a number of ways to alleviate the common good problem. One is to reduce costs. Thus, recommending an item should be as easy as possible. First, users should be able to make recommendations seamlessly from wherever they are working. This leads to the idea of KP-enabling various applications instead of having the Pump itself be a stand-alone application.

Secondly, the effort spent in making a recommendation should be as small as possible (but no smaller, to paraphrase Einstein). For example, for information types such as news articles, which have a very short shelf life, the cost must be very low. In this case, implicit ratings such as time spent reading the article play an important role (Konstan et al. 1997). On the other hand, for items with a longer lifespan, such as a description of a work practice or project documentation, a thoughtful review is too important to cut out.

The common good problem is also reduced if the benefits to providing reviews are increased. In fact, part of the beauty of automated collaborative filtering is that contributing provides its own reward: because of its statistical nature, the performance of the algorithm improves for a user with each contribution s/he makes. Furthermore, in an environment of peers, we can expect mutual reciprocity (Frenzen and Nakamoto 1993) and the possibility of enhanced reputation (Dichter 1966) to play important roles. Benefits can also be increased by providing explicit "rewards" for contributions. These rewards, of course, will be culture- and system-dependent. In an organizational setting, rewards could be given via performance appraisals. In contrast, in commercial settings, monetary rewards could play a very interesting role.

Finally, another approach is to modify the user's *perception* of benefits and costs over time, which can be very different from one-shot benefits and costs (Glance and Huberman 1994). For example, providing feedback from the Pump on average and individual activity (rate of recommendations received versus submitted, for example) may encourage the provision of recommendations over time, especially if additional incentives for submitting recommendations are provided initially.

A second important barrier to use for the individual is concern about personal privacy. At times, reviewers may be reluctant to sign their recommendations (or critiques). Allowing anonymous reviews overcomes this barrier but conflicts with the goal of enhancing the sense of community. At another level, users may be concerned about the overall picture of their activities that they give the system through daily use. In an Internet setting, this barrier can be lowered by associating a price to the usage data: people in some sense get paid for using the system (free information, for example) and in return reveal something about their preferences. In an organizational setting, the fear of "big brother" is probably harder to overcome and will likely result in any technology like the Pump being under-utilized. Guarantees that usage patterns will not be misused can hopefully alleviate these concerns.

The barriers to use for the individual are very significant, because the Pump, like any groupware system, suffers from the critical mass problem: it is a valuable tool only if enough people are using it. Like the telephone or the fax or e-mail, technologies like the Knowledge Pump will be used only if most people can be reached through it. In this sense, barriers to use at the individual level are the most important to overcome, although organizational actions can lower the barriers, as we will discuss later.

3.3.2 Designing for the Community

If technology like the Knowledge Pump succeeds, it will be for some of the same reasons that e-mail and Internet newsgroups have proved to be so useful: because they provide a standard channel for communication and information sharing; and because they provide a way to support communities.

Community is an over-used word currently, so it is worthwhile to state what we mean more precisely. Mynatt et al. (1997) define communities as social groupings which exhibit "in varying degrees: shared spatial relations, social conventions, a sense of membership and boundaries, and an ongoing rhythm of social interaction."

One of our goals with the Knowledge Pump is to support the community notion of membership and boundaries in ways not possible by e-mail or newsgroups. E-mail permits one-to-one or one-to-many asynchronous communication, where all participants must be listed prior to the communication. Diffusion through the social network of relationships is possible through forwarding, one step at a time. Newsgroups function like broadcasts, one-to-everyone, where individuals choose whether or not to be part of that everyone. Neither approach is the most effective way to reach all people belonging to the larger social network that are also members of a loosely-defined community.

There are several mechanisms that can be used to identify communities from the bottom up. One is seeding the system with user-provided lists of immediate contacts, or advisors—people whose opinion one tends to particularly value. This approach has been implemented in sixdegrees (URL) to reconstruct the broader social network on-line. Alternatively, the network of social relationships can be inferred automatically from Web pages, see for example Kautz et al. (1997a, 1997b). The person-person correlations calculated during automated collaborative filtering is another way to estimate the strength of social ties. These mechanisms can be combined to produce community maps, with the boundary horizon perhaps given as a parameter.

Recommendation systems that work on the basis of automated collaborative filtering reach all people likely to be interested, and thus go beyond the recommender's direct contacts. Social mechanisms can ensure that repeat recommenders become recognized as a core group of "gatekeepers" for the communities (reputation) and that repeat participants develop a sense of membership (common history).

An important aspect of community-centered collaborative filtering is that, if implemented properly, it should allow some "bleeding" across boundaries. While the permeability of boundaries can be considered a parameter, such bleeding permits cross-fertilization and identification of common interests among different communities.

3.3.3 Designing for the Organization

From the organizational perspective, the Knowledge Pump has the potential to bring a number of benefits. By mapping the many overlapping communities within an organization, it can connect disjoint communities into a larger one. It can also help uncover the web of compentencies of an organization's employees. These can be invaluable services for an organization, on top of providing new opportunities for knowledge sharing. However, an organization must take that the maps generated by the Pump adequately represent the organization's composition.

The cold-start problem of any groupware system is partly an organizational one. Marshall et al. (1994) speak of three stages in the lifecycle of community memories, which we hypothethize apply likewise to groupware systems like the Pump: seeding, evolutionary growth, and re-seeding. They have observed that seeding is necessary to make the system be perceived as useful. Then it can evolve on its own, until at some point re-seeding is required to organize, winnow, and re-order the accumulated collection and thus reinvigorate new growth.

The effort of seeding the system can best be supported from the top down. Part of a "Knowledge Pump Solution" should be a consultancy effort to provide preliminary mapping of employees' domains of interests and their social networks. We hypothesize that the optimal approach to mapping an organization is a feedback loop between human reconstruction and computational refinement.

Most vital is upper management support for a cultural environment that enables knowledge sharing. This may involve fashioning new types of incentives, or may instead mean changing some of the organization's objectives, focusing more on cooperation instead of competition between sub-entities, for example. The solution here is too dependent on the organization to speak in anything but generalities. Work like the design by Bell et al. (1996) of the Eureka process for the sharing of tips among field service personnal brings us closer to a methodology for finding solutions for individual organizations.

3.4 Implementation

In this section we present our first implementation of the Knowledge Pump. At the time of writing, we have a working prototype that we will soon be ready to deploy within a first group of users.

We had a few, basic initial design requirements: portability, ease of use, and immediate value. Portability meant one code set for all platforms, and suggested building something riding on top of the Web for a first implementation. Effectively, this pointed to Java, since HTML and scripting languages alone are too limiting. Portability also means not touching the browser: no plug-ins, for example, and no browser-specific capabilities, like cookies.

Ease of use meant near-zero installation cost, reliability, and seamlessness (rating capability integrated into the browser, for example). Low installation and maintenance costs again point to Java. Unfortunately, reliability (and quick response time) do not. As Java is a young language, we hope that these shortcomings will become less important over time. Seamlessness indicated modifying the browser, via plug-ins, for example; however, this interferes with portability, a higher priority for now. In future applications of the technology to specific settings, a uniform interface would permit better seamlessness. Also, because of Java's security restrictions, the interaction between the Pump, written in Java, and the browser is severely limited. Again, these restrictions could be removed in certain settings.

Immediate value means (1) providing a set of functionalities that are valuable above and beyond recommendations; and (2) seeding the system with a skeletal social network, a map of the organization's domains of interest and a collection of recommended items. To satisfy the first requirement, we have built in basic document management tools: search and retrieval over bookmarked items. The second requirement is the organization's responsibility, as argued in Sect. 3.3.3. For our first test, we will take on this role, in other cases, an organization will want to hire or contract consultants to do this work.

In choosing to connect first to the Web, we have joined a well-populated playing field of WWW filtering efforts. However, we doubt that collaborative filtering over such a large domain can work well in an organizational setting, as there are too many pages and too few reviewers. Our real goal is to connect to repositories which have Web interfaces. We are designing a plug-and-play interface to the Pump so that with minor modifications, any repository (Web front-end or no) can connect transparently with the Knowledge Pump. In the meantime, the Pump connects with any repository with a Web front-end in a less transparent, but still useful way. Currently, we are testing the plug-and-play principle by connecting the Pump with a first repository: Calliope (URL), an electronic repository of scanned journal articles.

3.4.1 Functionality: Document Management and Recommendation

The user's interface to the Pump, shown in Fig. 3.2, is through a small palette of functions. The *bookmark* and *search* functions are basic document management capabilities provided by the Pump. *Bookmark* allows the user to save a pointer to any Web page. S/he rates the document on a five-point scale from "irrelevant" to "one of my favorites," and optionally types in some comments. The user also classifies the documents into any of a number of the listed communities. Finally, the user can save the pointer as "private"—for his/her eyes only—or as "public."

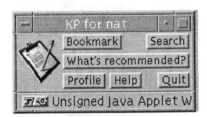

Fig. 3.2. The user's palette of controls

Complementary to the bookmark function is the *search* function, which allows the user to search for bookmarks classified into any number of domains according to date, title, author, rating, reviewer, and private versus public classification. The Pump delivers the search results as an HTML document to the Web browser. For each pointer satisfying the search criteria, the page includes the predicted or actual rating and provides a hyperlink to the comments associated with the pointer.

Preliminary user feedback indicated that these two functionalities were necessary to provide enough added value to the conventional Web browser to sustain usage of the tool, independent of the perceived value of the recommendation facility.

The *profile* function allows the user to enter or modify his/her personal profile. Here the user selects his/her "advisors" from the list of Knowledge Pumpers. Advisors refer to people whose judgement the user particularly respects—this list is used by the community-centered collaborative filtering mechanism described further in Sect. 3.4.2. The user also selects any number of domains of interests from the hierarchy of "communities." Recommendations by the Pump to the user will be sorted according to this identified set of domains.

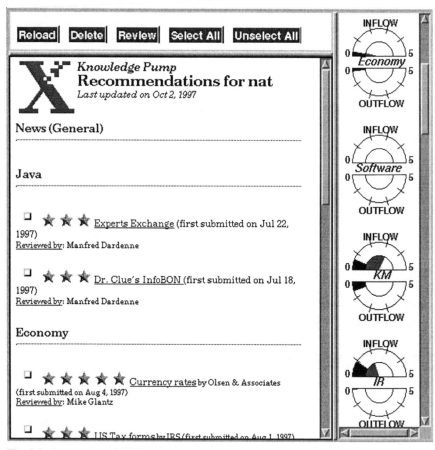

Fig. 3.3. An example of "What's recommended?" by the Pump

The *What's recommended?* function brings up the Pump's most recent personalized list of recommendations sorted by category as an HTML document in the Web browser. An example recommendations page is shown in Fig. 3.3. If the user keeps the recommendation page open in the Web browser, the Pump periodically and automatically updates it. In the current implementation, each recommendation takes the form of a pointer to a URL. The Pump only recommends items which the user has not seen before (not to the Pump's knowledge, at least) and for each item, displays the Pump's prediction of the user's interest as a number of stars, lists the names of all reviewers, and provides a link to their comments. The user can prune the recommendations page by deleting entries and can also review items directly from the page.

The panel to the right of the recommendations page contains a set of *gauges*, which provide feedback on usage. These gauges reflect the activity level of the Pump. There is a gauge displayed for each community to which the user belongs. The INFLOW half of the dial indicates how many recommendations are flowing in per person per week for the community. In black is the community average; in gray is the individual inflow. The OUTFLOW part of the dial indicates how many recommended links are being followed per person per week. Once again, black represents the community average; gray, the individual outflow. The gauges give feedback on how the average level of activity in a community fluctuates over time and give users a feel for how their level of participation compares with community averages.

Providing feedback serves two purposes. One is simply to inform the user and give the user an increased awareness of the collaborative nature of the Knowledge Pump. Another is to help stimulate community growth (and, when appropriate, community decline). We expect that users will be more likely to actively participate in communities that already demonstrate high or increasing activity levels, which will further stimulate growth. Likewise, we expect that users will be less willing to participate in communities whose acitivity levels are low or have declined, thus leading to further decline. Most significantly, we hypothesize that feedback mechanisms such as the gauges will encourage users to participate and to contribute more frequently to the more active communities. By providing aggregate information on both user and community activity levels we hope to encourage alignment between user and average community behavior: users of active communities will be incited to participate more and users of inactive communities will be incited to shift their efforts.

3.4.2 Technical Aspects: Community-Centered Collaborative Filtering

The Knowledge Pump uses what we call community-centered collaborative filtering to predict a user's level of interest for unread items in each of the user's domains of interest. This mechanism combines elements of social and content-based filtering.

For the moment we rely on recommenders to classify items into a commonly agreed upon classification scheme. This could be complemented down the line by automatic categorization via statistical classification algorithms.

The second layer of social filtering—matching items to people by first matching people to each other—lies on top of the initial classification by domain. It is important to filter by content first and by social relationships second because similarities among people tend to vary greatly across different domains. For example, the authors of this chapter have similar rankings of the most influential knowledge management gurus, but wildly different opinions concerning the best guitar players alive. Social filtering over all domains at once tends to wash out the differences in people's similarities to each other.

As mentioned earlier, social filtering via automated collaborative filtering is based on the premise that information concerning personal relationships is not necessary. In principle, we agree, because once an automated collaborative filter has collected enough information about its users, it can work very well. In practice, however, automated collaborative filters suffer from the cold-start problem: without large amounts of usage data, they work very poorly, which discourages the usage that would overcome this lack.

In contrast, in community-centered collaborative filtering, the collaborative filter is bootstrapped by the partial view of the social network constructed from user-input lists of "advisors"—people whose opinion users particularly trust. Bootstrapping the system in this way allows the collaborative filter to perform well from the start, weighing higher the opinions of his/her most trusted contacts when predicting the user's opinion on items. Over time, as more usage data is collected, the weight given to automated (statistical) portion of the collaborative filter can be increased relative to the weight given to advisors' ratings when predicting the user's interest in an item.

Additional statistical algorithms can also mine the usage data to automatically refine the Pump's view of the social network and visualize it for the users. This sets up a feedback loop between users and the collaborative filter: on their end, users collectively (re-)describe the social network; on its end, the Pump automatically refines and visualizes the social and community maps from usage data.

Of course, bootstrapping the Pump in this way only works in a setting where many members of the social network already know each other; thus, its relevance for information technology in support of knowledge management. Most significantly, community-centered collaborative filtering is a way to emphasize existing community structure while allowing the emergence of new communities, the evolution of old ones, and the combination of disjoint ones.

From a mathematical standpoint, collaborative filtering within a given domain can be viewed as matrix filling, where the rows of the matrix are items recommended into the domain, the columns are the people who have reviewed an item in the domain, and the cells contain the ratings submitted. An example is shown in Table 3.1.

The prediction algorithm used by the Pump is a weighted sum of three components:

- the average population-wide rating;
- the average over advisors' ratings;
- the correlation-weighted sum of all ratings.

The first two components are straightforward and are very important when ratings are very sparse, for example, when the system is first deployed. The second component uses the elements of the social network revealed from user-input lists of advisors.

Table 3.1. A sample user-item matrix of ratings

Item #	Alice	Bob	Chris	Dave
1	5	?	3	4
2	?	1	5	2
3	?	4	2	?
4	0	?	1	?
5	?	?	3	3

The third component is a standard automated collaborative filter (see Resnick et al. (1994), for example), which can be implemented in any of a number of ways. Our implementation first calculates person-person correlations from previous recommendations. These correlations indicate how much two reviewers tend to agree with each other on the items they both rated.

The collaborative filter automatically weighs more heavily the ratings of users that historically tend to agree with the user in question and discounts the ratings of those that tend to disagree. It is most effective when the user-item matrix is densely filled.

Currently, we use heuristics to combine the three components into one prediction. The heuristics take into account how long the system has been in place and the confidence level of each of the three elements. The confidence level is simply an ad-hoc estimate based on the density of ratings in the respective three populations. Once we have a user base established, we will be able to test the effectiveness of our approach and of the confidence level estimates and refine them for future use.

One last element of community-centered collaborative filtering is related to the user interface: users see the names of the people who have recommended an item and can read the publicly-available comments. This makes the boundaries between communities more permeable. A user can classify an item into any domain, regardless of whether s/he considers him/herself as a member of that community. Thus, members of a community can receive recommendations from people outside the community. Over time, the person can explicitly join the community by changing his/her profile or may become a de facto participant in the minds of its members.

3.4.3 Architecture: A Client-Server System

The architecture of the current implementation of the Knowledge Pump is shown in Fig. 3.4. The Pump is implemented as a client-server system. The client is written in Java and runs off a Web browser. It talks to the Knowledge Pump (Java) server which is responsible for a number of functions. The Knowledge Pump server provides an interface to system administration, periodically runs the community-centered collaborative filtering algorithm and builds the "What's recommended?" pages for each user. The pages are then saved and delivered to the user via the HTTP server.

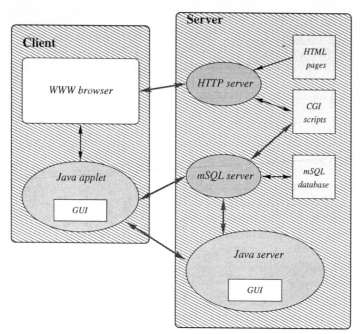

Fig. 3.4. Knowledge Pump client-server architecture

The data (user profiles, pointers to items, ratings and reviews, community members, etc.) is kept in a database. The database is accessed via yet another server. Both the Knowledge Pump client and server talk directly to the database through the database server. Alternatively, all communications to the database could have been routed through the Knowledge Pump server, which would have been cleaner but slower.

3.5 Summary and Outlook

As we discussed earlier in this chapter, we believe that the key to sucessful knowledge sharing is focusing on the community. We have implemented a first version of the Knowledge Pump that attempts to leverage community currency in the form of reputation, trust, and reciprocity to create incentives for sharing recommendations. At the heart of the Pump is a recommendation distribution mechanism we call community-centered collaborative filtering. This mechanism matches items to people by first matching people to each other, giving extra weight to trusted advisors.

The implementation of the Knowledge Pump as described in the previous section is a work in progress. Our first goal is to achieve proof-of-principle: to show that community-centered collaborative recommendation can indeed support knowledge sharing and improve community awareness and development. This first prototype is intended to provide the minimal set of functionalities sufficient to make it acceptable for use within an environment of early adopters.

However, understanding the environments in which the Pump could be used will be vital in order to tailor its functionalities and create incentives for use. For something like the Knowledge Pump to successfully support the flow and use of knowledge in organizations, it will have to become a seamless part of the way people do their work. The social aspects of use are perhaps the most fascinating and the most challenging.

Acknowledgments

The authors thank Daniele Pagani and Dan Holtshouse for inspiring this work and for their continued support. We are also grateful to Stefania Castellani, Antonietta Grasso, David Hull, Francois Pacull, Remo Pareschi and our other colleagues at XRCE for their suggestions and feedback.

Part III

Knowledge Cartography

4. Negotiating the Construction of Organisational Memories

Simon Buckingham Shum
Knowledge Media Institute, The Open University, U. K.

This chapter describes an approach to capturing organisational memory, which serves to ground an analysis of human issues that knowledge management (KM) technologies raise. In the approach presented, teams construct graphical webs of the arguments and documents relating to key issues they are facing. This supports collaborative processes which are central to knowledge work, and provides a group memory of this intellectual investment. This approach emphasises the centrality of negotiation in making interdisciplinary decisions in a changing environment. Discussion in the chapter focuses on key human dimensions to KM technologies, including the cognitive and group dynamics set up by an approach, the general problem of preserving contextual cues, and the political dimensions to formalising knowledge processes and products. These analyses strongly motivate the adoption of participatory design processes for KM systems.

4.1 Introduction and Definitions

In order to operationalise the concept of Knowledge Management (KM), numerous disciplines are now trying to analyse the processes and products of organisational knowledge, in order to clarify what tangible representations future knowledge managers might work with. These representations of the domain facilitate viewpoints and analyses of particular information-types from particular perspectives. This chapter describes one form of KM technology that has been developed over several years, which throws into relief a spectrum of human issues which are intrinsic to the process of designing and implementing KM representations—computer-supported or otherwise instantiated. This is particularly germane to the application of artificial intelligence (AI) techniques to KM, currently one of the most strongly represented disciplines in KM research, since the success of such approaches rests heavily on finding appropriate representations for knowledge modelling, ontology design, knowledge-based system building, and the subsequent reasoning that these activities are intended to support.

Let us begin by unpacking the concepts in the title, since several potentially ambiguous terms have been used. Firstly, meaningful *memories* are not simply retrieved according to some database model, but are *reconstructed* in the context of who is asking, and for what purpose. Bannon and Kuutti (1996) present an excellent introduction to the need to shift from a passive "storage bin" metaphor for organisational memory, to a more appropriate one of active reconstruction. We say different things to different people, varying the level of detail, emphasis, perspective, and so forth. Moreover, what is sanctioned as reliable knowledge depends on the community of interested stakeholders, who confer significance on certain sources (e.g. people), whether explicitly or implicitly. Knowledge is in that sense also *constructed*, serving particular needs at a particular time. When attempting to create a shared information or memory resource, we should not be surprised to find that *negotiations* about what is included, how it should be organised, and who has access to it, become key processes. This resource will itself be *constructed* over time as contributions are added to the digital corpus, and as its form and role within the project evolve.

This chapter introduces an approach to capturing organisational memory that takes into account the epistemological assumptions and collaborative processes implied by this framing of the problem. Teams use hypermedia groupware to construct graphical webs of argumentation and related documents as they discuss problems, recording aspects of their reasoning for future reference. This is a relatively mature approach which may be familiar to researchers in hypertext, computer-supported collaborative work (CSCW), groupware, and software design rationale. The purpose of this chapter is to contextualise it to the particular concerns of KM, and to use it to ground discussion of generic issues that KM technologies raise.

The chapter starts in Sect. 4.2 by characterising the *context* of "knowledge work"—if "knowledge workers" constitute an organisation's expertise, are there salient features of knowledge work that we can recognise? Section 4.3 introduces graphical argumentation as a candidate approach, with a particular niche in the design space of organisational memory systems. Section 4.4 introduces its representations for capturing group memory, Sect. 4.5 the appropriate supporting technologies. Section 4.6 then characterises the kinds of knowledge that can be captured with this combination. Section 4.7 briefly surveys studies of the approach's application, moving into a discussion in Sect. 4.8 of the hands-on practicalities of using it, taking into account cognitive, social and organisational level issues. Particular attention is paid to the problem of capturing adequate context. Section 4.9 closes the chapter by reflecting on the commitments that are made in adopting any representation, and the related issues of control and power that arise in managing knowledge about, and for, staff in an organisation.

4.2 Characterising Knowledge Work

The orientation of this research places a strong emphasis on the human dimensions to technologies for supporting organisational memory and expertise. The history of interactive computing shows repeatedly that it is the human issues which "make or break" new methods and tools at work. If we use the analogy of a river to describe the "work flow" at the level of an individual, team, or organisation, the designers of a new method or technology for organisational memory are placed in the role of "river engineers" seeking to change the flow of the river in some way. What they want to do is tap into the deep currents of the river, channelling it in new, productive directions. The question is, do they understand the hidden currents, eddies, and dynamics of that river sufficiently? If not, the result can be destructive "interference patterns" in the flow, or the force of the deeper currents may simply re-route around the changes.

It is, therefore, worth trying to clarify some of the salient properties of "knowledge work", given our intention to enter and change this fast flowing "river" with technologies. Two perspectives are considered: an empirical study of knowledge workers, and foundational work on characterising the properties of many real world problems.

4.2.1 A Study of Knowledge Workers

Firstly, on the basis of field studies of knowledge workers, Kidd (1994) has proposed several features which distinguish *procedural work* from *knowledge work*. All work is invariably a mix of the two, but increasingly, the procedural features are giving way to knowledge-based features. Kidd makes a number of distinctions, which are paraphrased below.

Knowledge workers are changed by the information in their environment, and they in turn seek to change others through information. Information is to be consumed, and once "digested", is often of little further value. Information resources which may have longer term use are often left visible and uncategorised (hence the frequent untidy piles and whiteboards), so that they can be quickly referred to. This is the antithesis of more procedural work (e.g. a secretary or administrator), whose work requires a lot of *filing* into *inflexible* structures—inflexible because the scheme is often standardised across the organisation, and because other staff also need to access those files.

Diversity and ad hoc behaviour patterns are common in knowledge work. New information is sought out, reused, and passed on in opportunistic ways, dependent on the changing context and interleaving of the worker's activities. In contrast, consistency of method and output is important in procedural work.

Communication networks are highly variable, with different patterns and use of media. Teams form and disband within the space of a day. The structure and job titles on an organisation chart are thus even less indicative than usual as to what someone does or with whom they work. Much of the knowledge exchanged is embedded in documents and email. Staff engaged in predominantly procedural work tend to have well-defined responsibilities and relationships, and the information flow that they maintain is more clearly defined.

These features provide a useful orientation to the domain of concern. They paint a picture of knowledge workers, and consequently their host organisations, as existing in continual flux as teams form and reform. In particular, the mobility of employees within and between organisations (coupled with "out-sourcing" to external contractors) creates conditions that can more easily lead to the fragmentation of any persistent shared memory within a team about lessons learned in projects. Furthermore, keeping track of discussions, decisions and their rationale is made harder when teams form on a project-specific basis, proceed to work interdependently but with substantial autonomy, and then disband. Experiences are not commonly recorded in conventional documentation, remaining locked in individuals' memories—individuals whose memories will fade, or who will take their expertise to other jobs. These are both motivating factors for, and militating factors against, the development of organisational memory resources. Collaboration tools which do not impose rigid models of membership or role, and which are able to integrate many diverse media types would seem appropriate in such an environment, discussed further by Kidd.

4.2.2 Wicked Problems

The second perspective on knowledge work comes from the formative work of Rittel (1972, 1973). Whilst the term "knowledge work" was not in currency in the late 1970s, Rittel identified crucial features of intellectual work which are highly pertinent to current concerns. Rittel characterised a class of problem which he termed "wicked", in contrast to "tame" problems. Tame problems are not necessarily trivial problems, but by virtue of the maturity of certain fields, can be tackled with more confidence. Tame problems are understood sufficiently that they can be analysed using established methods, and it is clear when a solution has been reached. Tame problems may even be amenable to automated analysis, such as computer configuration design or medical diagnosis by expert system.

Wicked problems display a number of distinctive properties that violate the assumptions that must be made to use tame problem solving methods. Wicked problems:

- cannot be easily defined so that all stakeholders agree on the problem to solve;
- require complex judgements about the level of abstraction at which to define the problem;
- have no clear stopping rules;
- have better or worse solutions, not right and wrong ones;
- have no objective measure of success;
- require iteration—every trial counts;
- have no given alternative solutions—these must be discovered;
- often have strong moral, political or professional dimensions, particularly for failure.

The connection between wicked problems and knowledge work should be apparent. Such problems are the typical challenges faced daily in, for instance, software design, government or social policy formulation, and strategic planning in organisations. It is also the case that wicked problems and lessons learned pose particular challenges for analysis and support by knowledge-based systems. What then is involved in supporting the capture of organisational expertise for such real world problems?

4.3 Negotiation, Argumentation and Knowledge Work

Let us develop the concept of negotiation, as introduced at the start. The claim is that knowledge work is dominated by communication, specifically *negotiation* and *argumentation*. There are several reasons for this.

- Firstly, much knowledge work is conducted in teams, and members have to communicate, increasingly distributed in space and time.
- Secondly, external factors often remove the control that a team has; the problem space is not stable. Goals, constraints and stopping rules are continually shifting. This demands a mode of working in which requirements, constraints and solutions must be regularly re-negotiated.
- Thirdly, Rittel concluded that wicked problems can only be tackled through what he termed an *argumentative* method (Sect. 4.4). Understanding how to frame a wicked problem is the key to finding solutions: what are the key questions? What are the key priorities?
- Fourthly, knowledge work is increasingly interdisciplinary. The different backgrounds, assumptions and agendas which members bring to a team can be extremely creative, but the inevitable conflict, debate, negotiation and compromise which is involved in reaching such creative solutions must also be acknowledged; this process can then be turned to the team's advantage.

In summary, an approach to capturing and representing organisational memory is required which is capable of supporting knowledge teams in:

- representing and reconciling multiple stakeholders' perspectives;
- re-negotiating project priorities in response to changed circumstances;
- communicating the rationale for decisions to others;
- recovering insights and solutions from past projects, to avoid "reinventing the wheel."

An organisational memory strategy which recognises the centrality of negotiation and argumentation in its employees' workflow (recalling the river metaphor) assumes from the start that the knowledge invested in a typical project is the product of much argument, compromise and the reconciling of different perspectives.

4.4 Visualising Argumentation

In *The Next Knowledge Medium* (Stefik 1986), Stefik proposes collaborative argumentation tools as one example of knowledge media. Such tools, "for arguing the merits, assumptions, and evaluation criteria for competing proposals" could provide "an essential medium in the process of meetings." "The languages provided by the tools encourage an important degree of precision and explicitness for manipulating and experimenting with knowledge", coupled with "augment[ing] human social processes." This conception of knowledge media lies at the heart of the representation and support technologies now proposed.

On the basis of his analysis of wicked problems, as introduced above, Rittel proposed the *IBIS* (Issue Based Information System) method, which encourages team members to actively discuss problems by raising *Issues* that need to be addressed, *Positions* in response to those Issues, and *Arguments* to *support* or *object-to* Positions. Conklin and Begeman (1988, 1991) developed a hypertext prototype called *gIBIS* (graphical IBIS) to support Rittel's IBIS method. In gIBIS, a team conducted its debates by building a graphical "conversation map." Figure 4.1 shows the gIBIS scheme, which illustrates how cumulative argument construction and critiquing can take place around a shared, graphical argumentation structure.

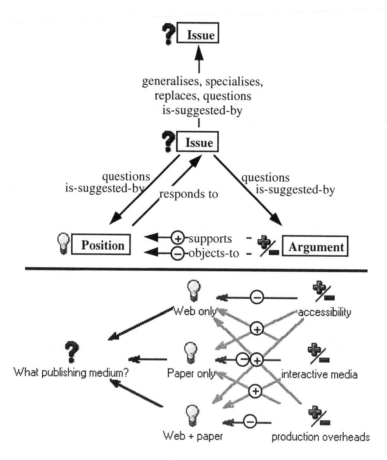

Fig. 4.1. The "graphical IBIS" (gIBIS) notation (Conklin and Begeman 1988) and an example showing how Issues, Positions and Arguments are combined to construct graphical argument spaces.

Many others have since developed variations on gIBIS. The complexity of the notation, and its visual layout rules (which vary with different approaches), determine how large and elaborate an argument can be expressed. For instance, a more expressive argument schema is shown in Fig. 4.2. The *Decision Representation Language* (Lee and Lai 1991) for supporting debate and qualitative decision making, introduces new constructs (e.g. the *Goal* node type), and allows participants to explore *Alternatives*, *Claims* backing them, and to contest through *Questions* and counter-*Claims* the relationships between these constructs.

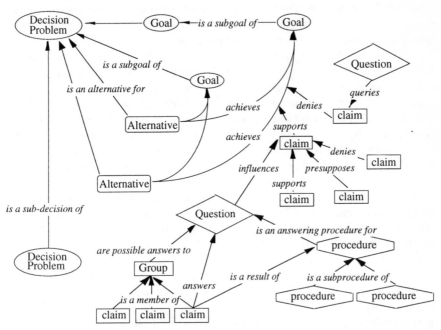

Fig. 4.2. The Decision Representation Language, one of the most expressive notations for capturing collaborative arguments (Lee and Lai 1991). A support tool (Lee 1990) provides graphical and tabular views of the underlying argument network.

This chapter focuses on notations like IBIS, which are "lighter weight" than DRL, the emphasis being on suitability for quick and intuitive use during meetings. A similar notation to IBIS is *QOC* (Questions, Options and Criteria) (MacLean et al. 1991), on which much of the usability evaluation work reported later has been based.

To summarise, having proposed that negotiation and argumentation are central to knowledge work, and having introduced the representation schemes which allow us to visualise such processes and products, let us now consider the technological support required. IBIS and QOC style representations have been used effectively with paper and pen, but computer supported argumentation is needed for easy editing, scalability and flexible linking, as discussed next.

4.5 Collaborative Hypermedia Infrastructure

Hypermedia is an ideal technology for capturing *informal knowledge types* with *inter-relationships which are hard to formalise*. This is in contrast to repositories that rely on more structured knowledge bases, requiring well-defined knowledge types and structures. The power that one gains from the latter comes at the cost of initial knowledge engineering effort, perhaps requiring a specialist. Moreover, as argued earlier, since the subject matter of most interest in knowledge work is often hard to formalise or continually changing, realistically, this encoding effort may be hard to justify even if it were possible in principle.

The evidence from cognitive studies of wicked problem solving points strongly to the importance of opportunistic ideas and insights. Hypermedia graphical browsers are well suited for linking together ideas without having to specify the precise semantics of their relations or roles (though see Buckingham Shum (1996a), Buckingham Shum et al. (1997) who reports that for certain types and stages of problem solving, even semiformal schemes can be too formal, impeding the creative flow).

Hypermedia is also well suited to organisational memory capture in a second essential respect: *media integration*. Debates, decisions and rationale do not exist in a vacuum, but in relation to ongoing work which relies on, and generates, many forms of artifact (e.g. faxes, email, reports, sketches, prototypes, simulations). It is crucial that these different artifacts can be integrated into the debates captured as semiformal argumentation. Hypermedia systems were designed precisely for this kind of media structuring, as exemplified in the the *QuestMap* hypermedia groupware system (Conklin and Yourdon 1993, GDSS 1996), shown in Fig. 4.3. This system is derived from the gIBIS research prototype described earlier (Fig. 4.1).

Finally, a review of the role of hypermedia cannot ignore the World Wide Web, the first truly global hypermedia system. In response to the need for tools to support asynchronous discussions between geographically dispersed participants, we are now seeing the emergence of Web systems to support argumentation of the sort illustrated above. One example is *HyperNews* (LaLiberte 1995), a system which supports discussions as textual threads through a combination of hierarchical indentation, augmented by icons which indicate whether a contribution is for example, an agreement, disagreement, or new idea. Figure 4.4 shows an example of argumentation on the Web (using a version of HyperNews), taken from an electronic journal peer review debate between an author and several reviewers, adopting an argumentation-based approach described by Sumner and Buckingham Shum (1998).

Such systems represent first generation Web argumentation tools. A similar textual outline representation was used in one of the most significant design rationale case studies (Burgess Yakemovic and Conklin 1990), summarised in Sect. 4.7. The Web is still a highly impoverished hypermedia system compared to many other systems, indeed, its simplicity is a major factor contributing to its explosive growth (Buckingham Shum and McKnight 1997). However, with richer hypertext models (Bieber et al. 1997), and the possibility of richer interactivity on the Web through

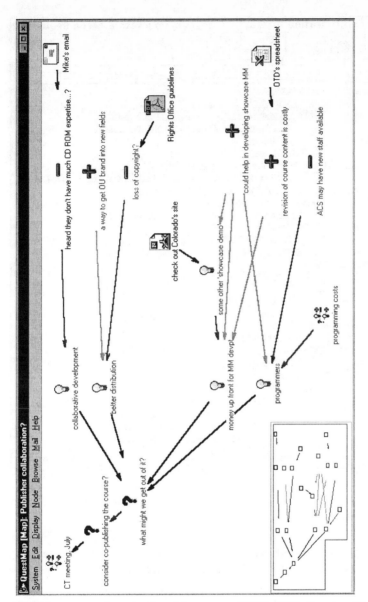

Fig. 4.3. A screen from the QuestMap system (GDSS 1996). Based on Rittel's IBIS argumentative model, this hypertext groupware system provides teams with a way to conduct synchronous or aynchronous debates. *Ideas* are suggested in response to *Questions*, and their *Pros* and *Cons* traded off against each other. New *Questions* can be raised by any element of previous discussion. Other media can be integrated into the web of debate through *Reference* nodes (e.g. reports, spreadsheets, video, presentations, code).

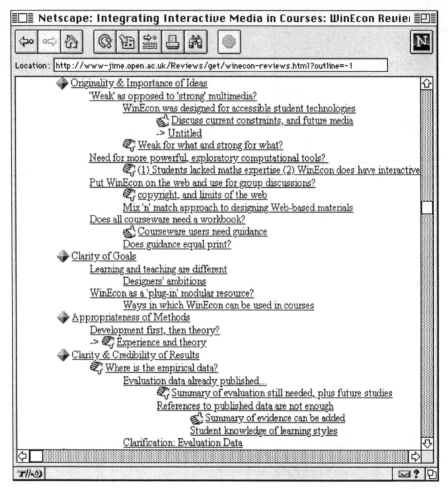

Fig. 4.4. Web-based argumentation in the context of journal peer review (Sumner and Buckingham Shum 1998)

developments such as Java and browser plug-ins, direct-manipulation graphical interfaces on the Web will become commonplace (e.g. Kremer 1996).

4.6 What Kinds of Knowledge are Captured?

The use of a tool like QuestMap (Fig. 4.3) allows teams to visualise their discussions, past and present. The following scenario may help to concretise how this might work in practice:

In June 1995, a meeting agenda is circulated specifying the *Questions* to be resolved. Over the network and in their own time, the multidisciplinary team members prepare by tabling their *Ideas*, beginning to critique these with *Pros* and *Cons*, linking in relevant reports, costings etc. In the meeting, the debate is projected onto a large wall to track the strengths and weaknesses of each idea as it is explored; following the meeting, team members reflect on the decisions made, and continue to discuss them, updating the map as new results and ideas come in. This map is emailed to others who were not present, who can quickly see what issues were discussed, which ideas were rejected, what decisions made, and on what basis. In September, several issues debated in June suddenly become critical. The relevant part of the map is retrieved, and it is realised that several Ideas rejected then are now valid. Moreover, links were created in June's meeting back to a previous discussion in May 1994, when a similar problem had been elegantly resolved. This provides a clue to the team as to how to resolve the current issues.

This scenario illustrates the affordances of an organisational memory resource coupling hypertext with argumentation. Firstly, it *supports the process* of discussion and negotation between multidisciplinary stakeholders. Secondly, it *captures the products* of those negotiations, providing the basis for an organisational memory. A team using such a tool builds for itself a form of intellectual trace which they can then draw upon. A group memory based on such a trace can help find answers to the following kinds of question:

- Have we faced problems similar to this before, and what was done?
- Who identified this problem/suggested this solution?
- What solutions were considered, but rejected, and why?
- If we change this decision, what might be affected?
- What led to this document being changed?
- What were the main criteria taken into consideration when that decision was made?

A resource based on this kind of approach clearly cannot represent all classes of organisational expertise; it should be seen as occupying one niche in the design space of tools to capture and maintain different organisational knowledge types. Some types of organisational expertise are without a doubt amenable to storage in more conventional databases, such as patents, procedures, employee qualifications, reports, etc. "Intellectual auditing"(Brooking and Motta 1996) can help to identify this kind of intellectual capital.

However, a strength of the approach described here (discussed further by Conklin 1996), is that the knowledge is captured *collaboratively*, and *in situ*, during the meeting or asynchronous debate, in the immediate context of one's work. Knowledge is represented, stored and indexed in relation to the real activities by which one's work is accomplished (as well as through some more abstract indexing system if so desired). Discussing *through* the medium of collaborative, graphical argumentation *eases the transition* from the messy, changing, contextualised, social, multimedia world, to their abstracted entry in an organisational memory system.

As entries are made in the organisation's long term memory, they bring with them (in the form of the web of discussion and work artifacts) important elements of the context in which they arose. Such cues are frequently used to recover memories (Eldridge et al. 1992).

4.7 Argumentation in Use

Collaborative, hypermedia argumentation has been tested since the mid-1980s to support knowledge work in a variety of contexts. Most of the earlier work on argumentation was taking place in research labs on the leading edge of the emerging technology of hypertext, for which graphical argumentation became something of an experimental "white rat" for testing technological flexibility. However, more recent research has placed an increasing emphasis on application to real, small-medium scale projects. This section points interested readers to more detailed reports of such studies. More detailed reviews of the research cited below can be found in Buckingham Shum and Hammond (1994) and Buckingham Shum (1996b).

Firstly, and not surprisingly, there has been a longstanding interest in the contribution that collaborative argumentation can make to complex, intellectual work where the quality of reasoning and accessibility of rationale for decisions are particularly important. Experimental fields of application have included government policy formulation (Conklin and Begeman 1988, Rittel and Webber 1973), scientific reasoning (Smolensky et al. 1987, VanLehn 1985), and legal analysis (Newman and Marshall 1991).

As hypertext matured as a technology, some of the most significant design disciplines began, and continue, to look at collaborative argumentation as a way to capture project/organisational memory, and manage the kind of changing environment and competing agendas described earlier. *Argumentative design rationale* is attracting substantial interest in *Human-Computer Interaction* (Carroll and Moran 1991, MacLean et al. 1989, Moran and Carroll 1996), *Software Engineering* (Conklin 1989, Jarczyk et al. 1992, Lee 1991, Potts and Bruns 1988, Potts et al. 1994, Ramesh 1993), *Knowledge Engineering* (Stutt and Motta 1995, Vanwelkenhuysen 1995), and *Knowledge-based Design Environments* (Fischer et al. 1991, Garcia and Howard 1992).

Thus far, the only financially costed benefits of this form of organisational memory come from a software engineering case study which introduced a textual version of IBIS argumentation, similar in form to the outline view provided by the HyperNews Web system (Fig. 4.4). This was used by a team working on a large commercial system development (Burgess Yakemovic and Conklin 1990). The study reports the discovery of eleven design flaws during the conversion of argumentation from outline to graphical form. The time savings gained for the project as a result were estimated at between three and six times greater than the time cost of converting the argumentation formats. It is evident that, as with any new tool, the success of IBIS in this case owed much to the enthusiasm of the team using it, in particular the maintainer of the issue base. Organisational practices and cultural differences in other teams were obstacles that prevented the uptake of the approach more widely (see Sect. 4.8.3). The availability of tools like QuestMap (Fig. 4.3) helps to make the approach more widely available, and in time should clarify the strengths and weaknesses of this particular approach in the context of different organisational cultures.

4.8 Hands-on Practicalities

In this section, attention focuses on the practicalities of using argumentation schemes. It is all too easy to propose new tools which should work in principle, only to find that insufficient account has been taken of the actual demands that they make in real work settings (borrowing our earlier metaphor, the force of the "river" may be underestimated).

4.8.1 The Cognitive Costs and Benefits

Organisational memory of any sort comes at a cost—someone must construct, index, and maintain it. There is no way for a knowledge capture enterprise to avoid this cost-benefit tradeoff. It is a question of how to negotiate it. Thus, minimal capture effort initially (e.g. video-record every meeting and store every document), simply shifts load downstream (how to recover the relevant records from memory?). In turn, the initial investment of knowledge encoding/engineering effort provides computational services subsequently.

Midway between these two extremes, the semiformal hypertext approach described here enables knowledge workers (not knowledge engineers) to structure their deliberations using a high level, reasonably intuitive vocabulary (e.g. Questions, Ideas, and Arguments). What are the overheads introduced by such schemes?

Analysis of the hands-on practicalities of using such a scheme (Buckingham Shum 1996a, Buckingham Shum et al. 1997) has highlighted four key cognitive tasks:

- *Unbundling*—teasing apart ideas which have been expressed together. A typical example would be when in one utterance someone raises a problem, and proposes a solution plus supporting reasons. Much time is wasted in meetings because a disagreement with one element in an argument is taken to be a dismissal of the whole argument. Graphical argumentation can clarify the different elements and hidden structure.
- *Classification*—deciding whether a contribution is, e.g. a Question, Option or Criterion. This is not always as simple as it sounds, because Options and Criteria may initially be expressed as Questions, or Criteria as solutions. A Yes/No Question can be asked about a particular Option, rather than clarifying the implicit problem to which that Option is one candidate solution. The task here is to cut through the surface form and recognise the "deeper content."

- *Naming*—how to label the new contribution succinctly but meaningfully. It can often be difficult to articulate ideas succinctly. The skill of doing so is nurtured over time, and the discipline involved can be helpful, although it can also be intrusive in a brainstorming mode of working. The overhead which naming creates is also dependent on the anticipated future use of the record, for instance, is it for colleagues present in the meeting, for a formal project review with a manager in three month's time, or for another team taking over from you? (Sect. 4.8.4)
- *Structuring*—how a new element relates to other ideas. Many meta-level representational and rhetorical decisions may arise at this point. For instance, what Question(s) does a new Option address? How does an Option trade-off against existing Criteria? Is this Question sufficiently similar to another in a different context, or should a new Question be introduced? Has this Criterion already been used elsewhere under a different name?

There is evidence that the intellectual rigour that this process encourages (e.g. being encouraged to ask "what really is the key Question here?") can focus team meetings about complex, wicked problems (Buckingham Shum et al. 1997). There is also evidence that when a problem is not in fact wicked, structured argumentation may not be helpful, slowing down discussion unproductively. It is therefore a case of choosing the right tool for the job; argumentation integrates well with certain cognitive and group workflows, but obstructs others. We have sought to alert practitioners to these hands-on issues when training them (MacLean et al. 1992-1994).

4.8.2 Modes of Groupwork

How can collaborative argumentation be used in a meeting? What role should it play in the project? There is a range of roles, depending on how committed a team wishes to be to capturing its intellectual investment in this way (see next section for factors that may militate against this). Figure 4.5 shows various points along a continuum which illustrate options which a team can adopt according to their work patterns.

A team will in fact move back and forth along this continuum for different kinds of meetings, and indeed *within* a meeting depending on the kind of problem that is being discussed (see previous section). We expect organisations, and within them individual teams and team members, to adapt these generic representations and tools to their own priorities and work patterns. Almost invariably, a new method or tool will be used in ways never originally envisaged by its developers; for instance, an innovative use of QuestMap for business modelling is described by Selvin (1997).

4.8.3 Organisational Culture

Understanding the human dimensions to a work representation cannot be restricted to the impact on cognition or group dynamics, critical though these are. As discussed in Sect. 4.9.1, representations take on political dimensions as soon as they are introduced into a workplace (Bowers 1991). Collaborative argumentation requires the adoption of a relatively open, transparent mode of communication, negotiation

Proactive role for argumentation

- Developing a coherent group record is a central, collaborative activity in the meeting. Debate is conducted *through* the graphical argument space. Ideas are edited and restructured as ideas evolve, resulting in a succinct summary of the key arguments behind the main decisions.

- An appointed 'scribe' records discussion, but other team members can see and use the emerging record as a shared representation to monitor their progress and guide discussion.

- A scribe privately records group discussion, which is then reviewed later by the team for erroneously recorded ideas, omissions, weaknesses in their reasoning, action items, etc. Argumentation plays a documentary role during meeting, but provokes reflection on review.

- A scribe privately records discussion, which is only referred to if information is later needed. No restructuring, purely documentary.

Passive role for argumentation

Fig. 4.5. Graphical argumentation can play a proactive or passive role in team deliberation. The more a team learns to interact via the graphical argument space, the more transparent it becomes—construction of the group memory becomes increasingly a co-product of the deliberation process, jointly owned by the team, and a living resource on which to build subsequently.

and accountability. Such an approach contrasts sharply with the harsh realities of some cultures, where there is distrust between employees and managers, and where efforts to improve meeting process, listen to all stakeholders', and make rationale more explicit are alien. Grudin (1996) and Conklin and Burgess Yakemovic (1991) have suggested that employees might, for instance, refuse to document who made a particular decision and why, for fear of recriminations in the event of an error. Moreover, certain stakeholders may perceive such approaches as undermining their power, since their arguments will be represented and treated on a more equal footing with other team members' views. Once displayed in the argument space, an idea is less tied to its owner, and more vulnerable to rationale critique. Conversely, for some stakeholders, this will be empowering.

Ultimately, we cannot escape the fact that organisational memory, certainly of the sort described here, requires a compatible working culture. There can be little doubt that even for team members who know each other well, there is a process of negotiating mutually acceptable conventions for maintainng the group memory (Berlin et al. 1993). This must take place on a correspondingly larger scale to prevent an organisation-wide memory from dying through neglect or subversion, as seems to be the fate of so many new methods and tools which do not sufficiently appreciate the organisational dynamics they seek to change.

One may hypothesise that current excitement within the organisation and business literature about the shift to "learning organisations" will create work cultures who will look favourably on collaborative argumentation tools. One may also hypothesise that the dynamic of change is two-way, and that in the hands of a committed team able to demonstrate its relevance to the organisation's business, collaborative argumentation tools could work from the bottom up as agents of change.

4.8.4 Negotiating the "Context Paradox"

Information becomes useful knowledge once its significance in its original context is understood; divorced from its context, information is open to misinterpretation. In engaging in the enterprise of constructing organisational memory, therefore, we are faced with the challenge of effectively capturing sufficient context to accompany entries in the information base. What can be termed the "context paradox" is the possibility that more context will be needed to interpret whatever contextual information has already been provided. Attempts to provide richer, more extensive contextual information through, for instance, audio/visual multimedia commentaries, or more complex hypertext webs of information are still prey to the reinterpretation problem. A related irony is that the more contextual background there is to digest, the less likely it is that busy staff will do so.

The degree to which additional context is needed to interpret information correctly clearly depends on who the recipient of this information is. In creating what is intended to be a reusable resource, careful thought needs to be given to the user groups one is serving. For instance, colleagues who are co-present in a meeting have established a rich context in that time and place for intepreting each others' contributions. A video recording may help an outsider recover important elements of this, although not everything is captured on camera, and of course, prior knowledge of the context of the meeting may be critical to make sense of it. Tools are now being developed to assist in capturing important moments in meetings, and managing that corpus of material (Moran et al. 1997).

As the intended user base of a group memory system expands from the core team, to encompass wider circles of staff, the common ground which can be assumed decreases, thus increasing the amount of implicit knowledge that needs to be made explicit. One way to think about this process is as the evolution from a group memory for *unstable, provisional information* kept for the core team's own use, to a memory for more *stable, consensus information*. This corresponds to shifts from implicit to explicit knowledge, from being a private to a public resource, and from being a one-off entry (e.g. to facilitate a single meeting), to being a reusable resource of wider interest. Berlin et al. (1993) have also described how the group's process must adapt when they commit to maintaining a group memory, even for themselves, as individual styles of entry must be held in tension with establishing agreed conventions.

How does the context paradox translate with respect to the particular approach presented in this chapter? Graphical argument/document networks of nodes are quite terse compared to textual documents. They capture the essence of discussions, leaving the original participants to "fill in the gaps" with their own memory—the network is a resource to cue them. There is some empirical evidence that outsiders can have difficulty in making sense of someone else's graphical argument structures when they have not been involved in the original discussions (Bellotti et al. 1995, Buckingham Shum 1993). As emphasised earlier (based on evidence such as these studies), one solution is to tightly integrate the argumentation with the relevant documents, making it very easy to bring up a relevant document. Open hypermedia systems (e.g. Microcosm) make it easy to link from point to point in any desktop document running in Microsoft Windows, and Webcosm extends this to Web documents (Multicosm 1996).

Another approach is to enrich the argumentation with expert commentary from one of the original team, who can introduce the discussion, much as a colleague might set in context some documents that they are handing over. With off-the-shelf products such as ScreenCam (Lotus 1996) for instance, one can easily record commentary to accompany a visual walkthrough of a map to introduce a particularly complex analysis, and for instance, bring out nuances behind particular arguments that are invisible. Subsequent users would play this guided tour first, to get an overview of the discussion they are about to step through in detail.

The key information design task is to design for different user populations, and to use different representations of context appropriately. Graphical argument structures have different cognitive affordances to time-based media. The latter can be very effective in conveying subtle information that is hard to express in graphical/textual summary form, whilst the latter provides an overview of the discussion space, and as a shared representation, supports collaborative reasoning about a problem. Detailed analysis of the individual and group cognitive affordances of graphical argumentation in a design context is presented by Buckingham Shum et al. (1997).

To conclude this section, as the context paradox emphasises, efforts to supply richer context are still open to misinterpretation, and unless carefully designed, may be ignored due to information overload. If well designed, however, fewer people will lack important context, since the circle of readers who now share key common background knowledge has been widened. It is worth re-iterating that if a group memory is successful in providing contextualised information, what the reader will come to share with the team is not only an understanding of what they did and why, but also an appreciation of the tensions and trade-offs that set the context for those decisions.

4.9 "Knowledge (Management) is Power":
Ethical and Representational Issues

This chapter has intentionally focused on technologies embedded in contexts of use, seeking to elaborate scenarios of organisational memory usage as a way to highlight future possibilities, and to identify obstacles to uptake. This foregrounding of the human dimensions to knowledge technologies is extended in this final section to issues of power and control over *what* gets represented and *how*, *by whom*, and *for what purposes*. Our starting point is the fundamental issue of *representation*.

4.9.1 The Politics of Formalisation

> In selecting any representation we are in the very same act unavoidably making a set of decisions about how and what to see in the world. [...] A knowledge representation is a set of ontological commitments. It is usefully so because judicious selection provides the opportunity to focus attention on aspects of the world we believe to be relevant. [...] In telling us what and how to see, they allow us to cope with what would otherwise be untenable complexity and detail. Hence the ontological commitment made by a representation can be one of the most important contributions it offers (Davis et al. 1993)

> Classification systems provide both a warrant and a tool for forgetting [...] The classification system tells you what to forget and how to forget it. [...] The argument comes down to asking not only what gets coded in but what gets read out of a given scheme (Bowker 1998).

The above two quotes, the first from knowledge engineers, and the second from an ethnographer of organisational memory, draw attention to the filtering function that a representation provides, and the problem that through the process of simplifying a domain in order to describe it within a formal scheme, we may also be systematically factoring out certain classes of critical information simply because they are hard to formalise.

Whenever an authoritative body (e.g. corporate management, or a research funding council) declares an interest in certain concepts, it is inevitable that its dependents (e.g. managers, or researchers seeking grants) will seek to align their activities with these concepts in order to maintain a presence. The first point, therefore, is that the introduction of systematic KM (whether or not technology is involved) creates a new *economy of knowledge* and a *knowledge vocabulary*. Any group and their work will remain invisible and thus unresourced unless they can represent themselves within this new economy, using the right language. Bowker presents an illuminating analysis of the impact of "professionalisation"—systematic classification of skills and courses of action, and management of these via technology—on a profession in which expertise takes the form of hard to codify tacit knowledge and craft skill, in this case nursing:

> One of the main problems that [...] nurses have is that they are trying to situate their activity visibly within an informational world which has both factored them out of the equation and maintained that they should be so factored—since what nurses do can be defined precisely as that which is not measurable, finite, packaged, accountable (Bowker 1998).

This illustrates clearly the political dimensions to formal classification. The names and labels one uses unavoidably emphasise particular perspectives (see also Suchman (1993) on the politics of computational categories in CSCW).

Knowledge-based systems require the systematic decomposition and classification of expertise; a knowledge-base unavoidably "holds" an ontological view of the

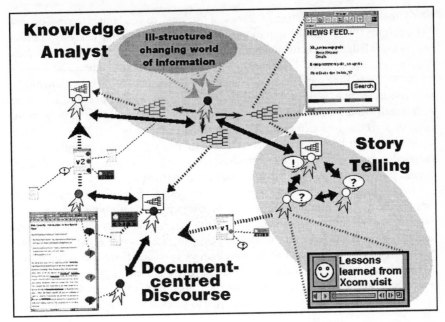

Fig. 4.6. Pro-active knowledge analysts, technical "story-telling" amongst staff, and document-centred discourse are three ways in which knowledge is shared within organisations. Media that are now emerging within many organisations to support these processes are illustrated—Web intranets integrated with agents and broadcast media, desktop audio/visual recording tools, and document-discussion environments. Their integration with AI techniques is discussed more fully by Buckingham Shum (1997a).

world (ontology with a small "o"). More recent knowledge-sharing initiatives and other research devoted to formal Ontologies make more explicit the issues faced in knowledge modelling, independent of any particular symbolic implementation as a system. One question that the ontology community may be able to help answer is how to manage the inevitable incompletenesses and inconsistencies in an organisational knowledgebase, due to uncodified, or uncodifiable knowledge. If ontology building is to form part of AI's contribution to KM (as some argue), how can we ensure that areas of uncertainty or incompleteness are made explicit in the ontology, *and* carried through to the implementation and user interface of any KM system based on that ontology? If the KM system is to be used by the organisation's managers, then they must be sensitised to the limitations of the tool's ontology, as a check and balance to the seductive sense of control that manipulating clean computational abstractions offers. What training is required in order to wield such tools intelligently?

We have argued elsewhere (Buckingham Shum 1997a), that some of the most robust forms of knowledge sharing and communication that we know occur in organisations are socially based, and their content is extremely hard to formalise. These include the discussions that endow documents with significance (Brown and Duguid

1996), the informal recounting of technical "stories" to colleagues to pass on new insights (Orr 1986), and the importance of dedicated knowledge analysts to maintaining knowledge resources, and both persuading and assisting staff to access them (Davenport 1996). Figure 4.6 schematically illustrates these three processes.

As illustrated, the representations and technologies that should be considered for such processes may well be rather different to the knowledge-based technologies with which we are currently familiar. (As an aside, there appeared to be a strong sense at a recent symposium on AI's role in KM (Dieng et al. 1997) that formal representation of knowledge seems to have a limited role to play in organisational knowledge management, with the emphasis shifting to supporting the social, coordinated *processes* through which knowledge is constructed.)

To conclude this section, the representations we use shape the world we can see through them. All representations are simplifications; the question is are they *over*-simplifications? The baseline assumption in the argumentative approach is that there rarely is one correct view of the world to begin with; the first step is to take seriously the different viewpoints, and to then seek ways in which these can be expressed and resolved. As discussed above in relation to the context paradox, however, no representational scheme is immune from the danger that it becomes too simplistic, too terse to be useful, or too decontextualised to support meaningful interpretation.

4.9.2 "Participatory KM" Based on Stable, Sanctioned Knowledge

Dear Employee,

In order to maintain and increase KnowTech's competitiveness, an intellectual audit is to be conducted on your department in the coming month, as part of a corporate wide strategy. This will provide Strategic Planning with a better understanding of your skills, communication networks and contributions to KnowTech's business. This will enable them to ensure that you are receiving the right information at the right time, and that we make the most of your valued expertise.

The Management

Software design is the process of moving from vague requirements to executable, computational models. Participatory design approaches to interactive system development emphasise the many stakeholders in a system development project, and the need to involve the system's end-users in order to co-design software and work practices. This final section draws on the participatory design perspective to examine the particular challenges that KM technologies face if they are to be collectively "owned" by the staff whose knowledge is being managed. We return again to the foundational theme of representation that runs through this chapter, identify the stakeholders that a participatory approach should involve, and then propose a heuristic measure for deciding when to commit to formally representing knowledge processes.

Knowledge-system design, as a particular form of software design, is the construction of computer-manipulable representations of domain knowledge. The process of *formal representation* raises a host of issues, some of which this chapter has considered. From a participatory design perspective, three of formalisation's most significant features in a KM context are as follows:

1. *Representations can become less flexible*, that is, as layers are added, dependencies on old structures increase, and the whole structure becomes harder to change in response to changes in understanding, or of the domain being modelled. Representations tend also to become less tolerant of incompleteness, inconsistency, or ambiguity. This is of course useful for highlighting weaknesses in an organisation's KM, but it may also be a significant limitation, since the models that different parties hold of a domain may be equally valid, but shaped by competing priorities. It may not be possible to satisfy these with one elegant representation. The cost of formalising too early, even semiformally as hypertext, is that it may be too much effort to revise a representational scheme that turns out to be wrong, so it is left as part of the system. Clearly, the art is in knowing when to formalise.

2. *Representations become less comprehensible* to staff who are not knowledge-engineers. One of the consequences of formalisation is that the contents become increasingly inaccessible to the majority of stakeholders. It is of course common that a profession's language and representations are opaque to outsiders, but extra care needs to be taken in KM-system design, due to the legitimate interests of different stakeholders in knowing what is to be encoded in the system, and what role this is playing in management decision making.

3. *Representations support automated analysis.* Clearly this is the main purpose of formalising, so why should this be a problem? Problems arise when the processes of decomposition and abstraction, required to create a representation capable of supporting automatic analysis, result in models which strip out important contextual details which are in fact critical to understanding the domain (see Sect. 4.8.4 on the problem of "capturing" context). Models of employees' skills, work processes and interdependencies may not adequately express the true nature of their expertise and coordination of work. If the representation is too incomplete (it will always be incomplete to some degree), then the most powerful manipulations and analyses are meaningless. This of course is not a novel insight, but organisational dynamics are particularly difficult to model.

It is rare to find knowledge modelling papers that explicitly recognise the informal and social knowledge processes in the organisations (real or imagined) for which they are designing (though see Euzenat (1996), van Heijst et al. (1996), Vanwelkenhuysen and Mizoguchi (1994) for exceptions). Combining social and computing disciplines in this way is surely a fruitful area for further multidisciplinary work, as exemplified by Fischer et al. (1995). The formality and accessibility of knowledge representations are central to a participatory KM approach.

Who are the main stakeholders in a KM initiative, and what are their concerns? Obviously, management want to know how can they make the most of their investment in quality staff and hope that systematic KM will give them views and benchmarks on the organisation's state. For a company's information technologists, this may represent an opportunity to rationalise and upgrade the IT infrastructure. For the personnel/human resource division, this may be the opportunity to move towards a more "learning organisation" culture. As for the staff whose knowledge and expertise is so central to the whole enterprise, and who may be expected to participate in the capture and subsequent use of any technology, they may be hoping to reduce wasted time trying to get information from other groups (it will now be online), reduce the need to handle the same queries repeatedly, and benefit from innovations elsewhere that they never hear about. All of these perspectives are interdependent. None can be examined in isolation except in an artificial, decontextualised way.

There are a number of questions, set out below, that can be asked of any proposed approach to organisational knowledge capture and re-use. These draw attention to the interdependencies between economics, technologies, work practices, and the power and responsibility that controlling knowledge repositories brings. As such, they may help to pre-empt the development of approaches which privilege any single set of concerns to the neglect of the others.

1. *What classes of knowledge/expertise are addressed by this approach?*
   There are many different classes of knowledge and expertise residing in an organisation. Relevant dimensions include tacit-explicit (see also Fig. 1.2, p. 6), procedural-declarative, tame-wicked, cognitive-cultural. Obviously, these vary widely in the extent to which they can be made (i) explicit, and (ii) formalised and structured in digital repositories. A central challenge for organisational knowledge is to develop a better understanding of the most appropriate media for different kinds of personal and organisational knowledge/expertise. It is likely that the knowledge represented by some points in this multidimensional space cannot be formalised, without in the process invalidating it.

2. *What representational scheme is proposed, enabling what kinds of analysis and computation, with what justification?*
   What computational services over these repositories are proposed, in order to solve what kinds of problems? How does the repository reflect the changing world? Does analysis of such representations make idealised assumptions which do not hold in the real world embodiments of the knowledge/expertise being modelled? Such justification is needed when the contents of the repository relate to staff and their work practices.

3. *Who are the stakeholders? How will knowledge encoding and re-use impact their work practices?*
   Who is responsible for entering information into the repository—a knowledge engineer; each staff employee? Does one have control over one's own area, e.g. one's "skills profile?" Is it mandatory for all staff to keep their areas up to date; if so how is provision made for this? How does the system change interdepartmental relationships, since one's knowledge profile in the repository is now public, and therefore social? Do staff trust the system? If not, on what basis can the management?

Elsewhere (Eisenstadt et al. 1996), we illustrate how these questions can be used to critique a system. If one takes seriously the complexity of modelling knowledge processes and products, one will approach the task of constructing organisational memory, or for that matter any KM resource, with some caution. As a heuristic approach which translates this caution into appropriate action, let us consider two related principles which can be summarised as:

KM technologies should formalise only knowledge which is **stable** *and* **sanctioned**.

Stability refers to the rate of change in the domain being modelled, relative to the speed with which these changes can be detected (either by knowledge analysts, or automatically by the KM system), and the underlying knowledge representation then updated. Thus, as organisational structures change, as teams change, as individual's skills change, how will these be reflected in the KM system? This relative notion of stability implies that in principle, as advances in the flexibility of knowledge representation are made, the linkage between the model and the domain being modelled (organisational, group and individual cognitive processes) could become tighter, so that more dynamic classes of knowledge can be managed; the domain will be relatively more stable in relation to what the KM system can cope with.

Work practices become stable because they are *sanctioned*—sustained by the relevant stakeholders. How can stable, sanctioned knowledge be identified? There is a relevant urban-planning practice to call upon here: after laying a fresh area of grass, wait for the main paths to be trodden down; it is then that one builds proper paths to bear the heaviest traffic. In other words, in domains where consensus is unclear, formalisation should wait until the daily practices and routines of the organisation—some of which may be too complex to predict in advance—reveal the important, stable patterns that are in most need of support. These might include: regular transformations of knowledge from one medium to another; transfer of knowledge from one party to another; filtering functions; interdependencies between two or more schedules; checklists of action items that always need to be addressed whenever a certain event occurs.

The concept of sanctioning knowledge not only emphasises the right to know about and participate in any modelling of one's work domain, but also the right to know how one is represented in the KM system that results. This might take a number of forms, varying in the strength of the "right to know" policy, and the technical complexity of implementing it:

- the right to know the form and content of one's entry in the knowledge base (e.g. skills, networks, workflows, responsibilities);
- the right to know if automatic analysis or inferencing by the KM system forms the basis for management policy (appropriate questions can then be raised if there are concerns about the sufficiency of the representation or reasoning);
- the right to view, or even update knowledge stored about oneself (accessible user interfaces are required here), or to transform knowledge in one medium to another (e.g. from a video story to a textual summary, or vice versa).

At this early stage, it is hard to predict the implications of a truly established "knowledge economy" (Stefik 1986) operating within and between organisations. It is proposed that participatory KM design is a promising perspective to adopt: it involves all the relevant stakeholders in the complex business of modelling people's work practices and skills; it is appropriately cautious in recommending that representations be used only for stable, sanctioned knowledge processes; it emphasises the conflicts and interdependencies between the different agendas that the move towards systematic KM raises, in particular the political dimensions to controlling knowledge repositories and the legitimate concerns that this raises.

4.10 Conclusion

Dialogue between the AI community and other relevant disciplines such as human-computer interaction, collaborative computing, workplace ethnography and organisational learning is essential, in order to begin developing the detailed organisational scenarios of use that are at present conspicuous by their absence. From there, the first design iteration needs to be completed with empirical evidence of the success or failure of knowledge management technologies in action. Some might respond that it is too early in this field to see serious inter-disciplinary dialogue; each discipline is still struggling to formulate its own views on what The Knowledge Management Problem is. Historically, however, the evidence from more established domains of interactive system design is that the relationship between computing, human and organisational disciplines is complex, and that each is changed through its dialogue with others. This chapter has tried to illustrate how the human and computing sciences can productively engage with each other to analyse the domain, develop appropriate representations and technologies, and reason about scenarios of use from the many perspectives that interactive knowledge management technologies require.

Acknowledgements

The author is grateful to Geof Bowker, Enrico Motta and Tamara Sumner for feedback on earlier drafts. The ideas in this article also benefited from discussions with delegates at the 1st International Conference on Practical Aspects of Knowledge Management, Basel 1996, and the AAAI Spring Symposium on Artificial Intelligence in Knowledge Management, Stanford 1997.

5. A Technology for Supporting Knowledge Work: The RepTool

Brigitte Jordan[†], Ron Goldman,[‡] and Anja Eichler[ℓ]
† Xerox PARC and IRL, Palo Alto and Menlo Park, CA, USA
‡ Bell Atlantic Science and Technology and IRL, Menlo Park, CA, USA
ℓ Witten-Herdecke University and Xerox PARC, Palo Alto, CA, USA

In this chapter we report on the RepTool,[1] a computer based tool for the collection, analysis, and presentation of data about "workscapes." Users of the tool collect relevant information about workplaces and workpractices in a central data structure on which the tool provides different views. Physical, social, and cognitive spaces in users' or customers' environments can be represented and analyzed. The RepTool supports systematic data collection and collaborative data analysis that can help people at all levels of an organization build a shared view of the formal and informal work processes they participate in. A tool for collaborative knowledge management, it nurtures intra- and inter-team conversations that can lead to an empirically grounded, shared view of current realities and potentially necessary changes.

5.1 Introduction

Knowledge work characteristically takes place in multi-person work groups such as collaborative work teams, communities of practice or other kinds of social units. The activities of such groups are located in "workscapes" or "work ecologies" that include the totality of affordances and constraints provided by particular physical settings, social relationships, endogenous work practices, official work processes, and the customary artifacts and technologies that are instrumental in accomplishing the work at hand.

At present, most representations of work are prescriptive and process-oriented. In particular, work groups and their often informal work practices are not well captured by current tools. As we attempt to go beyond sequential workflow modeling and look at knowledge work with a holistic workscape perspective, we need tools that support this perspective.

Ideally such tools would show a number of specific characteristics. Minimally, they should:

- be equally useful for workers, analysts, and managers
- be usable by non-specialist participants under field conditions
- be tailorable and adaptable to the requirements of different users

---

[1] The RepTool is patented jointly by the Institute for Research on Learning and Bell Atlantic.

- support systematic data collection
- make data available synchronously and asynchronously
- allow collaborative data analysis
- foster collective inquiry by building team-shared views of conventional or virtual workscapes
- produce representations that can act as "boundary objects" conducive to reflection among stakeholders
- support a collaborative (re)design of work processes, work places, and work technologies.

When analyzing workscapes from a holistic perspective many different kinds of information might need to be considered. Workscape analysts might want to be able to investigate such issues as:

- What is the physical space like: Who inhabits it; what objects and technologies are located in it; how much physical space is available to carry out the work at hand.
- What are the social relationships between people: Who reports to whom; who works with whom; who goes bowling with whom; who asks whom the questions no M&P manual answers; who supports what projects.
- What are the relationships between the various communication and computing technologies present in the workplace: Which workstations have access to which servers; which workstations share the same software; which computers are linked to which printers; or whose desktop conferencing setup can connect to whom.
- What is the cognitive space for this work setting like: What sorts of projects, ideas, enterprises does it contain; where are they located; who works on them; what technologies do they require; what other projects or ideas are they linked to.

We have designed a representational tool, the RepTool, to help investigators explore these kinds of questions (Jordan et al. 1995). As a tool for the collaborative collection, analysis and representation of information, it can aid knowledge workers and analysts of workscapes to better understand and shape particular work settings. Since the systematic representations that are produced when using it can be dynamically updated and shared among stakeholders, the tool supports reflection-in-action and facilitates conversations leading to collective interpretation and sense making.

Michael Schrage (1990), in *Shared Minds: The New Technologies of Collaboration*, predicts that collaborative tools will "converge to create new collaborative environments" and that "people will discover new modes of interaction, new styles of creativity and conversation, and a new desire to work with people to solve problems and craft innovations". The RepTool is intended as a step in that direction.

5.2 Views provided by the RepTool

The RepTool offers a variety of different views on a tailorable, central data structure in which users/investigators collect information relevant to their concerns. What makes working with the RepTool data structure different from working with many other kinds of databases is:

- A high level of tailorability allowing users to change the structure of the information they are collecting on the fly.
- Ability to provide different views on the information collected: Printing or otherwise displaying the central data structure presents a verbal view of the data. A visual graphic view is provided by the fact that the same information can be displayed as a map that shows the objects of interest, be they artifacts or people, and optionally the relationships between these objects.
- A highlighting function that supports the combination of verbal and visual spaces: It enables the user to run queries on the data structure and display results on the map as highlighted objects or by drawing arrows and lines to indicate relationships. Thus different views can be explored that may lead to new insights.

Users typically will want to have information on the physical space, the social space, the technology space, and the cognitive or idea space of the workscapes they are concerned with.

The physical space: Users of the tool might want to see the physical layout of a workplace in a map-like representation, complete with desks, doorways, windows, people, documents, and relevant technologies. This would allow them, for example, to highlight the office locations of all persons who work on a particular project in order to study the effects of collocation. When trying to understand activities on a production floor, they might want to see all locations through which a product travels.

What differentiates these representations from conventional sketches and maps is that each object in such a representation is "alive", that is to say can be associated with a record in the central data structure that contains additional information about the object.

The social space: At the same time, an analyst might want to generate a representation of the work-relevant social relationships that exist in the workplace, be they friendship networks, mentoring relationships, kin networks, trade relations, coresidence, bowling team membership, alma maters, or current and previous work associations. The RepTool can represent reciprocal (e.g., friend/friend) relationships as well as complementary ones (e.g., supervisor/subordinate). In addition to formal reporting relationships expressed in an organization chart, analysts might want to understand such things as who gets advice from whom; who says they work with whom; who mentors whom; who are the informal leaders that people go to when they are stuck with a difficult problem, and the like. This kind of analysis can be used to examine an organization from many angles in order to identify key players, bottlenecks, communities of practice, communications between teams, and social networks (Stamps 1997).

Simultaneously representing the social and the physical space allows investigators to map the movement of various kinds of objects through the company. One could, for example, look at the distribution of documents in relation to the people who need access to them, at the movement of hoarded spare parts through the social channels of a service organization, or the informal exchange of favors, factors that lead to a better understanding of how an "informal economy" is constituted in the workplace. By examining what is normally invisible in the organization, it becomes more possible to see how the organization really works and to show these findings to others in a convincing way—as printouts on paper, as overheads, or in live electronic form.

The technology space: A representation of the infrastructure consisting of computing and communication technologies such as fax machines, scanners, computers, speaker phones, computerized whiteboards, video conferencing setups, and the like allows investigation of which machines are connected to which other machines, which computers run what software, or who is connected to whom through what kinds of communication devices. This might be useful for such things as tracing breaks and impasses in information flow in the company.

The cognitive space: Non-physical spaces can be represented in the RepTool as well. For example, managers might want to map out a company's "project space" in order to identify project success factors or cross-division connections over projects; corporate lawyers might want to represent a company's patents together with known infringements in a "patent space"; and researchers might want to model the emergence of particular ideas across a research lab.

In sum, since the RepTool allows us to map out all manner of physical, social, organizational, and idea spaces it should prove useful in all cases where investigators need to understand what kind of formal and informal situated knowledge work goes on in their own workscapes and those of their customers.

5.3 Technical Details

The RepTool consists of an object-oriented database connected to a drawing tool. The user gathers information about a workplace, stores it in the database, and then creates multiple graphic views, or maps, to represent different aspects of the work. Values and relationships in the database are then used to highlight the objects displayed in these graphic representations and to draw lines between them.

The RepTool is designed to be easy to learn and to be easy for the user to tailor to his or her needs. We have been using an iterative, participatory design process for its development. After identifying user needs, new features are designed and implemented. Every four to six weeks a new prototype is released for more testing and the process is repeated.

5.3.1 The RepTool Database

The RepTool uses an object-oriented database with no inheritance. The database consists of one or more record types, each of which is made up of a list of data fields and a number of individual records of that type. For example a database may have records for people, computer systems, and projects as shown in Fig. 5.1. The record for a person might contain their name, position, phone number, and pointers to all of the projects they are involved with.

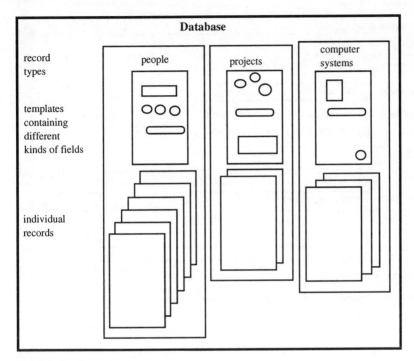

Fig. 5.1. Database structure

The fields in each database record can contain one of the following types of data:

- text—this can be a short string, like a name, a multi-line comment, or a longer text note that will appear in a separate window
- number—this can be a simple integer or one with decimal digits (e.g., 3.14)
- date/time—this consists of the date (i.e., day, month, year) and/or time of day (i.e., hour, minute, second)
- Boolean—this is for yes/no or true/false values
- multiple choice—this can be either one or several choices from a set
- pointer—this is a pointer to another record in the database; a pointer field can point to one or several other records

Figure 5.2 is an example of a record for a fictional employee showing how the fields appear when displayed.

The database is designed so that it is easy for a user to add new fields or edit old ones at any time. All of the records in the database are immediately updated with the new fields.

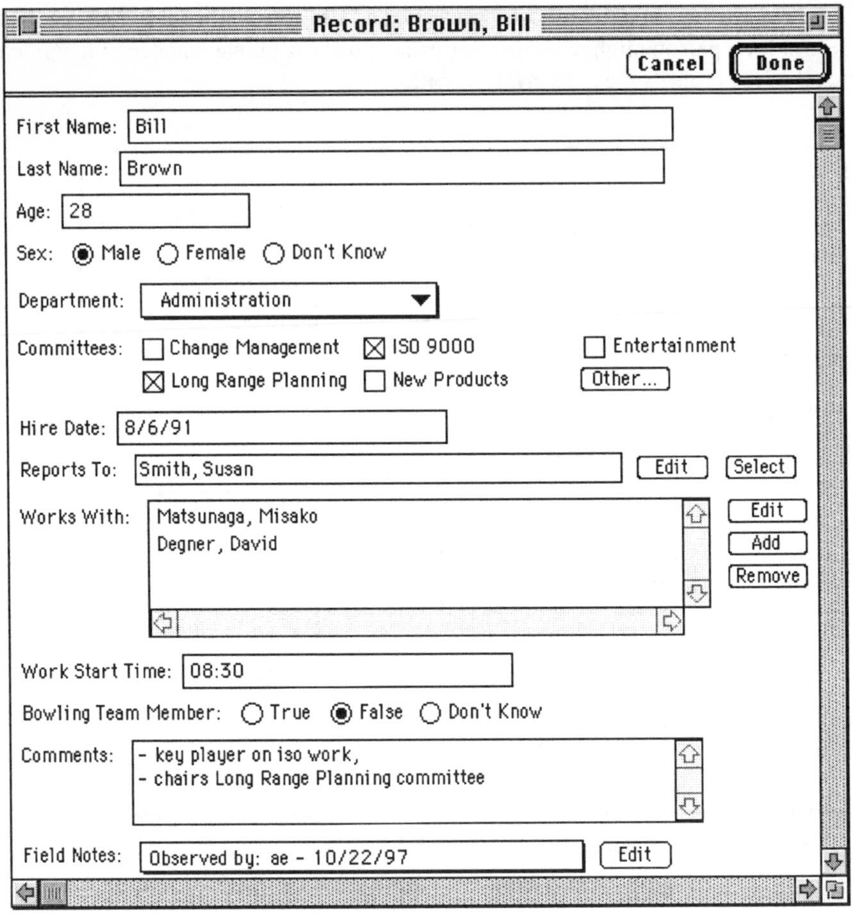

Fig. 5.2. Sample database record

The RepTool also allows the user to describe relationships between records in the database. These relationships are shown graphically as lines connecting the objects associated with the records. This is useful for showing relationships such as who reports to whom, which databases a computer system has access to, where a technician goes for help on questions, etc. The information connecting the records is stored in pointer fields in one or both of the records.

Currently the database is memory resident and only supports one user or team at a time, though it supports merging of records from one database into another. Eventually we intend the RepTool to support simultaneous use of the shared database by multiple users or teams.

5.3.2 Graphic Views and Maps

To create a graphic representation the user can select an object and place it on a map. Objects can be moved, rotated, resized, duplicated, etc. Text labels can be added as can notes, which appear like a yellow post-it note and when clicked on open a separate window for longer comments. The display can be zoomed in or out.

Figure 5.3 is an example of a simple office map created with the RepTool. The circles represent people. Double clicking on the note labeled "Fieldnotes 9/22/97" would open a window containing the text of the fieldnotes.

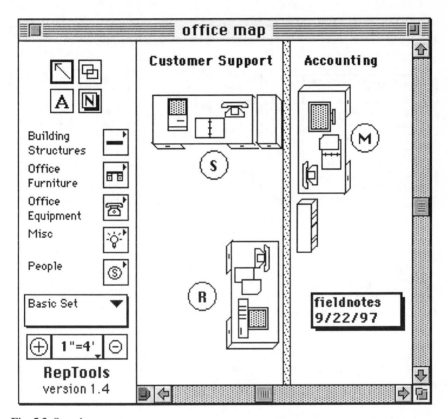

Fig. 5.3. Sample map

The RepTool currently comes with about three dozen predefined objects such as walls, desks, tables, telephones, computer terminals, and employees. When additional objects are needed they can easily be defined by the user. Objects are made up of simple drawing primitives such as lines, rectangles, ovals, arcs, polygons, and text. For those objects that are associated with a record in the database, the text displayed can be the value of one of the record's fields.

Each map is stored in a separate file and consists of a list of the objects in it and information on how these objects are to be highlighted (described below).

Slide shows can be constructed specifying a series of maps to display. Each "slide" specifies what part of the map to display, what scale to display it at and what highlights to use when drawing the objects and relationships between them.

5.3.3 Connection between the Database and Graphical Representations

After creating a database and a map the user can associate objects on the map with records in the database as shown in Fig. 5.4.

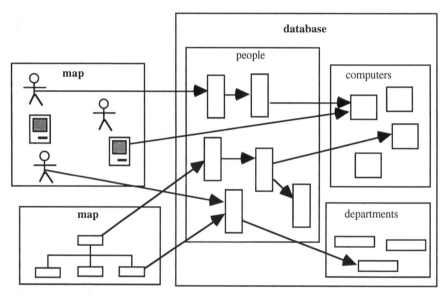

Fig. 5.4. Connecting maps and the database

These objects can then be connected by lines showing the relationships between the records they are associated with. For example, in Fig. 5.5, the lines show the flow of orders through four legacy computer systems. The single circle "R" shows a customer representative who must take orders from the SOP system and manually enter them into the WFA-D system—a potential bottleneck where system through-put might be improved.

The RepTool can selectively highlight objects based on the value of fields in the associated database record. This is done using a special highlight editor to specify the color to use and the record fields to examine. Using this editor both simple and complex queries into the database can be created. A simple example is shown in Fig. 5.6.

For example, we might highlight in red all those employees who have worked more than seven years for their company and highlight in green all those who have

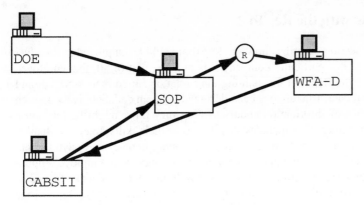

Fig. 5.5. Displaying relationships between objects

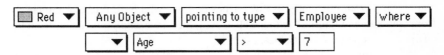

Fig. 5.6. Simple database query

worked there less than three years. Relationships can also be selectively displayed. For example, we might ask the tool to draw lines between each of the technicians and the people they go to for advice on technical problems; and specify to draw the line in red if the other person is also a technician and draw it in blue if the person is an engineer.

It is this ability to easily alter the graphic display based on the underlying database that distinguishes the RepTool from similar applications. Conventional drawing/presentation programs, such as PowerPoint or Visio, provide greater graphic possibilities, but the resulting representation is static (what you see is all you get). Geographical information system (GIS) software has an underlying database and can highlight objects, but cannot display or represent relationships between the objects. The RepTool can use the information in the database to both highlight objects and show relationships between them. As we continue to develop the RepTool we will be building on this strength to allow users to create new types of graphic representations based on information stored in the database.

5.3.4 System Requirements

The RepTool currently runs on Macintosh computers. We are looking into porting it to the PC. It is written in C++ using Symantec's Think Class Library. It requires at least 2 megabytes of memory.

5.4 Working with the RepTool

The following section describes how the RepTool could be employed in an advertising agency. In this particular company it is notable, first of all, that employees consciously use the RepTool for defining their relationship to their work community. The central data structure has been designed by them collaboratively and represents categories of information about anything they think might be relevant to their working together. This includes such things as their skills, likes and dislikes, past projects, education and professional background, hobbies and anything else they want their colleagues and management to know about them. Employees update their entries whenever changing interests and developing expertise make that advisable. They are free to fill in fields in templates or leave them empty. On occasion, there is a proposal to rename, delete, or add new record types and those decisions are always made collectively. The RepTool and its associated views of the company have proven especially useful for newcomers, who have profited immensely from being able to familiarize themselves with their new environment and from the challenge to represent themselves.

Beyond this mirror on the company, teams within the company also use the RepTool very effectively as a tool for generating shared views and organizing their thinking about particular issues as they come up. In the following sections we are going to look at the use of the RepTool in detail by exploring two different settings: The first shows potential RepTool use in a client-focused campaign in the agency; the second revolves around the ways in which the tool can support the planning and decision-making activities involved in the agency's day-to-day operations.

5.4.1 Supporting Teams in a Client-Focused Campaign

A team of five people plans to work on an advertising campaign for winning a new account. For the first meeting the following people are present: Andy Nord, head of the graphic design department, Loraine Martins, graphic designer, Marco Terrotti, the account manager, his assistant Marc O'Brian, and Lindy McShirly, an intern. The purpose of this meeting is to share what information they have individually, such as which people they know in the target organization, the work of the agency that has been in charge of the client's product campaigns so far, what kinds of campaigns the client prefers, and the like. It turns out that collectively they already hold a lot of information, but what they have resembles a patchwork quilt rather than a systematic data collection effort. In order to build a winning strategy it will be necessary to get a shared view on the situation. But which is the relevant data? The team engages in a lively discussion about what they need to know that they don't know yet and explore what skills and other resources they might need.

Working on the data already assembled, the group first tries to figure out which are the major issues they need to be concerned with. The first record type they make up in the RepTool's data structure concerns their potential client. They start to define several fields which are going to capture the client's profile: The name and address of the company, the type of business in which it is engaged, and other items are entered into the data structure. After this the team pulls down an organizational chart of the client's company to check if they already have contacts to anybody in important positions. It turns out there are two persons who they know already.

Marc O'Brian suggests creating a new record type named "contact persons" to gather information on this issue. But Andy Nord is opposed: He wants to be able to have a look at these data in close connection to the information concerning the client. Marco Terrotti proposes to connect the two records through a pointer field. A double click on this field would switch between the two records. Andy Nord agrees. The team goes on to discuss what kinds of information about contact persons might be relevant to their campaign and how to collect it.

After they have done this, they take a few minutes to look back on what they have accomplished so far and what they need to do next. Lindy McShirley asks "What about the client's former advertising? Who is our competition and what have they been doing?" Marco Terrotti proposes they analyze the three latest campaigns which everybody thinks is a good idea. For a few moments several people talk at the same time until Marco Terrotti intervenes with the suggestion to make up a new record type named "Former campaigns" which contains records for each campaign. Thus they would be able to gather information more systematically.

During their conversation, Loraine Martins has already scribbled down some ideas for the new campaign which she now presents to the group. A lively discussion starts. After a few minutes of brainstorming, the group has developed four competing ideas on how they might design their campaign. One member of the group proposes to make up a new record type named "envisioned campaign" in the central data structure to capture their ideas. This record type will be the template for the four proposals on what the envisioned campaign might look like. Again the team has to decide what information might be relevant to capture their emerging ideas. They decide to give a short description of the idea and to gather some data about the resources they would need for carrying it out. Marco Terrotti and Loraine Martins start to work on budget estimates for the different proposals. Finally, the team adds a comment field where they can collect further ideas as they emerge before their next face-to-face meeting.

The group is now about to finish their first session. Marc O'Brian raises the question of how they can make their strategy clear to people who are going to join the group in the future. After some silence Loraine Martins suggests making up a RepTool map to explain how they proceeded in building up their strategy. She sketches her idea on a piece of paper as she talks about it. The other team members think her sketch represents their ideas well and she maps it in the RepTool. Figure 5.7 shows the result.

The RepTool supports the process of systematic, collaborative data collection as it structures the course of discussion between team members. The team needs to discuss what information is important for their particular purposes in order to configure the tool's central data structure appropriately. When in former meetings the exchange of opinions and views had sometimes been chaotic as everybody had contributed what came into his or her mind, team members now try to fill in the

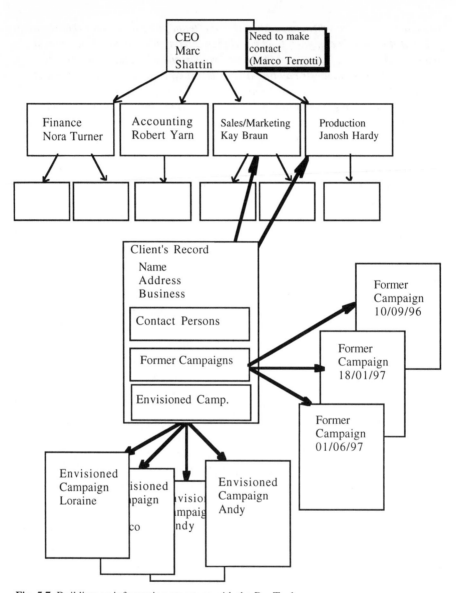

Fig. 5.7. Building an information structure with the RepTool

fields they have jointly defined as relevant. The RepTool supports the group in brain-storming ideas, organizing ideas, evaluating ideas, and as a result of theses activities, generating an outline for the envisioned campaign. It thus helps the group shift the character of their discussion from merely exchanging information to building up a shared view. Furthermore, as all records of a certain type share the same template, the RepTool supports the group in collecting data systematically. This allows the team to gain new views and insights, as it benefits not only from the analyses of each individual campaign but from a comparison between them.

In the future course of the project, the RepTool will enable them to share their data with people who could not attend the first meeting but who will carry out important tasks. Moreover, the RepTool makes the gathering of additional data more efficient and more systematic. If team members go out to visit the client, they can use RepTool-generated representations to check their perceptions of client needs with the client. In such sessions, the templates in the records will remind team members of the data they still need to collect. Finally, the resulting information collected by different team members, possibly at different times and in different locations, will be directly comparable. In fact, it will all go into a single database which will make it easy to share field data among team members. In the next session, team members' attached notes will be a good starting point for generating a joint discussion.

In the following section we will see how the RepTool supports people in running the advertising agency in its daily operations.

5.4.2 Supporting Operational Work

A few steps away from the conference room where our team is working on the outline of their emerging campaign, Robert Lurry, in charge of facilities, is sitting in front of his computer. He is studying space utilization on the second floor. The group of Andy Nord, the head of the graphic design department, has acquired several new members and thus needs more space. In the past, problems had occurred each time people and groups had to move. Sometimes they found that after the move they didn't have enough space to spread out their working tools in their new environment or additional cables had to be pulled through the whole building to give people access to their network. And often people complained after a move that they now had to cover long distances to maintain face-to-face contact with other teams they were collaborating with.

This time Robert is going to find out how Andy's group uses their current workspace and with whom they are collaborating before he is going to make any plans for moving them. The RepTool supports him in doing spot observations on the second floor and mapping them to see how the various work spaces are used and by whom. He also queries the central data structure to see which other groups Andy Nord's team is collaborating with. On the screen, he provisionally tries to move the graphic design department to the third floor and notices that this does not seem to be a good idea. As he had mapped all facilities to scale he can see that the cubicles on the third floor are too small to accommodate the technical equipment of the group. Furthermore, Andy Nord's group collaborates with a team of texters on the second floor, the people who create the text for his advertisements, so that makes a third floor location even more undesirable.

Robert looks for other possibilities and finally decides to make a proposal for moving the accounting department from the second to the third floor. He quickly sends email messages to several people: Andy Nord, Sandy Simmon, the head of

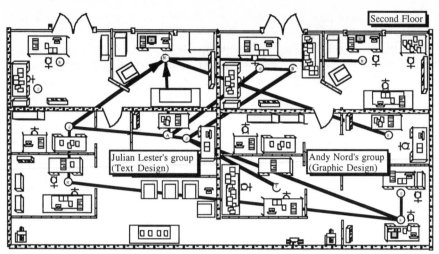

Fig. 5.8. Representing working relationships between people with the RepTool

the accounting department, and Alice Turner, the computing infrastructure analyst, asking them to pull up the proposed solution in a RepTool map and comment on it.

Alice Turner, the computing infrastructure analyst, routinely uses RepTool maps for resource analysis. She has just got Robert's mail and checks out if she has enough workstations for the new members of Andy Nord's team. She uses a map on which she can display all employees and all computer terminals and data structures. With the help of the map she wants to look at which computer systems Andy Nord's team uses. She starts a query with RepTool's highlight function. She first highlights all terminals on the second floor that are actually used by someone. She finds out that in one of the rooms there is a workstation nobody seems to be working on. In a second step she highlights on her map which databases can be accessed by this computer terminal and queries which databases the members of Andy Nord's team use. It turns out that the computer system is not connected to the databases Andy Nord's team uses. Alice attaches a note to the map referring to this and sends an email message to Robert to ask him about solutions. Maybe it would be easily possible to connect the free terminal with the server for the needed databases.

In the meantime Robert Lurry, the facilities man, got feedback on his proposal for the move. Andy Nord agrees, but Sandy Simmon, the head of accounting, is pretty upset about the idea of moving to the third floor. She claims moving would cost her department many days of work. Furthermore, she states that the art directors' clique is always given priority space whereas the work of her department is constantly underappreciated. She proposes that Robert Lurry himself with his staff should move to the third floor. Sandy also used RepTool maps to support her argument regarding the best solution to the space problem. Robert decides to arrange a meeting between himself, Andy Nord, Sandy Simmon, and CEO Leigh McMiller. In this meeting he wants to discuss the reasons why he thinks that moving the accounting group might be the best solution to solve their space problem. To support his argument he will also show other possibilities for moving people around the building, which seem to him to be even more undesirable than moving the accounting department. Robert prepares further maps and compiles them in a slide show. He hopes that it will be possible to eliminate some of the rancor that has been creeping into their exchanges by inviting everybody to a face-to-face meeting where they could refer to the objects on the map and the information associated with them. During their conversation, it will be possible to show different views and to highlight objects and show relationships according to the individual questions of each. Thus the RepTool might help to keep these discussion on a factual level and prevent them from getting personal and emotional.

As the RepTool provides its users with multiple views on the data they have collected, it merges the processes of data collection, data representation, and data analysis to expose patterns and relationships. RepTool's central data structure is designed to be shared amongst team members so that it also provides them with the ability to reflect on different data sets collected from similar environments, possibly by multiple investigators at different times, thus facilitating agreement on important patterns and relationships. It supports building an empirically grounded, shared view of the work practices, physical spaces, and social relationships that define the workscape. Thus it becomes a tool for learning in organizational team settings.

Even though our example dealt with an advertising agency, the RepTool is of course equally useful for other organizations that need to go beyond the official documentation of work processes to understand how work actually happens in real work situations. The following sections suggest other work environments in which the tool might be of use.

5.5 Using the RepTool

We believe that the RepTool would be extremely useful in all situations where a quick, principled, assessment of the important features of a work site is necessary. In particular, the RepTool allows representing the often neglected but nevertheless crucial informal aspects of work, such as who seeks advice from whom; who is collocated with whom; who went to the same school, and the like. Since the database is built up by the user with locally relevant information, it supports asking locally relevant questions. This gets us beyond the generic "plain vanilla" approach of most workflow tools. We anticipate that the RepTool could substantially improve the productivity of individuals and teams who need to make decisions for which a detailed knowledge of particular workscapes is essential.

Imagine the following situations:

– a sales team strategizing about a new account
– a group of software designers worried about an application's fit into users' ongoing work
– a facilities manager having to relocate several teams
– a sales team preparing for a new account presentation

- a department manager trying to figure out where to locate a new employee
- a reengineering team consolidating different functions in a central call center
- professional ethnographers collecting data in the field
- customer analysts reviewing customer needs
- management consultants preparing feedback to their clients
- real estate agents answering potential customers' questions about properties

5.6 RepToolian Visions: The RepTool in the World

5.6.1 Views of Knowledge and Knowledge Management

There appear to be two paradigms for knowledge management. The one that has the greatest currency at this point is concerned with managing information contained in some kind of depository or other, be that a set of electronic databases, a professor's collected lecture notes, or a company's archives going back 37 years stored in a stable that nobody dares dispose of because of fear of a law suit. This archival paradigm is well represented in corporate processes, management consultants' expertise, and a variety of tools. The second paradigm for knowledge management has to do less with the administration of existing information than with the creation of new knowledge and knowing practices and the construction of workscapes where knowledge is generated. This is management *for knowing* rather than management *of knowledge*. This kind of knowledge management to date is poorly understood and ill-supported by methods and tools.

Another productive way of thinking about the role of tools in knowledge management is to consider what sorts of knowledge and knowing practices are readily visible in an organization, are easily identifiable, and attract in general the greatest effort. In Table 5.1, they appear in quadrant one. They are concerned with all those things that information systems have dealt with since time immemorial, from accountants' ledgers to university libraries to training modules stored in three-ring binders and CBT modules. This quadrant is well supported by current information technologies, search engines, access control algorithms, and the like.

The second quadrant is concerned with what an organization knows it needs to know but doesn't currently, the knowing practices that deal with updates on the current state of the organization and its environment, market intelligence, information about suppliers, and so on. Here, too, we have fairly well established methods and tools.

The third quadrant becomes more problematic. It deals with what is there but often invisible to management and outsiders, the tacit knowledge present in communities of practice where the real work gets done. Given that the very existence of this kind of knowledge is overlooked in most organizations, there is little support for it except by default.

Finally, the fourth quadrant concerns the sphere of the unimaginable, the conditions and states an organization doesn't even know it might want to know about.

Beyond futures scenarios as a way to open up this dimension, there is no support there at all.

Table 5.1. Knowing and not knowing

	What we know	**What we don't know**
We know	**Answered questions:** what we know that we know (expertise in hand) – *Depositories* – *Archives* – *Data banks*	**Unanswered questions:** what we know that we we don't know ... but have ways of finding out about; expertise we know we have to get – *Market intelligence* – *State of the organization*
We don't know	**Unquestioned answers:** what we don't know that we know – *Local knowledge* – *Tacit knowledge and practice* – *Competence in invisible communities of practice*	**Unquestioned questions:** what we don't know that we don't know – *The unimaginable* – *The questions we never thought of asking* – *An evolutionary quantum jump*

The RepTool has a number of characteristics that allow it to address at least three out of the four quadrants and maybe even provide the foundation for productively thinking about the fourth. Let us summarize then, some of the ways in which the RepTool can support knowledge management.

5.6.2 RepToolian Data Collection: Systematic and Relevant

It is difficult to manage patchy, irrelevant data, though that is what most organizations have to deal with much of the time. The RepTool is designed in such a way that the categories for data collection have to be determined in each case by the analyst (or team of analysts) as they decide what information is important for their particular purposes. Since they themselves decide how to configure the tool appropriately (by setting up records and making templates), only data relevant to the group will be assembled. Given that the tool makes it easy to display which fields have no entries, it also becomes possible to see where data is lacking and to remedy that situation. The tool also eliminates duplication of effort since individual investigators' data structures can be merged so that all team members have access to the collective effort. Organizational theorists have long argued that practically all corporate data collection efforts suffer from too much data—data that is, to boot, often irrelevant and unlikely to get acted on (Feldman and March 1981). The RepTool enforces thinking through what might be required in a particular situation and then keeps track of the extent to which that goal has actually been achieved.

5.6.3 RepToolian Conversations

A central feature of the RepTool is that it easily produces electronic and paper representations that can act as conversational "boundary objects" (Star and Griesemer 1989); that is, they can support a variety of conversations among users, stakeholders, and outsiders who have an interest in the particular workscape and its issues. One great advantage is that the e-representations, viewed either on a screen or, for a larger audience, projected onto a wall, are "alive"; that is, if questions arise, it is easy to click on an object and pull up relevant contextual information from the data structure or to switch to a different view altogether. For presentations, a slide show can be assembled which has the same advantages.

Clearly, e-representations have the greater functionality, but we have found that even paper printouts of RepTool-generated views can be a powerful conversation stimulator that brings agreement to the surface and makes differing perceptions of reality visible for resolution. That is as true for internal discussions among analysts as it is for checking the quality of the information collected with inhabitants of the workscape.

The RepTool also facilitates participation of workers in the design process. On-site workers can be actively drawn into the data collection and analysis process through the representations created.

5.6.4 Support for Participatory Knowledge Management

Field conversations facilitated by RepTool maps provide important validity checks but also establish a relationship between analysts and the people in the workplace that gives workers a stake. In some cases they may become involved in data collection themselves, suggesting new records and fields and even taking over data entry. This gives the analyst a more valid, co-constructed picture while workers gain a comprehensive picture of their own worksite and begin to own the representations of their work as they are drawn into the data collection and analysis process. Workers thus acquire the necessary skills for documenting the realities of their own work and that of their peers, to represent *their* view of work practices, social relationships, and productivity impasses to relevant others such as managers, system designers, technologists, and decision makers.

Using the RepTool to its greatest benefit in organizational settings probably means giving employees continuous access to what information the central data structure contains about them, so they can update it with information they want their peers, managers, and the organization as a whole to have about them and the workscapes they are a part of. The RepTool thus can play an important role in generating a common, shared, and in some sense more "accurate" view of the distribution of resources and skills. It can generate shared knowledge about the state of the organization that is "owned" by the community as a whole, thereby building employee morale and involvement. Such a tool can also stimulate and enable conversations between different levels of the organization, from front-line workers to senior management, thereby nurturing cross-organizational conversations that build a shared view of current realities and necessary changes. For example, a printout of an organization's formal reporting structure juxtaposed to a worker-assembled view of informal leadership in the workplace may generate fruitful discussions about how these two kinds of structures can profitably interact.

As Senge et al. (1994) have proposed for dialogue, we would suggest that the RepTool can serve as a tool for improving organizations, enhancing communication, building consensus, and solving problems. As people work with the tool, they learn how to think together, not just in the sense of analyzing a shared problem, but also in the sense of occupying a collective sensibility in which the thoughts, emotions, and resulting actions belong not to one individual but to all of them together.

Acknowledgements

The RepTool was developed in a collaboration between IRL and Bell Atlantic (formerly Nynex Science and Technology).

Part IV

Communities of Knowledge Workers

6. An Environment for Cooperative Knowledge Processing

Wolfgang Prinz and Anja Syri
GMD, Sankt Augustin, Germany

This chapter describes the realisation of and experiences with two complementary tools for the support of cooperative processes: electronic circulation folders and shared workspaces. Circulation folders support structured work processes, shared workspaces provide a working environment for less structured processes. Both approaches are complementary and their combined usage provides new and very flexible ways of telecooperation and cooperative knowledge management. The components are integrated in the POLITeam system which is developed for the support of cooperative processes between the separated ministries in Bonn and Berlin.

6.1 Introduction

The CSCW research area has yielded numerous groupware applications for cooperation support. Most groupware applications focus on the support of special aspects of cooperative work, such as workflow coordination, document sharing, or video-conferencing. However, cooperative processes are not limited to a specific pattern. Thus, the integration of different groupware functionalities is needed to span and support a range of different cooperation patterns.

This chapter presents selected components of the POLITeam[1] system: electronic circulation folders to support workflows and shared workspaces to support document sharing. Electronic circulation folders offer a functionality similar to their concrete counterparts. Users can add documents to a folder, specify the path the circulation folder should take on its way through an organisation and forward it along this way. Circulation folders provide a good facility to support structured cooperation processes, but offer enough flexibility for exceptions and the support of ad-hoc workflows. Shared workspaces support less structured cooperation processes. They provide their users with a shared working environment, a place to store common working documents and tools. The seamless integration of both tools in a cooperation support system provides users with easy means to switch between both tools. Their combined application allows for new ways to structure and organize cooperative processes and knowledge management.

---

[1] POLITeam is funded by the German Federal Ministry of Education, Science, Research, and Technology in the POLIKOM framework. A general overview of POLITeam can be found in Klöckner et al. (1995).

The design of the POLITeam system is based on an evolutionary process, in close cooperation with selected pilot users working in a German federal ministry, a German state ministry, and for a car manufacturer. Starting with an existing groupware system the pilot users are supported by this system in their daily work. Their experiences are gathered, new requirements derived, and considered for the next design cycle. We will reflect this process in the course of this chapter.

First, we present an application scenario from the federal ministry. This provides an understanding for the environment in which the POLITeam system is used. Furthermore the scenario reveals requirements which have guided our developments. Then we introduce the POLITeam components electronic circulation folders and shared workspaces in more detail. We present a design concept for CSCW systems which supports the design of flexible CSCW systems allowing to combine different basic CSCW functionality and to provide the end-users with the possibility to configure this functionality. Finally we show how both tools allow for an easy switching between different work patterns and how their complementary use supports new work practices.

6.2 Application Scenario

This section considers the scenario of preparing a speech for the minister without computer based cooperation support. It is meant to provide an understanding for our application environment and we will use it later to derive design requirements for POLITeam.

The request for the speech is issued by the minister's office. Together with the request additional background information that is useful for the preparation of the speech is collected in a circulation folder. The minister's office addresses this folder to the head of the department responsible for the speech topic. It is also common practice that the minister's office already prescribes the sequence of addressees down to the unit level of the ministry.

Figure 6.1 illustrates that the processing of this request involves several hierarchical levels. The managers at the department and subdepartment level are each supported by a secretary, who performs additional tasks on incoming or outgoing documents. For example, this includes the sorting of incoming folders according to their priority, which is indicated by three different colours of the circulation folder. The manager at each level acknowledges the receipt of the folder, i.e. the speech request, and additionally provides comments or advice for further processing. As a speciality the comments and the signature are performed using a coloured pen. The colour corresponds to the role and position of the manager in the hierarchy.

Even though the subsequent addresses of the circulation folder are already predefined by the minister's office, the manager may reroute the folder or inform subsequent recipients about the process as the situation demands. Before the circulation folder is received by the units its contents is registered by the registry.

At the unit level of the ministry the speech is prepared in a cooperative process between different people of the same unit or different units. This process is

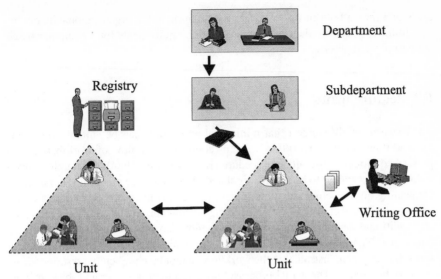

Fig. 6.1. The flow of a circulation folder in a ministry

not determined by any particular order. The person who initiates the cooperative process decides who should or must be involved in the production of a document, or whether contributions to the document are collected in a sequential order or in parallel. Members of the unit level are supported by a writing office that types the handwritten or audio-taped drafts they produce. The cooperation process is characterised by a frequent exchange of documents between the members and the writing office if the modification of a draft requires the production of new versions.

After the creation of a typed draft version, it is sequentially processed by the managers of the unit, sub-department, and department. Each manager reviews the speech and additionally annotates the document with own comments to the proposal. Before the proposal is forwarded to the next higher level the managers approve the cover note that is attached to the proposal with their signature. Again coloured pens are used for that purpose. If necessary the manager may return the proposal to the preceding recipients, but more often questions or comments to the proposal are discussed by phone.

After the proposal for the speech has been finally commented and approved by the minister or his assistants it contains a lot of handwritten comments. This document is then retyped by the writing office. Often its members use the previously stored draft version of the text and modify this according to the handwritten annotations on the paper document.

This scenario briefly discussed the major steps of the preparation of a speech for a minister. Although this describes just a special process out of large number of different processes that are handled by a ministry, it is typical in the sense that most processes are treated in the same way: a top-down processing of documents through the organisational hierarchy, a cooperative production of a document at the unit level, and then a bottom-up approval process through the organisational hierarchy. The following section identifies some essential requirements for a computer based support of such processes.

6.3 Requirements

The scenario might suggest that ministerial procedures can be suitably supported by workflow systems. Workflow systems coordinate the flow of work based on a prescribed model of the office procedure (Kreifelts et al. 1984). Although ministerial workflows appear to be strictly regulated, they cannot be predefined completely. Depending on the actual situation, the employees involved in a procedure may return the documents to the last station, change recipients, add an additional recipient, add additional documents, or temporarily remove documents to discuss them with colleagues. These are just a few examples of possible actions on a workflow document, but they demonstrate that the workflow cannot be completely prescribed from the very beginning. The actual processing of a circulation folder and the contained documents thus depends on the current situation. Therefore a workflow system that requires the complete prescription of a workflow and that does not allow the modification or circumvention of a given procedure would not be applicable for our purposes. As a primary requirement we can identify that a flexible coordination medium is required for the electronic support of ministerial workflows. The flexibility should encompass easy means for the modification of the workflow route and the ability to transport arbitrary documents that can be easily added and removed from the circulation folder.

Further requirements for the workflow support can be identified by a more detailed look at the document processing at the various steps. It happens that managers receive up to 30 or 60 folders, three times a day. In the case of documents that are further processed by the units this pile of folders is processed within 15–20 minutes. This requires that an electronic solution must provide means for a rapid browsing and annotation of documents. Documents that are produced by the units must be approved by the managers. This requires secure electronic signatures and the possibility to reconstruct the document history to identify the changes and annotations made by the managers at the different levels. To support the discussion of a document between a manager and a unit member it is feasible to include a video-conferencing and application sharing functionality. However, we do not assume that all processes will be handled electronically. In many cases a procedure will consist of electronic and paper documents. Thus, a solution for the combination of non-electronic media with the electronic information processing is necessary.

With regard to the cooperative production of documents by several members of the unit supported by the writing office, we can offer electronic support by providing shared workspaces. The scenario reveals several requirements that are to be considered here. The process involves different persons of the same unit or different units. Neither the persons who should contribute to the process nor the individual steps of the process can be prescribed in advance. The person who initiates the process decides on the participation. As a consequence a workspace should offer the possibility to declare a person to be "supervisor" of the workspace. This person is allowed to decide on the membership of the workspace and—since the membership is subject to changes—to invite new members or to exclude persons during the existence of the workspace. Nevertheless each member should have the possibility to finish participation and to leave the workspace. Furthermore the supervisor should be allowed to hand over privileges to another person.

The order of contributions to the cooperative process cannot be predetermined but follows from the activities of the cooperation partners. Therefore it is very important that each of them has access to the latest versions of the documents. The workspace provides its members with an environment where they can store all documents belonging to the cooperative process and access the documents worked on by their cooperation partners. By these means each person has the possibility to get an overview about ongoing activities and the progress of the cooperation.

The next sections present our approaches to satisfy basic requirements to the cooperation tools and some experiences with their use by the application partners.

6.4 POLITeam Solutions and Experiences

It is the primary goal of POLITeam to base the system design on requirements that are derived from user experiences with the actual use of a groupware system in a ministerial working environment. For this purpose it is necessary that a groupware system is available and used by the application partners that provides a basic support for the users cooperation needs. We have chosen LinkWorks, an object-oriented, client-server groupware product by Digital (LinkWorks User Manual, Digital 1995) as the start-system for the requirement analysis and as platform for our developments.

This process of implementing POLITeam at the pilot partners site started with the installation of a first basic version that provides general support for the individual and cooperative work. Based on the user participation the system is then iteratively enhanced to become more appropriate for the daily work and more specific for ministerial environments. A detailed description of this design in work practice and the methods that we apply can be found in a paper by Pankoke-Babatz et al. (1997).

The following section presents solutions for a flexible support of ministerial processes as described previously with the support of electronic circulation folders and shared workspaces.

6.4.1 Circulation Folders

POLITeam provides electronic circulation folders, similar to Karbe et al. (1990) as a flexible workflow coordination medium. It corresponds to the paper- circulation folder that is described in the previous application scenario as the document transport medium. With that cooperation tool we aim to support the cooperative processes in the ministry by the provision of a user tailorable cooperation medium and not by the provision of predefined cooperation mechanism (Bentley and Dourish 1995, Grudin 1994). More sophisticated workflow coordination mechanisms (Schael and Zeller 1993, Glance et al. 1996) are not applicable in this organisational environment since these would require an over-specification of the cooperation process.

The next section describes the basic functionality of the circulation folder. Afterwards we describe various extensions to this functionality to satisfy the specific needs identified previously.

Basic Functionality. The electronic circulation folder is capable of transporting arbitrary electronic documents, e.g. spreadsheets, presentations, audio, or video objects. It is fully integrated into the POLITeam electronic desktop. Users add or remove documents by simple drag and drop operations between the folder, the desktop, other folders, and containers. Access to the documents is controlled by access rights that determine the operations that users can perform on the folder (e.g. the removal or inclusion of new documents) and its contents (e.g. reading or modification of documents).

The route of the circulation folder is described with a configurable circulation slip. It sequentially lists all recipients of the circulation folder. If a specific workflow requires parallel processing of a document this can be expressed, too. The contents of the circulation slip can be modified easily by the recipients of the circulation folder. This allows users to react flexibly on situations that require a change to the described route of the circulation folder.

Figure 6.2 illustrates the symbolic representation of a folder on the desktop, its contents, and the attached circulation slip.

Extensions. The electronic circulation folder supports the flexible routing of arbitrary electronic documents. To satisfy the specific requirements of a ministerial environment a number of additional functionalities needed to be realised. These include electronic signatures, information about status and locality of a circulation folder, the integration with paper documents, an interface for fast browsing through a pile of folders, and the integration of a video conferencing system.

Electronic Signatures. The support of workflows that span different hierarchies requires a solution for secure signatures to electronic documents and the ability to reconstruct the complete history of modifications to a document made by the users involved in the workflow. In particular the latter is required to clarify responsibilities for political decisions. In POLITeam the secure authentication of signatures is realised by the integration of SecuDE, the Security Development Environment (Schneider 1993) into the base system LinkWorks. With the SecuDE integration it becomes possible to sign electronic documents with digital signatures according to the RSA technique (Rivest et al. 1978).

The user interface design of the electronic signature list adopts the structure of the cover note that is attached to each workflow. It supports the repeated commenting and signing of a text according to a signature list. This list contains the persons

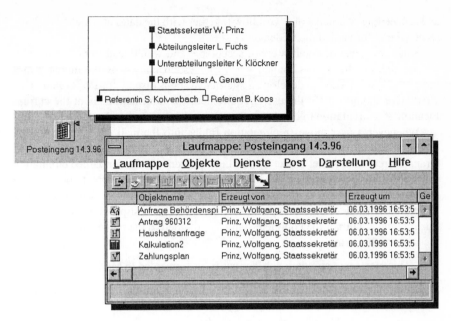

Fig. 6.2. An opened circulation folder and its circulation slip

who are expected to sign the document row by row. By selecting a row of the signature list that contains a signature, the version of the document is displayed that has been signed by the appropriate person. The repeatedly signed document is stored in different versions to ensure that the version a user has signed can be easily retrieved for control purposes. Thus a user who receives the document can ascertain the history of the document before the signature is performed. After a user has supplied his digital signature, his name, date, time and a comment are listed. The name of the signing person is read from a SmartCard that is used for the digital signature. This allows substitutes to sign a document and it indicates that a circulation folder has been processed via another route than the one that was specified when the signing process was initiated. The signature list is integrated with the electronic circulation folder such that it is ensured that all members of the signature list are automatically included into the circulation slip. Thus the members of the signature list determine the minimal contents of the circulation slip. It can be easily extended to include further or alternative recipients if this is demanded by the actual situation. A more detailed description of this solution can be found in (Prinz and Kolvenbach 1996).

Status and Locality. The capability of a workflow system to provide up to date information about the current state and location of a workflow is often considered as a major advantage compared to a paper based workflow processing. Our pilot users consider this functionality as very useful because they often perform time consuming searches for the current location of a folder. However, the detail of information that is provided by the standard LinkWorks workflow status window can be easily (mis-)used as a control instrument, because it provides a listing of the preceding and succeeding recipients of a workflow together with the dates at which users have received and forwarded the folder.

Since this level of detail was not acceptable and would lead to problems with the members of the works council when the system is used by the ministry in a larger scale, we needed to develop an alternative status display for POLITeam. This alternative should satisfy the users requirement for information about the current location of a circulation folder, but it should not display further details.

Whenever a user moves a circulation folder into the mail outbox, a so-called "shadow object" of that folder is created in the mail outbox. This shadow object wraps a circulation folder object by holding a reference to the forwarded circulation folder. Via this reference the shadow object can retrieve the current status of the circulation slip from the original electronic circulation folder. Thus whenever a user accesses the shadow object the status of the circulation slip is retrieved through this reference, but not the complete status is provided to the requesting user. Just a message of the form

"This electronic circulation folder has been forwarded to Mr. Smith"

is displayed. No further details are provided which can be misused as a control instrument.

Integration with Paper Documents. While POLITeam aims at supporting users working with electronic documents, it still has to provide support for documents printed on paper. As an example, it is necessary to deal with incoming non-electronic documents. We propose a different approach to integrate paper documents with the electronic system than the obvious scanning. Documents which it is not feasible to scan (e.g. books, large plans) are still distributed in a paper circulation folder as before. The only difference is that a bar-code label containing a reference number is attached to every circulation folder. Every time a user receives a circulation folder, he can easily find the corresponding electronic version by simply using a bar-code scanner in combination with a search tool integrated into the POLITeam environment. A circulation folder therefore consists of a non-electronic and an electronic part linked together by the bar-code. The two parts contain different documents, the first contains just the documents that are not available electronically, the second all others.

Ideally, the usage of electronic documents will increase over time when more users move towards using POLITeam for their daily work. We also expect that the preference of paper documents over electronic documents will change as soon as more departments are geographically separated.

Fast Browsing and Annotation of Process Documents. A department manager receives a pile of 30–60 incoming documents three times each day which are processed within 15–20 minutes. This indicates that an electronic support must provide means for a rapid browsing through electronic documents. Although the incoming documents will be of different types, e.g. scanned letters, fax, or email, the flow of work should not be disrupted by the need to start different applications for each document type.

Figure 6.3 presents an HTML-based interface for the presentation of and inter-action with electronic circulation folders (Gräther et al. 1997).

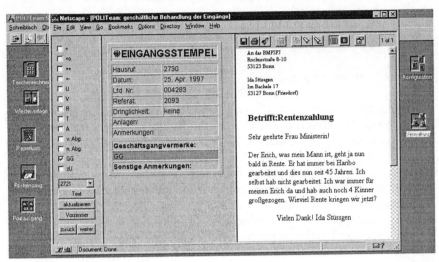

Fig. 6.3. The HTML interface for electronic circulation folders

This interface allows the browsing of incoming documents of different formats (right part), the provision of comments and advices for the further processing of the document (left part) and offers an overview of meta-information of the document, and comments provided by predecessors of the document (middle part). We have chosen an HTML-based interface that is enhanced by various Java applets since this provides flexible ways for the modification of document and workflow attributes and for the integration of viewers for different document types. Furthermore it allowed a design that is close to the appearance of the paper based process documents.

Integration of a Video Conferencing System. The main goal of POLITeam is the support of asynchronous cooperation. However, the application scenario identifies a need for the provision of tools that allow synchronous discussion of documents. In particular users at the management level that is still located in Bonn demanded a support function that allows the discussion of documents with members of units in Berlin. This support function has been realised by integrating a commercially available video conference and application sharing system that is based on ISDN or LAN connections into the POLITeam system. This provides a basic means of communication, e.g. to clarify questions arising during the processing of documents contained in an electronic circulation folder.

A more sophisticated integration which includes a customised access to the video system from various components of the POLITeam system is currently under development. This will allow users to record video sequences and to include these as video-objects in the electronic circulation folders. Effectively, this provides a simple form of video mail.

In this section we presented the design of an electronic circulation folder that integrates various extensions as a tool to support ministerial workflows. The following section describes the functionality and experiences with shared workspaces, a complementary cooperation tool.

6.4.2 Shared Workspaces

Whereas electronic circulation folders are mainly used to support structured cooperation between the different levels of the hierarchy, shared workspaces (Agostini et al. 1996) support the cooperation among members of a unit or different units and the writing office. The POLITeam workspace provides its members with a virtual space for cooperation and communication. We differentiate between a person responsible for the workspace and "ordinary" members. For initialisation the user creating the workspace is responsible for it, but may delegate this task to another member of the workspace. Only the responsible person is allowed to invite new members to the workspace or to exclude an existing member by withdrawing the share. The decision to leave a workspace is left to each member.

Since the coordination of the activities within a workspace is not prescribed, it is important that other means of coordination support are integrated into the workspace. The POLITeam notification and information service provides its members with shared feedback about ongoing and past activities of their cooperation partners as far as cooperation issues are concerned (Sohlenkamp et al. 1997). This information allows the members to react on the activities of each other. An integrated video conference tool facilitates further coordination of asynchronous activities and even allows the transition to synchronous cooperation. The integration of task lists allows the imposition of more structure on the cooperative process by introducing subtasks and assigning responsible persons to these tasks. The following sections give an overview of the different design cycles for the shared workspace component we ran through in the POLITeam project.

As described earlier, the development of the POLITeam system is based on the groupware product LinkWorks. In order to share a document with someone else, the user creates a share (which is a further access point, a handle to the object) to the document and sends this via e-mail to the user to be invited. Using the original LinkWorks solution, the user gets no information about who else has got a share to the object. Members that have once been invited cannot be excluded from the cooperation process afterwards. They even have the possibility to invite further members. Since this procedure is very difficult to explain to users that are not familiar with the underlying mechanism, we decided to hide it and provide our users with a different interface to the sharing facility. Different design rationales were important to us: the sharing functionality should

– be easy to understand and easy to use,
– allow the transition from single-user objects to shared objects, therefore no explicit shared workspace objects were introduced,

- focus on the sharing of container objects which contain further objects that are accessible to different cooperation partners and
- allow limiting the shared usage to a certain period of time.

The shared workspace component was designed and developed according to these requirements. The user of the POLITeam system can select an arbitrary container object on his desk and specify the users that are to be invited. If the access right to the container object does not allow a cooperative usage, the user is notified by the system and gets the chance to assign a suitable access right. The invited persons are notified about the invitation and find a share to the object in their mail inbox. They can move the icon representing the object to their preferred location on their personal desk. A special dialogue (shown in Fig. 6.4) tailored to the needs of our users informs them about who else is using the workspace.

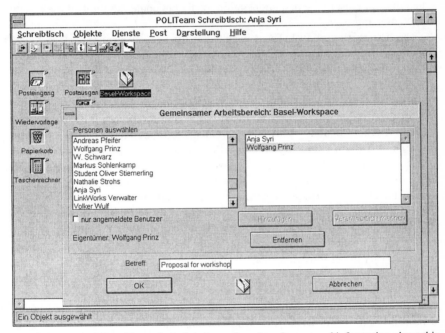

Fig. 6.4. A typical POLITeam desk showing a shared workspace and information about this workspace

Different design alternatives were discussed within the group of designers: *What is the best place to hand over a shared object to a new member?* Two locations were discussed: the personal desk or the mail inbox. Placing a new object share on the desk of the user did not seem to be appropriate because of two reasons. First it results in modifying his personal desk and second it might be difficult for the user to detect the workspace on the desk. We decided in favour of the mail inbox being an entry point for incoming documents and equipped with a notification facility that announces changes to the user.

What is the best place to place a shared object? Here again the same problem occurs: when a user moves a shared object into a private container on his desk. The exclusion of the workspace member by the responsible person is no longer possible, since this would result in a modification of the private container. We decided not to restrict the users in their interaction with the system, but recommended not to store shared objects in private ones. The rest is left to the social protocol.

Extensions to Shared Workspaces. At the beginning of the POLITeam project we interviewed our application partners. These interviews helped us to get into closer contact with them and to gain some insight in their daily work. The answers to our questions should help to configure the first version of the system. Being asked if they could imagine using electronic circulation folders or shared folders, the users stated their interest in the first cooperation media but could not think of the benefit of the latter approach.

The first version of POLITeam installed at the sites of our users offered electronic circulation folders as well as some predefined shared folders. The shared folders were used to exchange documents between the unit and the writing office. The first experiences with these shared folders revealed two things. First, the users made use of these folders and discovered the advantages despite their disapproval of the shared workspace approach stated in the first interviews. This shows how difficult it is to articulate needs or requirements without having the possibility to experiment with a system (Kyng 1994). Second, the interaction of the users with the shared workspaces showed that they were not really aware of the shared usage. Some users moved documents out of the shared folder in order to edit them on their personal desk, not realising that their cooperation partners had no longer access to these documents.

The next version of the workspace component provided the users with an easy facility to create new workspaces. Additionally the members of the workspace had the possibility to get more information about the state of the workspace. After the installation of this version and some months of usage, we discussed the component and their experiences in a workshop. A vivid discussion revealed that our application partners required some conventions that frame their usage of shared workspaces (Mark and Prinz 1997), as the following examples show.

Editing documents within a workspace. The application partners committed themselves to edit exclusively within the workspace in order to overcome the problems mentioned above.

Deletion of documents. Since the deletion of a document affects all members of the workspace, the application partners decided in favour of the following policy: Only the owner of a document is allowed to delete a document. One has to inform the other members of the workspace about this intention by mail and is only allowed to continue if no objection is raised within a certain amount of time.

Structuring the contents of a workspace. Since different persons have different preferences concerning the structure of a container, it is difficult to specify a common structure for shared workspaces. Whereas members of the units want to structure the workspace according to the different work processes, the writing office is mainly interested to gain an overview of the different types of texts at first sight. Furthermore there are different preferences according to the hierarchical structure of a workspace: whereas some members of the unit prefer to store all documents on the top level of the workspace, others like to make use of deep hierarchical structures.

These examples show that the introduction of a groupware system not only requires training of persons on the functionality of the system, but additionally analysing work processes, making cooperative processes visible to the users, and showing how these processes can be supported electronically.

Our system should not only consider and realise the conventions mentioned above but offer a range of conventions. Different policies preventing the users from misusing the system are possible. Activities (as moving a document out of a shared workspace) can be forbidden, accompanied by a dialogue box making the user aware of the consequences, or handled in a different way (e.g. creating a copy of the document within the workspace). These examples show that it must be possible to configure the behaviour of shared workspaces to reflect the usage patterns and conventions of a group. The next section introduces a design concept that allows to configure shared containers and to bind a specific set of conventions to them.

Design Concept. In order to react on upcoming new requirements the underlying system has to allow stepwise refinement of functionality and offer possibilities for configuration. A comparison of the development cycles of the two different cooperation tools, electronic circulation folders and shared workspaces, shows that extensions to the basic components are of different nature. Circulation folders were mainly extended by further functionality, such as electronic signatures or the HTML interface. The usage of shared workspaces has demonstrated the necessity for means that allow a flexible configuration of their behaviour.

The object-oriented paradigm promises to support software design of complex systems since it allows encapsulation of functionality into objects. Reusability of functionality is supported by the mechanisms of inheritance and polymorphism. Several groupware systems are developed in an object-oriented programming language. Their underlying class hierarchy contains classes that support individual work practices (like documents, filing facilities, or tools) as well as classes that support cooperation among the involved partners (as circulation folders or shared workspaces). Some of these groupware systems provide a programming interface to their functionality. The design of specific cooperation support functionality within such a system is usually done by refining these basic classes in derived classes. This approach reveals several disadvantages: Every implementation of a specific cooperation tool results in the extension of the class hierarchy. A flexible reaction to new user requirements is only supported when the underlying programming language allows modification of the class hierarchy during runtime of the system.

In the following we propose a different approach which is mainly based on the object-oriented concept of composition. This approach provides an infrastructure that allows to enrich the functionality of object instances. The main components are

- *CSCW enablers* which are service objects that provide basic cooperation support functionality and
- *CSCW mediators* that encapsulate the interaction of enables attached to an object.

The functionality of an object (like a container) can be configured and extended by attaching enablers to the object that realise additional cooperation support functionality. The mediators role is to administer all enablers belonging to the target object.

The concept offers a broad range of cooperation support functionality each encapsulated in enablers. Just to mention some examples, there are enablers that provide communication facilities or support coordination among different users of the object. This can be done by explicit methods (like access control and locking) or implicit methods (like awareness mechanisms). Further enablers support object sharing or are used to introduce conventions into the system.

Regarding the example of a shared workspace mentioned earlier, a container object designed for the "single-user-case" can be realised with the help of different enablers:

- an access control enabler controls access to the container,
- a member administration enabler allows to invite new members or exclude current members,
- a communication enabler provides communication facilities,
- an event enabler notifies current members of the workspace about ongoing events,
- a history enabler records past events,
- a shared workspace (sws) enabler informs users about the "publicity" of further actions after having entered the workspace,
- a privacy enabler suppresses information about private modifications of objects in the object history,
- a "create-a-share" enabler is activated when a user drags objects out of the container. It informs the users that removing objects out of the container results in withdrawing access for the other members and proposes to automatically leave a share to the object in the container.

Figure 6.5 shows how the invocation of the add-method of the container object is delegated to the different enablers via the mediator (numbers indicate the sequence of calls). As the example shows, some enablers are activated before the method on the target object are called (like access control). The method on the target object is only invoked in case of a positive result of these pre-processing enablers (access is granted and the user has confirmed the entrance of the shared workspace). Other enablers should only be activated when the method on the target object succeeded (as event notification).

One part of the enabler interface is constant: this part corresponds to the interface of the enabled objects. Its methods specify how the semantic of object methods

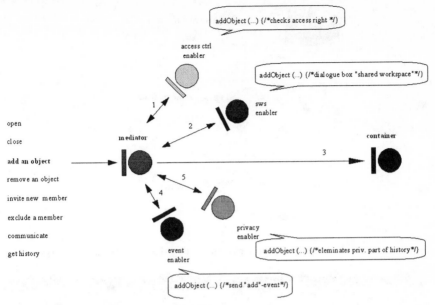

Fig. 6.5. Enablers attached to a container object

on the target object are enriched. They therefore allow specification of cooperation support functionality to specific access situations (when someone opens a document, modifies the document, etc.).

Enablers can enrich the functionality (e.g., by sending an event notification), stop execution of the called method (when access is not granted) and invoke new methods.

We introduce the CSCW mediator as the component which encapsulates the interaction of the different enablers. Whenever a method on the target object is called this call is first delegated to the mediator. The mediator maps the incoming method call onto a corresponding method of the enabler interface and iterates through all enablers attached to the target object. Since a modification of the target object also results in a modification of its context, the mediator takes this context into account. Figure 6.6 shows the example of deleting a document within in a shared workspace. The deletion of a document results in removing the document from its context formed by its containers. The mediators invoke the corresponding enablers.

This concept allows the configuration of the cooperation support functionality on different levels: the introduction of further enablers allows to adapt system functionality to the work setting, the combination of enablers allows to configure a target object and by deactivating single enabler methods, more fine-tuning can be done.

Figure 6.7 shows the configuration dialogue to attach enablers to target objects. This dialogue, too, allows the configuration to be made visible to every user that has access to this object. In this way, the behaviour of the shared workspace is not

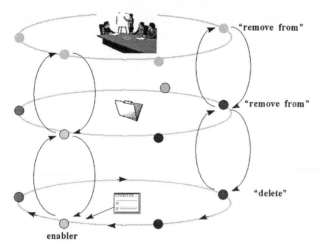

Fig. 6.6. Enablers of a target object (memo) and its containers (folder, shared workspace)

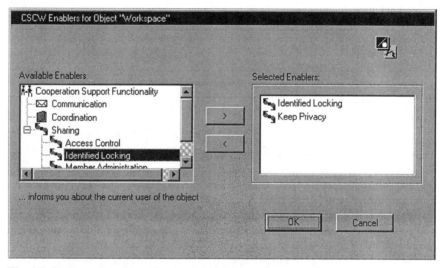

Fig. 6.7. Configuration of an object by combining enablers

hidden anymore in the system but is made apparent to its users. Further information is given by Syri (1997).

The example has shown how a shared workspace can be realised with this design concept. The introduction of further coordination supporting enablers may even introduce a turn-taking mechanism and to-do lists in the workspace. With this mechanism we can realise the complementary use of circulation folders and shared workspaces that is proposed in the next section.

6.4.3 Integrated Use of Both Cooperation Tools

Having introduced both cooperation media—electronic circulation folders and shared workspaces—this section shows how both tools complement one another.

The cooperation media realised in the POLITeam system provide each support for a certain type of work process. However, the scenario shows that both types of work are interweaved. For example documents received by a circulation folder need to be discussed or must be supplemented with contributions from others. Thus, both electronic cooperation media must provide easy means to switch between each other and to exchange documents. The combination of both tools provides further possibilities to structure and organize cooperative processes. In the following we will illustrate how shared workspaces can be extended by electronic circulation folders and vice versa.

Electronic Circulation Folders Structure the Work Flow in a Shared Workspace. Two application areas exist for this. Let us first consider a group that coordinates the production of a document by the use of a shared workspace. Although each member of the group wants to have unlimited read access to the documents in the workspace, they want to coordinate the modifications to the document. This is important when the task requires a sequential order of activities because the input of one user depends on the input of the precessor. To achieve this a share to the document is placed in an electronic circulation folder. The circulation folder is then routed between the members of the workspace (Fig. 6.8, left side). By convention or by the configuration of appropriate access rights, only the user who currently accesses the circulation folder is allowed to modify the documents. With this application the circulation folder provides a turn-taking mechanism for cooperation within the shared workspace.

Fig. 6.8. Circulation folders route workspace documents

The same technique can be used to involve people who should not receive full access to the whole workspace. In this case, shares to relevant documents of the workspace are added to a circulation folder and forwarded to the person not being member of the workspace. This allows the use of both tools on the same document to distinguish between users who have unlimited access (the workspace members) and users who receive only limited, sequential access, e.g. for approval processes. This is illustrated in Fig. 6.8, right side. It shows the participants involved in the process who are coordinated by the electronic circulation folder and how selected documents are processed by additional participants.

Electronic Circulation Folders Extend Shared Workspaces. A circulation folder can be added to a workspace in order to involve persons for a limited period of time and ask them for a certain contribution. This allows further persons to become involved without affecting the circulation path. The sequential cooperative process is extended and cooperation on the content of the circulation folder can take place in parallel (see Fig. 6.9).

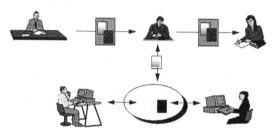

Fig. 6.9. Extending the sequential flow of a circulation folder by a shared workspace

For example this enables a user to share a received circulation folder with other users. These are then able to contribute documents that provide additional information to the process. By the provision of a temporary common access to the previously sequential medium, an acceleration of the process can be achieved, if the sequential order is not required at this stage of the process.

Furthermore this technique can be used to give read access to a person during the complete flow of the circulation folder, not limiting the access to a certain stage of the folder. This provides an overview of the ongoing activities.

In this section we have discussed the combined usage of the two POLITeam cooperation media. It is interesting to see that this combination maps to the four modes of knowledge conversion proposed by Nonaka and Takeuchi (see Fig. 1.2, p. 6).

Workspaces can be seen as a "free" field of interaction. They allow the users to "socialize" around a process and also to move the tacit knowledge to explicit knowledge. This requires means for the externalization that are provided by the elctronic circulation folder. Thus the workflow component can be regarded as a means of enacting the explicit knowledge contained in the process maps of organizations.

The first example can be seen as using the circulation folder to move from tacit knowledge (every one in the shared workspace knows how the documents have to be produced in terms of content structure and approvals) to explicit knowledge in a circulation folder describing which are the steps the documents must follow in the organizational structure. The second example allows to add to the process a space where to externalize further tacit knowledge not described by the explicit procedure described in the circulation folder.

6.5 Summary

This chapter focussed on the two cooperation media provided by POLITeam: electronic circulation folders and shared workspaces. Whereas the first medium is especially suited to support structured work processes, the latter can be used for less structured ones.

We have presented a ministerial application scenario and shown that most cooperative processes embrace structured as well as unstructured parts. In order to provide suitable cooperation support, both cooperation forms have to be considered.

We have shown that electronic circulation folders and shared workspaces are complementary. Circulation folders can be used to structure subtasks within shared workspaces and to ask non-members for a contribution. Shared workspaces allow to interrupt the flow of a circulation folder for a while and to do work in parallel.

The combined usage of circulation folders and shared workspaces allows a smooth transition between structured and less structured processes. Together they offer a very flexible support of cooperative processes and provide new means for the organization of cooperative processes. Although the requirements for the development of the basic tools as well as the various extensions were derived from the practical use of the POLITeam system in a German Ministry, we believe that the solutions presented are applicable for other applications of cooperative knowledge management too.

Acknowledgements

We give special thanks our POLITeam collegues and to the reviewers for their valuable comments on this chapter.

7. Ariadne: Supporting Coordination Through a Flexible Use of Knowledge Processes

Carla Simone[†] and Monica Divitini[‡]
† Universita' di Torino, Italy
‡ Norwegian Univ. of Science and Technology, Gloshaugen, Trondheim, Norway

Knowledge of the cooperative work processes characterizing an organization is a fundamental patrimony not only for people involved in their automation but also for the whole organization in performing its everyday activities. This chapter focuses on workflow technology as a set of tools both supporting coordination and enhancing management of the knowledge of work and learning processes within a group of people coordinating their own activities. We present a framework for the construction of coordination mechanisms whose design principles and tools make them a technology enabling the sharing of knowledge about processes and the incremental learning of people within the organization. These claims are illustrated through a working example.

7.1 Introduction

Workflow technology has been proposed as a means to support cooperation in terms of coordination of activities and exchange of information and documents. Since its appearance it has been questioned because of its rigidity, inability to adapt flexibly to changes in the surrounding organization and relative demands. Thus from initial proposals focused on the definition of strictly formalized work processes (e.g. Kreifelts et al. 1991b) and the first generation of commercial workflow management systems) the trend shifted toward proposals based on the opposite idea: namely, questioning the suitability of work processes formalization, as if everything was an unique event needing to be re-defined every time it occurs (e.g. Kreifelts et al. 1993, Fuchs et al. 1995, Trevor et al. 1993, Fitzpatrick et al. 1996). The latter proposals provide little support to process definition in the hypothesis that one shared working space can be sufficient. More recently, other authors have been tackling the problem by proposing specific process representations claiming that they are suitable for the users or for at least adequately supporting flexibility (e.g. Shepherd et al. 1990, Kaplan et al. 1992, Malone et al. 1992, Swenson et al. 1994, Glance et al. 1996, Dourish et al. 1996). We consider the above extreme positions equally inadequate in dealing with real user needs: this point has been raised and sharply discussed by Bowers et al. (1995) and Schmidt (1997). Our position is somewhere in-between (see also Chapter 6), not because we look for a simplistic or opportunistic compromise, but because we believe that serious consideration of the position supporting diverse user needs demands technology flexibility above all in relation to users' capabilities and interests. We examine this in greater depth here below.

First of all, the term "user" is often taken as a stereotype characterizing users either as naive actors incapable of doing anything with the work processes and related technology, or as skilled actors very efficient in organizing their work in cooperation with colleagues and in designing the related technology. Obviously, we are considering here not minor short-term activities but work processes where the coordination effort is constitutive by nature. Our first claim is that users are of different kinds, possess different skills and cultures, have different interests and attitudes, play different roles within the organization. Moreover, the above properties may be related to the work process at hand: that is, each (instance of the) work process might define different values of these properties. Finally, the above properties can change according to the evolution of the user experience in participating in organization life. In other words, the users are embedded in a continuous learning process in which they participate with different moods, possibly in a discontinuous way, but in which they must participate if they want to feel part of the organization's social system. Thus the technology, and in particular the systems supporting the coordination and execution of work processes, should be conceived of and designed neither as a prescriptive set of rules (possibly to be violated) nor as a tool to build ad hoc supports for temporary or specialized situations. On the contrary, it should be conceived of as a tool enabling the above mentioned learning process. This is the specific viewpoint from which we approach the theme of knowledge management within organizations. In fact, we are aware that it is impossible to deal with all aspects at the same time: they are too many, involve too broad a range of disciplines and tools for managing their inherent complexity. We focus on the knowledge managed by people when dealing with the coordination of their work processes: a specific component of people's work that has been called *articulation work*. In so doing, we focus on how the technology supporting articulation work can serve as an enabler, among the other technologies and organization strategies, of the mentioned learning process.

The second point is that the technology can play this strategic role if it is based on some design principles that make it a flexible and useful tool. By adopting the evocative terminology used by Bowers et al. (1995), the introduction of workflow technology requires us to find a delicate balance between a *from within* and a *from without* the work process perspective in its design. The former perspective puts emphasis on the current work practices, the latter on the organization demands relative to what the authors call *(inter-organizational) accountability*. This consideration leads to the definition of a basic requirement for the technological support: namely, the capacity to take into account both perspectives and their interaction in a flexible way, that is, allowing for a dynamic shift of the borderline between the two. Our approach tries to fulfill this requirement by providing the means for *partial specification* and *incremental design* of the work process support. These means have strong relationships with organizational knowledge management, in terms of both memory and learning. In regard to memory, partial specification allows the organization to record and make available the conditions of satisfaction a work process has to meet in order to be harmoniously inserted in its environment. These conditions are what make the actors safe in their work as they constitute a frame of reference where their autonomous choices are not source of problems for other organizational components. On the other hand, incremental design is what makes autonomous choices possible, because in addition to the specification of information that cannot be anticipated before the actual process instantiation it allows actors to select the operational behavior most suitable to the contingent situation according to the local working practices. We must emphasize that this view is not based on the unrealistic hypothesis that the interplay between constraints and autonomy is an easy achievement. To the contrary, as anticipated, it is the outcome of a dynamically adaptive process in which the necessary choices within the possibility space induce a recurrent re-thinking, sometimes a re-negotiation, which is the stimulus and outcome of a continuous learning process (see also Chapter 2). An effective and timely shift of borderline between constraints and autonomy can be made possible by other two basic requirements: on the one hand, the tools for the partial definition and incremental design of the workflow support are under actors' control; on the other hand, this control is governed by the actual network of organizational responsibilities. In turn, these requirements imply the full *accessibility* and *visibility* of the tools by the actors, and the capability of the tools to take into account the dynamic relationships between the work process and its *organizational context*. The latter is another type of information entering the organizational memory associated to the work processes. The main issue here concerns the way in which the organizational context plays an active role not only in the execution of the work processes but also in the evolution of their definition and instantiations. Finally, the focus on the work practices and the need for continuous adaptation in the various interpretations illustrated above have an impact on the internal structure of the work process support. First of all, the workflow technology is based on the modularity and compositionality of the various work process components, at any level of granularity, in order to govern the modifications and their impacts. Secondly, these components are identified so as to make sense to the actors using them. That is, they are not generic (low level) objects; instead, they are *categories* at the semantic level of *articulation work*. Lastly, the technology supports the interoperability between components, at their different levels of aggregation, by providing *communication primitives* supporting both articulation work and interoperability. These principles have been incorporated in a computational notation, called Ariadne; and in its implementation in a multi-agent architecture, called ABACO. Through a working example we illustrate how the features of Ariadne can be used for designing coordination mechanisms able to enhance the management of knowledge related to processes and the process of learning within the group of people coordinating their activities. We conclude with a short description of the implementation of Ariadne in ABACO.

7.2 Ariadne: A Description of the Framework

The conceptual framework underlying Ariadne has been presented by Schmidt and Simone (1996). Ariadne's notation has been described in detail by Simone et al. (1995) and Divitini and Simone (1996), where a comparison with other approaches can be found. Since the focus here is on how Ariadne can be used in supporting users with varying needs and experiences within the organization, we briefly sum up the used terminology (see Fig. 7.1) and move on to how this framework can be used for the construction of flexible workflow systems.

Cooperative Work is constituted by the interdependence of multiple actors who interact through changing the state of a common field of work.

Articulation Work is constituted by the need to restrain the distributed nature of complexly interdependent activities.

Cooperative Work Arrangement: an ensemble of actors engaged in a cooperative effort in relation to a common field of work.

Field of Work: the part of the world affected by actors work; in the case of a computational coordination mechanism, the data structures and functionalities of the application.

Coordination Mechanism (CM): an integral construction consisting of a coordinative protocol and of an artefact in which the protocol is objectified.

The protocol: an integrated set of procedures and conventions which stipulate the articulation of distributed interdependent activities. The protocol reduces the complexity of articulating cooperative work by providing a precomputation of task interdependencies which actors for all practical purposes can rely on to reduce the space of possibilities.

The artefact is an information structure which objectifies the protocol and gives permanence to the coordinative protocol so that its stipulations are publicly accessible. The artefact of a coordination mechanism represents the state of the execution of the protocol and serves as an intermediary between actors that mediates information about state changes to the protocol. The material format of the artefact conveys stipulations and provides a "shared space", structured according to key aspects of the protocol, for mediating changes to the state of the protocol.

Computational Coordination Mechanism (C^2M): a software device in which the artefact *as well as* (aspects of) the protocol of a coordination mechanism are incorporated in such a way that changes to the state of the protocol induced by one actor are conveyed by the computational artefact to other actors according to the protocol.

Fig. 7.1. Key concepts of the Ariadne framework (Divitini et al. 1996)

Ariadne provides the designer of workflow systems with features that are described in the following sections where the different elements of Ariadne will be presented in a frame-like notation. In the frames, words in italics denote concepts that will be described in subsequent sections.

7.2.1 The Notion of Coordination Mechanism

The notion of Coordination Mechanism (CM) is the unit of analysis of the target reality and the corresponding Computational Coordination Mechanism (C^2M) is the unit of technological support of the target workflow system. These notions represent a first step toward the fulfillment of the adaptability requirement which is at the basis of a creative use of the technology. First of all, the notion of Coordination Mechanism drives the designer to pay attention to the current work practices, in terms of both protocols and (paper-based) artefacts actors have invented to manage the complexity of the articulation of the activities they are involved in. Then the technological support is built on top of these practices. Secondly, the concept of C^2M allows the designer to tailor the target system into sub-systems in a way that makes sense to the actors as these sub-systems are identified from the work practices around artefacts. Thirdly, the inherent modularity and the related communication requirements give the target system a structure suitable for supporting its partial specification and incremental design. According to the definition in Fig. 7.1, a C^2M can be specified as in Table 7.1.

Table 7.1. Specification of computational coordination mechanism

Attribute name	Attribute type
name	Identifier
Active artefact	*Informational structure*
Protocol	*Partial order relation* $\subseteq$ CAW $\times$ CAW
Under the responsibility of	Role
Defined by	<Role, policy>
Adapted by	<Role, policy>

The attribute "under the responsibility of" specifies the Role responsible for the activation of the mechanism. The attributes "defined by", "adapted by" specify by whom and in which way the mechanism is defined and modified. A policy can be either a set of rules or an invocation of another C^2M. These attributes define the organizational constraints to modifications. The type of the attributes "active artefact" and "protocol" has to be understood as references to appropriate frames that will be presented later on.

7.2.2 The Categories of Articulation Work

The components of a C^2M are expressed in terms of categories of articulation work (CAWs) (which are shown in Fig. 7.2 together with their semantic relations); and of some formal relations which are expressed as a special interpretation of graphs to represent non-deterministic relations, and of partial-orders to express causal relations among CAWs. The set of basic elements was derived from studies of how artefactually imprinted protocols are designed and used by actors in everyday work activities, as reported by Schmidt and Simone (1996). They represent the minimal set of elements required to express the C^2Ms examined in these field studies. However, it must not to be considered as definitive: it can be enriched if and when new needs emerge from the experimental use of the notation. Distinguishing the CAWs according to their *nominal* and *actual* status (as indicated in Fig. 7.2) identifies categories pertaining respectively to the definition and specification of C^2Ms. This distinction plays a role in adaptability: in fact, the *nominal* status defines the categories in order to express the constraints to what can be dynamically and incrementally specified by means of the *actual* status categories.

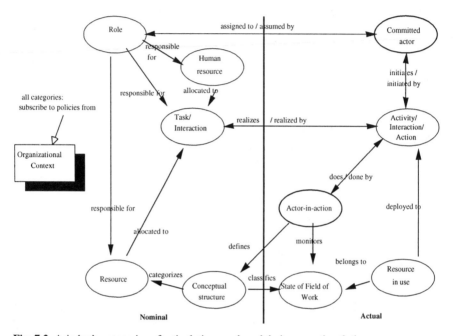

Fig. 7.2. Ariadne's categories of articulation work and their semantic relations

As for the formal relations, the field studies show that the possibility of representing relationships among entities is central to a notation for the design of CMs: e.g., causal relationships among tasks in workflows, part-of relations in classification schemes and so on. The literature provides several types of formalisms that serve exactly the purpose of expressing such relationships in an unambiguous way. At the current stage Ariadne contains the following relational structures: labeled graphs, as a very general purpose formalism to represent non-deterministic relationships; labeled AND/OR-graphs and different classes of labeled Petri nets, as a way to represent causal relationships in presence of concurrency (Bernardinello and de Cindio 1992). All are grounded in a sound mathematical theory providing algorithms for animation, simulation and analysis that can be exploited in the construction of a C^2M. All structures have associated labeling functions to express the interpretation of their constitutive elements, mainly in the set of categories of articulation work (CAW). We briefly describe a class of labeled Petri nets that emphasizes modularity, namely Superposed Automata nets (de Cindio et al. 1982), since it will be used in the working example:

Labeled SA nets $::= [name_1 : SM1 \|.... \| name_n : SM_n]$

where $name_i$ are names of objects that can be selected in the CAW (e.g., a Role); SM_i are labeled state machines where only transitions carry a label; and finally, "$\|$" is the parallel composition based on the synchronization of sending/receiving messages. Without entering into the details of SA nets' semantics, we recall that the semantics of any concurrent systems can be different in relation to the strategy adopted in executing the sets of concurrent actions: *full concurrency* semantics when all possible actions are executed in one shot; *step* semantics when any subset of possible actions is executed in one shot. This subset can be identified by means of arbitrary criteria (priority, common property of the labels, and so on); and finally, *interleaving* semantics: when just one action at the time is selected and executed in a fully non-deterministic way. Details about this and formal definitions can be found in a paper by Pomello et al. (1992) in relation to Petri-net languages. These various semantics can be formulated equivalently in all formalisms representing concurrency.

7.2.3 The Ariadne Environment

The modularity (both in analysis and design) discussed in Sect. 7.2.1 provides the designer with the possibility of considering processes with different characteristics in a systematic and coherent way. This means that each identified C^2M can be constructed by combining a protocol with different characteristics and eventually an artefact. While the modeling of the latter can be dealt with by exploiting classical data structures in combination with communication capabilities (see Sect. 7.2.4), the modeling of the protocol requires a more specific argumentation. In fact, all approaches to workflow modeling (either explicit or implicit into a specific technological solution) propose a single language, that is, a restricted set of basic categories and relations that allows the designer to represent workflows in a unique way: as a sequence of things to be done, as a flow of documents, as a negotiation of commitments. These issues have been discussed in Chapters 3 and 6 in some detail.

In some cases, the language allows us to consider resources too. Very often this makes the modeling activity a sort of translation from a hypothetical language closer to the target reality (for example, during the analysis phase) into the language imposed by the considered technology. Ariadne aims at providing the designer with the possibility of adopting within the same framework a variety of modeling approaches by combining CAWs and formal relations. This richness has the obvious drawback of imposing an undue effort for whoever is defining each single C^2M, since the selection of the combination of components suitable for a specific work process is not an obvious task. Hence the Ariadne interface is organized so as to reduce this overhead of effort by providing a place where such combinations (more formally called *grammars*) are defined, stored by and made available to the authorized actors. When a user enters the Ariadne environment she has available three integrated levels (the central part of Fig. 7.3): one for the definition and modification of grammars (γ level), one for the construction of C^2Ms in terms of protocols and artefacts (β level), and one for the activation of the C^2Ms (α level). Each framework is tailored to the specific needs of its potential users.

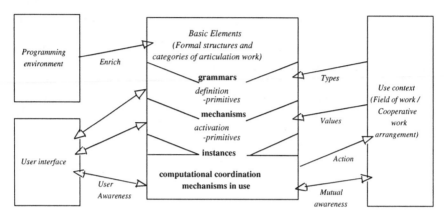

Fig. 7.3. The structure of the Ariadne environment and its contexts of development and use

Building a grammar, at the γ level, means determining the expressive power of a language for defining a class of C^2Ms as well as the operational semantics associated to the elements of the grammar. The "possibility space" within which grammars can be defined at this level is determined by the set of categories of articulation work and by the available formal relations (the basic elements of Fig. 7.3). As an example, let us consider the definition of a grammar,[1] called CONV_GR, for the construction of different types of conversation models (Winograd and Flores 1986) that are traditionally described by means of a labeled graph. Then the definition of CONV_GR assigns to the protocol an L-graph whose arcs are labeled in the set of interactions.

CONV-GR ::= (|| protocol)*
protocol ::= Role ⟵ structure of interaction
structure ::= L-graph
interaction ::= see related frame

This is realized by making available an interface where L-graphs can be edited and the related arcs labeled in the set of the interactions. The arc labeling function is not arbitrary. Indeed, it has to follow some semantic constraints: for example, the fact that an "accept", "counteroffer", etc. must follow a "request"/"offer." This property can be represented in the notation by suitable predicates that are defined together with the grammar.

---

[1] The definition of grammars is given in terms of production rules. The starting symbol is always the name of the grammar while the other non-terminals are taken in the set of component of the notation. || denotes parallelism; X^* denotes an arbitrary sequence of elements of type X.

As a second example, let us consider the definition of a grammar called WF_GR for the construction of workflows that the designer wants to represent by a formalism describing distributed states and actions. Then, the designer chooses to base the description on Superposed Automata nets.

WF_GR accesses a framework where labeled SA nets can be edited and their transitions are labeled either as a task or an interaction. The names of the constituting state machines are defined as the name of a Role extended by the acronym of the current CM. The formal specification of the grammar is as follows:

GR-WF ::= ($\parallel$ protocol)* $\parallel$ Active Artefact

protocol ::= Role $\longleftarrow$ structure of Task/Interaction

structure ::= Labeled SA nets

Active Artefact/Role/Task/Interaction ::= see related frames.

At the β level, the user can then define (or modify) the C^2M itself according to the chosen grammar. In this context, the user can determine the allocation of functionalities between human actors and C^2M, select the degree of partial specifications, and make permanent changes to an existing C^2M as part of its evolutionary design.

Finally, at the α level, the user can instantiate and activate the C^2M in a particular situation and do so in an incremental fashion; moreover, at this level the user can make local changes to the C^2M instances in order to deal with ad hoc needs.

While the two levels of definition and activation of C^2Ms can be recognized in almost all recent CSCW applications, the first level, where it is possible to define grammars, is unique and allows for the desired flexibility in work process modeling. The different levels of Ariadne are typically accessed by users with different skills and needs. At the β and α levels, the use of the notation merely requires the ability to select and combine predefined items according to the rules of a relevant grammar and the associated semantics. These levels are typically needed by end-users who, as part of their everyday work activities, use, adapt and in some circumstances define coordination mechanisms. The γ level, on the other hand, is typically the realm of the "application designer" or, in our framework, of actors who define grammars needed by a particular community of end-users for defining their protocols. The full visibility and accessibility of the three levels, while preserving their specific context and functionality, is the basis of what has been proposed as an incremental approach to customization (MacLean et al. 1990). Thus, in the following, user and designer are to some extent synonyms.

7.2.4 The Role of Communication Features

In Ariadne the role of communication is crucial in many ways. First of all, the categories of articulation work and the active artefact are equipped with communication features allowing them to show a reactive and proactive behavior. Let us consider how an active artefact is specified (see Table 7.2).

The attribute "visibility" specifies the access rights of the roles involved in the C^2M. The attributes "update/read requests", "coordination" and "awareness" specify the actual behavior of the artefact and in which sense it is *active*. In particular,

Table 7.2. Specification of active artefact

Attribute name	Attribute type
Name	Identifier
Content	Data-frame
Visibility	<Role, data-type>*
Update/read requests	<Role, request>*
Coordination	<Condition, out-trigger>*, <In-trigger, function>*
Awareness	<Condition, out-trigger>*, <Condition, in-trigger>*
Defined by	<Role, policy>
Adapted by	<Role, policy>

"coordination" and "awareness" deserve some explanation. The first attribute tells under which condition or incoming communication the artefact reacts either by issuing a communication or starting an internal data manipulation. These activities are mandatory, in the sense that they are a constitutive part of the protocol the artefact is participating in as a *partner*. On the other hand, the communication associated to the attribute "awareness" is used to allow the artefact to participate in the construction of the so-called "awareness information" which is not intrinsically part of the protocol but is recognized as playing a relevant role in effective coordination. Awareness information can be filtered in input and in output as specified by the guards expressed by the conditions. The attributes "coordination" and "awareness" appear with the same purpose in all CAWs' specification.

Secondly, the distributed nature of the protocols contained in the C^2Ms requires communication capabilities that can be expressed by the CAW called "interaction." The next section will illustrate this aspect in depth. Finally, the mentioned possibility of making C^2Ms interoperate is based on the communication across C^2Ms that characterizes their Interfaces. Actually, the modularity of Ariadne and its features allowing for communication among and across its components at any level of aggregation is implemented through a multi-layered architecture of agents whose behavior is characterized by their communication capabilities (Divitini et al. 1996). In this architecture, which will be described in Sect. 7.5, C^2Ms interfaces play the fundamental role of filtering and managing the communication across C^2Ms.

7.3 Ariadne at Work: A Working Example

The working example is a simplified version of a real case presented in greater detail by Divitini and Simone (1996): here the details that are not essential or relevant in this context are omitted, since the description is functional to an intuitive presentation of the different elements of the notation and of its use in supporting cooperation.

We start with the presentation of the scenario and then we simulate the construction and activation of the required C^2Ms.

7.3.1 The Scenario

In the following we will analyze two coordination mechanisms that we have observed in an organization, let's call it Alfa, whose mission is to promote the constitution of consortia for the development of targeted projects.

The development of the projects is achieved through a set of processes of different nature that are both autonomous and coordinated. When Alfa was established, the only computer-based support provided to its members was a simple communication system (basically, e-mail and moderated conferences) connecting the various people. This solution was acceptable at the beginning but became inadequate with the increase in size of the organization, in terms of numbers of both members and sponsored projects. Then the problem was to find a technological framework where the various ongoing processes, and in particular their interactions, could be supported. In fact, the loose organizational structure characterizing Alfa was the source of a low cohesion of its members and of a reduced mutual visibility. We will consider how Ariadne has been applied for the construction of a mechanism supporting the management of the various projects and the related research area.

Each project that is approved by the devoted committee is classified as belonging to a specific research area. Each research area is under the responsibility of a Research Area Coordinator (RAC). The management of a research area and of the related projects has many obvious goals, among which we will consider only what is related to the timely submission of the project reports and the implementation of the decisions taken during the periodical review meetings of the above mentioned committee. When Alfa was established, the management of an area was seen only as the juxtaposition of the management of the single projects belonging to it. At this stage the RAC was responsible simply for delivering the decisions of the committee to the appropriate project leader (PL) and for handling exceptional situations that could arise during the development of one of the projects belonging to her area. As the complexity of the projects increased, the RAC became more operative, assuming relevant tasks concerning the coordination of the management of the projects: among the others, the responsibility for the preparation of the project reports that have to be delivered to the committee in order to verify the status of a project. In fact, one of the recognized difficulties in the review process concerned the different levels of quality and timely delivery of the reports: this made their comparative evaluation difficult.

Both Project Management and the Research Area Management work processes are obviously quite complex and could be analyzed from different points of view and supported in many different aspects. As already said, the focus here is mainly on the interaction protocols needed to synchronize the action with the activities performed in the Review Meeting process: the production of the documents to be approved and the management of the impacts of the decisions taken during the review. As project teams are composed of several actors, loosely coupled in terms of organizational structure, the problem was to define a protocol among them which could guarantee the timely propagation of the decisions and the consistency of the distributed actions according to them. Then, a "detailed map" should be drawn, to serve as a reference point for all the involved roles.

In the following subsections we will describe the project management in greater detail in order to exemplify the various elements of the notation. Description of the research area management will instead appear in Sect. 7.4. There we will see how Ariadne can support its users in introducing new mechanisms for overcoming the inadequacies of existing ones in dealing with a changing situation.

7.3.2 Constructing Computational Coordination Mechanisms

In order to construct a C^2M the user has to specify the requisite CAWs and select the appropriate grammar. CAWs are specified by instantiating the templates provided by the notation. Let's consider, as an example, the roles involved in the described scenario. The project management involves a project leader and a variable number of designers who can be classified as senior or junior. Senior designers assist the project leader and are in charge of the revision of specification, while junior designers have a more "operative" role. In Ariadne we can specify these three roles starting from the template that it provides, as described in Table 7.3.

Table 7.3. Specification of role

Attribute name	Attribute type
Description	Data-frame
Responsible for	Resource*
Responsible for	Task*
Responsible for	C^2M^*
Involved in	C^2M^*
Precepts	Set of rules
Assumed by	Actor*
Defined by	\<Role, policy\>
Adapted by	\<Role, policy\>
Coordination	\<Condition, out-trigger\>*, \<In-trigger, function\>*
Awareness	\<Condition, out-trigger\>*

Each "role" is defined through a set of *responsibilities* for "tasks", "resources" and "C^2Ms." In the considered scenario, the role senior designer, for example, is responsible for revising the specification and appointing their implementation to a junior designer, for assisting the project leader in planning and for working with junior designers in the preparation of the required reports. The project leader is responsible for the whole mechanism. Role responsibilities are established in the Organizational Context by the role mentioned in the attribute "defined by." The definition of a role can be changed by the role mentioned in the attribute "adapted by", still in the Organizational Context. A role can be "assumed by" one or more actors. The rules in the attribute "precepts" regulate the assumption of the role by an actor and the behavior of the actor that assumes the role. For example, a role can be assumed only by people carrying a certain experience or possessing some formal property (like a Ph.D.) and its behavior has to obey some legal constraints. In the case under analysis, for example, the role of project leader is normally assumed by the main contractor of the consortium, and by default by the research area coordinator.

The definition of a role, as well as the one of the other categories, can proceed in an incremental fashion and can be interleaved with the selection of the grammar and the definition of the needed protocols and active artefact.

The grammar is selected by using the primitive *access*(Grammar-set), where Grammar-set contains the grammars constructed at the γ-level. If we consider the grammars defined in Sect. 7.2.3, then Grammar-set = {WF_GR, CONV_GR}. If no adequate grammar is available, the user can (ask some authorized person to) define a new grammar using the primitive *define-Grammar*(X), where X is the name of the new grammar.

The analysis of the work processes in Alfa led to the selection of the grammar WF- GR. In fact, it was evident that the overall structure of the project management is influenced by the presence of a paper-based artefact the project teams introduced to support coordination among participants in the project. When computerizing the coordination mechanism, it was decided to let the computer based artefact manage the same type of information and in addition assume an active role in promoting coordination and awareness. Then, the "data frame" of the "active artefact" is a structure of project modules: information about each module is expressed by some attributes with the related access rights. For example, the attribute reporting the state of the project can be updated only by the project leader; junior designers have access to all the pieces of information recorded in the artefact but cannot change them. Its communication capabilities make the "active artefact" an active component contributing to the protocol supporting the articulation work necessary to manage (the considered aspects) of the project management.

The protocol coordinating the members of the project team was naturally expressed by a structured and distributed flow of "tasks" and "interactions" across the involved "roles", in order to represent not only the related responsibilities but also the causal order in which they have to be fulfilled. Then, a formal structure is needed for representing this relation. It is important to notice that interaction is a category of articulation work that does not simply model the exchange of a message among the various components of the mechanism, but allows definition of specific communicative protocols, possibly activating devoted mechanisms. For example, if necessary it is possible to activate a conversational protocol (Winograd and Flores 1986) (constructed by means of CONV-GR) for dealing with the undertaking of a commitment between the communicating actors.

The designer can define all the above mentioned components of the C^2M by means of the primitive *define*-$C^2M(X)$, where X is the name of a C^2M. Specifically, the protocol, including the communication capabilities of the active artefact, is visualized[2] in Fig. 7.4 with the following conventions: for sake of conciseness, all message content implicitly refers to the project the PL is leader of; all labels are either "tasks" that can be described in detail as in the case of the other CAWs, or "interactions"; synch(roles, info) denotes a special kind of task which has to be performed jointly by the mentioned roles and has to produce the mentioned resource. The way in which this cooperation is performed can be established, dynamically and/or incrementally, by specifying the task attributes such as the activities realizing the cooperation or by the activation of a specific protocol, i.e., of another C^2M. By default, synch(...) opens an interaction space where the joint behavior can be performed. Finally, CALL(...) denotes the invocation of a function of the Field of Work that is not specified here.

Once the C^2M is defined, two primitives help the designer in verifying its properties: *animate*(X) and *simulate*(X), where X is the name of the C^2M. These primitives provide the user with the possibility of "playing" with the C^2M to verify its behavior. Simulation is an animation with the additional computation of predefined parameters expressing good performances. These functions have an obvious value during the definition of the C^2M because they allow the designer to test different possibilities and then choose the best one. Moreover, they can be successfully exploited also for increasing the awareness of the actors potentially involved in the execution of the mechanisms. In fact, through an animation (or a simulation) the users of the mechanism can familiarize themselves with it before actually starting to act within the organization.

This is a very good way for newcomers to learn the protocols that are established in the group they are entering and to understand how their actions are going to impact on the overall cooperative effort.

Another important primitive is provided by Ariadne at this level: *access*(C^2M-set). This allows users to access to the mechanisms that have already been defined, of course respecting the privacy criteria that are defined through adequate policies. The availability of this kind of knowledge is essential for users when they have to define a new mechanism. In fact, the C^2M-set together with the history of their evolution managed by the primitive *history*(X) where X is a C^2M name, constitutes an elementary form of organizational memory on processes and, as such, it allows members of an organization to take advantage of the experience gained by other people. Even if there is no mechanism that can be exploited directly for the purpose at hand, the recorded information can provide a precious source of examples from which to learn. The importance of this kind of knowledge has been pointed out, for example, by Malone et al. (1993).

---

[2] The use of this formal language is just limited to giving a graphical representation of the causal relations to complete the conventional way of describing C^2Ms. This does not mean that this language is proposed to visualize them in the real user interface.

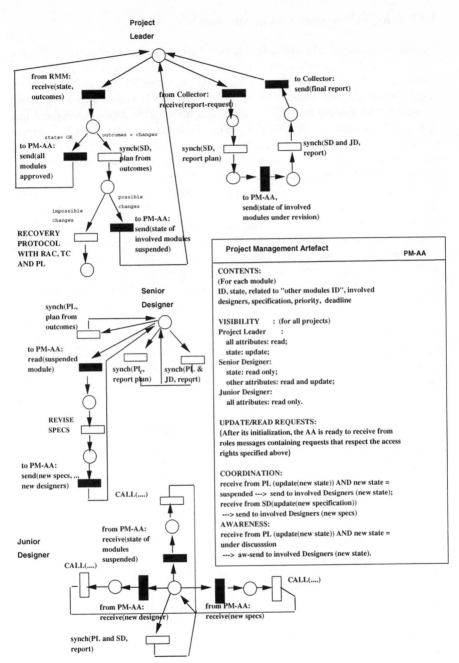

Fig. 7.4. The C^{2}M project management (gray transitions represent interactions)

7.3.3 Using a Computational Coordination Mechanism

The execution of a C^2M requires an additional effort in order to complete the partial specification provided at definition time. This effort is mainly in charge of the actor(s) assigned to the role responsible for this C^2M: to this aim they use the primitive *enact-instance*(X, Y), where X is the C^2M name and Y is the instance identifier. Obviously, the amount and type of additional information depend on the existing specification, on the time of activation, on the contingent situation. Here below some examples are sketched in the hypothesis that each additional piece of information can be added at any time with the only constraint that it is available when it becomes mandatory for the execution of the C^2M.

The person responsible for a C^2M, putting it to work for the first time, has to define which actors will play the roles mentioned in the C^2M. For example, the project leader can define her team by selecting which actors will play the roles of senior and junior designers, and maintain it, by default, for all the subsequent activations of the project management C^2M. Obviously, at each instantiation the team can be modified, within the constraints stated by the role assignment policies. For example, the person responsible can delegate some of her duties to other actors after a negotiation with them and/or an authorization by some role playing as supervisor.

The assignment of roles to actors makes real activation possible: basically, this act determines the start of the transition from the nominal to the actual status of the C^2M. The activation can be done either under system control, when it depends on some external event: for example, a specific event signaled by the clock, or an incoming communication which plays the role of trigger of the protocol constituting the C^2M; or under actor's control by means of the primitive *activate*(Y). During execution of the C^2M, the Ariadne environment asks the actors to provide the missing information: for example, a "task" can be accomplished by executing some "activities." The partial specification can contain some activities from which the actor can select the most appropriate one for her current needs; when no activity is mentioned, the actor can define it, on the fly, or be satisfied with a weaker support by the environment. In fact, in this case the latter opens a working space where the actor is totally in charge of the control. A similar reasoning can be done for all the attributes characterizing a task.

The possibility space for incremental design is very rich, and the above examples provide only a taste of what the Ariadne environment aims to support. The main point we want to make is that this environment, thanks to the flexibility with which it can be used, supports not just the execution of a work process but also the definition of many ways to realize it and the selection of the coordination support it requires in the current situation. As mentioned in the introduction, each actor, each process, each instantiation can pose different demands. The selection process allows the actors to range from a conservative approach which relies on some existing effort and experience, typical of the unskilled/inexperienced/ill-motivated actors, to the most creative one, typical of the most innovative and self-confident members of the organization.

Since work process definition and selection can be conceived of as cooperative efforts supported by specific coordination mechanisms (e.g., the already mentioned conversation patterns for negotiating them), they can become a means for the propagation of experience and skill. Moreover, the environment makes it possible to record some definition and selection which resulted particularly effective and thus worthy of becoming a shared patrimony. This is achieved through the primitive *MakePermanent*(Y, new-name) which transforms an instance Y into a permanent C^2M that will be referenced by the new-name and then accessed through the primitives mentioned in the previous section, for design, learning and training purposes. A similar functionality is provided in, e.g., EGRET (Johnson 1992).

7.4 Modifying a Computational Coordination Mechanism

Simply selecting from among a set of possibilities or inventing a new C^2M or some of its components is not enough for managing all demands. We already mentioned the use of the repository of C^2Ms for reuse and adaptation. This opens the fundamental topic of how to support the modifications of existing C^2Ms as well as of existing grammars.

The modifications can pertain to each of the three levels of Ariadne's environment. First of all, at the γ level, a grammar can be modified in some of its components through the primitive *modify*(G, modification-type), where G is a grammar identifier. In this case, the type of modifications can be in relation to either alternative CAWs or alternative formal relations. For example, *modify*(CONV-GR, structure) allows the user to change the structure used in the grammar: Labeled SA nets whose transitions are labeled in the interactions could be substituted for the labeled graph, in order to allow for the definition of multi-party distributed conversations in addition to the standard dialogue patterns. The modification could act also on the labeling functions by modifying the type of the objects constituting the labeling sets. For example, in the WF_GR we can allow only tasks as labels of the transitions and change the names of the protocol from roles to generic labels. It is possible to modify also the semantics of a component of the grammar and not the component itself. For example, in the case of relational structures modeling concurrency one could select one of the alternative associated semantics. As mentioned in Sect. 7.2.3, the γ level is the domain of the so called "application engineers" who have the skill for dealing with the formal aspects of the notation and for defining suitable combinations of the various basic elements to be used to construct a class of C^2Ms.

At the β level, Ariadne provides its users with the possibility of specifying in the attribute "adapted by" who has the right/duty to modify each specific component and/or their aggregation up to a whole C^2M, of the work process description. The value of this attribute can be either a role or a whole C^2M: this is a way to account for the recursive nature of articulation work (Schmidt and Simone 1996) since the component under modification becomes the Field of Work of a C^2M (as defined in Fig. 7.1) governing the modification process. Notice that people responsible and the modalities for the modifications can be totally different from the people responsible and the modalities for the definition of C^2M. This holds in general for all components of the C^2M. The environment provides the authorized actors with the primitive *modify*-$C^2M(X$, modification-type) where X is a C^2M name.

The question about modifications of a C^2M, as well as its definition, is not just about what is syntactically possible; rather, it is also about the correctness of the new description and of its relations with the descriptions of the work processes interacting with it. The environment provides the *define* and *modify* primitives with (interfaces to) tools for verifying the correctness of the new C^2M by exploiting checking techniques based on the formal relations contained in the notation, since the latter have an internal representation in terms of Petri Nets. This idea has a long tradition: it was present in Domino (Kreifelts et al. 1991a) where Petri-nets algorithms are exploited (Brauer et al. 1987); in the proposal contained in Ellis and Wainer (1994) where proving correctness of a modification of ICN (Ellis and Nutt 1980) exploits the theory of graph grammars (Ehrig et al. 1983) as ICNs are based on AND/OR-graphs; and finally, in more recent proposals collected by de Michelis and Pareschi (1996).

The identification of a tool supporting the check of correctness with other interacting processes introduces the crucial problem of how to manage the *propagation of changes*: this latter can be realized in different ways, depending on the type of modification. A first step is to evaluate whether or not the modifications have any impact on other C^2Ms.

This point opens one of the most challenging research areas to the improvement of adaptability in Ariadne, as it constitutes one of the main weakness of nearly all proposals. The modularity and focus on communication characterizing Ariadne suggest we look for support in verifying the consistency of the work process from the communication point of view. Although it is not integrated in Ariadne's framework, we worked on a tool for the semi-automatic verification of observational equivalence (Milner 1980, Pomello et al. 1992) in concurrent systems. We can illustrate the idea in the scenario. If for some reason, the protocol of the project management C^2M is modified in terms of the involved "roles", structure of "artefact" and assignment of "tasks" to "roles", then the only constraint is the "communication interface" with its environment, namely the communication with the Review Meeting C^2M (not discussed here and described by Divitini and Simone (1996). If all the "tasks/interactions" not involving this communication are considered as unobservable, then the interface just specifies the communicative events with the environment and their causal relation. Once in the new solution the internal behavior and communication are again made unobservable, then the modification is not affecting the other C^2Ms if the new interface is equivalent to the old one. That is, the communicative events with the environment satisfy the same causal relation.

The illustrated case is trivial since most of the communication is internal and therefore unobservable. The general case can be quite complex: our claim is that a computer support interacting with the designer who decides the correspondence of the old communicative events with the new ones could provide an invaluable support that can be applied uniformly to all components of a C^2M.

If the modification does not have any impact on the other C^2Ms then propagation of changes involves how to deal with the active instances of the modified C^2M: there are two possibilities here. An easy solution is to let them terminate according to the old definition and to consider the new one just when new instances are activated. If this is not the case, then the responsible person mentioned in the policy associated to the attribute "defined/modified" by has to deal with the definition of a new state from which to start the execution of the new C^2M. We will come back to this point later on.

If the modification does have an impact on other C^2Ms then propagation of changes is dramatically more complex. In fact, beside the problem mentioned above, propagation of changes has to deal with the alignment of the behavior of all the involved C^2Ms, possibly at both instantiation and definition levels. If the impacts can be filtered by the modified C^2M interface, then the problem is just to act on this interface so that the new C^2M appears unmodified to the external world: this case will be discussed later on. Otherwise, all the responsible roles have to be involved for realizing the alignment. Ariadne does not provide any "panacea" for this problem: rather it makes the responsible roles visible, supports the cooperative redefinition by means of an ad hoc C^2M (specified in the policy associated to the attributes "defined/modified by"), and in principle could support the evaluation of the external impacts just applying the technique based on the above mentioned observation equivalence.

Let's go back to the scenario. In Sect. 7.3.1 we said that when the organization was established the management of a research area was seen simply as a juxtaposition of the management of the single projects belonging to the area. The research area management C^2M can therefore be described in the following way:

Research area management ::=
        project management$_1$ $\|$ ... $\|$ project management$_k$

where *project management$_n$* is the mechanism whose construction has been illustrated in Sect. 7.3.2. These mechanisms are fully independent.

In a subsequent stage, the two considered C^2Ms had to be modified as the outcome of an evolution of the organization demands. As the complexity of the projects increased the RAC responsibilities became more operative, in particular in the attempt of guaranteeing a uniform quality (and timely delivering) of the reports submitted to the periodic review meetings where the organization monitors the status of the on- going projects. Then, the research area coordinator (RAC) became not just a reference in case of exceptional situations (namely, the handling of impossible changes, as illustrated in Fig. 7.4); rather, it had to play an active role in guaranteeing the quality of the process by synchronizing its behavior with that of the people involved in each project management, for fully anticipated tasks. In this view, the research area management C^2M was no longer to be considered as a set of juxtaposed project management C^2Ms, but as a structure of independent mechanisms that have to synchronize at some points through the communication with the role responsible for the structure. The new C^2M, still called *research area management*, "contains" the others in the sense illustrated in Fig. 7.5. An artefact is introduced:

its structure was defined according the new responsibilities of the RAC. We are not giving here its detailed components: for our purposes it is just worth mentioning that it contains the references to the project management C^2Ms. In our experience, this is a quite recurrent situation that arises whenever there is the need to harmonize the parallel execution of different instances of a same mechanism. This is why we think that this situation could be defined as a predefined pattern of information structure and communication capabilities to be provided by Ariadne and specialized by the designers.

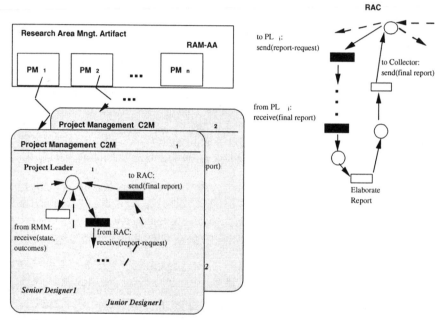

Fig. 7.5. The new C^2M research area management

The (part of the) protocol governing the new RAC behavior explicitly states a communication with the various project leaders for preparing the reports. This has an impact on each project management C^2M (within the research area management mechanism): the only required modification is the change of source and destination of the communication about the report preparation. In fact, what before had to be communicated to the role responsible for collecting the reports (the Collector mentioned in the "interactions" of the project management mechanism) is now communicated to the research area coordinator. This modification should have some effect on the C^2M supporting the review meeting (again, not considered here) because it implies the modification of one of its role. The decision about how to realize this modification was the outcome of a discussion among the people in charge of the reorganization: the main concern was about how to manage the related impacts.

Two strategies were considered. The modification is to be considered either as a re- organization internal to the research area management process or as part of a more global reorganization, as a "must" coming from outside the process itself. In the former case, the Collector remains fully unaware of this modification. Collector sends out report-requests and waits for the reports from the project leaders. From the technical point of view, the interface managing the external communication of research area management C^2M has to take care of the "translation" of these addresses. In the second case, if the modification has to be part of an explicit re-organization, then Collector in the Review Meeting process has to be explicitly involved too: that is, here the communication with the project leaders has to be changed accordingly. Various factors, among which the small size of the organization, led to the selection of this second possibility.

If we abstract from the specific scenario and consider a more complex situation, then the people in charge of the reorganization could adopt a strategy which is a combination of the two in order to better manage the propagation of changes. In fact, considering in the first place a modification as an event local to a process (C^2M) allows us to test its consequences locally before making the modification a public event explicitly involving other processes. When the solution is satisfactory, then the other processes are modified with a greater level of confidence. The process originating the modification will remain stable for a while.

This way of proceeding can have a positive impact in supporting the active involvement of everyone in modifying work processes, avoiding the delegation of all changes to the management. In a highly dynamic working environment, in fact, the modularity of Ariadne allows experimentation of new solutions locally, so that the lack of impact on the external world can increase the creativity of the people directly involved in the process execution. In this way, changes are the result of experiences gained "in the field:" people learn to work together and adapt their interaction in order both to meet changing demands in the environment and to perform more effectively. This is not to deny the importance, within the organization, of more global changes that can be addressed only by people with an overall vision of the organization and the evolving market requirements. A system like Ariadne, we believe, can provide a smooth integration between changes coming from the bottom, and therefore "situated" in a specific working setting, and ones coming from the top, and therefore "enlighten" by a global vision of organizational needs. We want to underline that this is a possibility provided by Ariadne, the extent to which this possibility is actualized within the specific organization depends on the policies defined within the organization itself.

Finally, at the α level, the modifications concern temporary changes of an activated mechanism in face of some unexpected event or of events whose handling strictly depends on the current situation. Two are the primitives available to this end. The primitive *modify-instance*(X) allows for structural modifications of the instance: for example, if its source C^2M exploits graphs as a formal structure, *modify-instance*(X) allows the insertion/deletion of arcs and nodes and/or the change of their labeling functions. These modifications affect just the current instance while the source C^2M remains unchanged. As for the case of the permanent changes at the β level, the primitive *modify* can interact with tools for the verification of the consistency of the modified instance. Of course, if the changes have an impact outside it, then the alignment to the new configuration has to be negotiated among the interested actors, possibly by means of a C^2M supporting negotiation. The decided alignment can be "enforced" by the following primitive.

The primitive *enforce*(X, new-configuration) makes an instance to proceed from a new configuration with respect to the current one. For example, if we consider a graph-based formalism, the configuration is made of the current node; in the case of Petri-nets based formalisms, the configurations are the markings; in the case of an active artefact the configuration is the current set of values. Then, the primitive allows us to change node, marking and values, respectively, in a way that is independent of the previous configurations. As discussed by Ellis et al. (1995), enforcing a new configuration poses serious consistency problems and requires ad hoc tools for guaranteeing a consistent future behavior. Beside the techniques they propose for Petri nets-based descriptions, we would like to mention the possibility of using the notion of state equivalence of Petri nets (Bernardinello et al. 1996), a notion allowing two net systems to be compared through suitable morphisms relating their structure and their state spaces. In this way, a designer can check if the new state leads to a configuration from which an anticipated behavior can start again.

The already mentioned primitive *MakePermanent*(X, new-name) which allows us to transform an instance into a permanent C^2M that will be referenced by the new- name can be used after the activation of the primitive allowing for structural modifications that are becoming recurrent so that they can be made permanently available for future uses.

In the scenario, an example of modification of the current state is generated by the "task" Recovery Protocol in the project management C^2M: this task is activated when the review process requires changes of the project that are considered as impossible in the current situation. In this case, there are two possible outcomes: either the project is forced to a final state or all the current activities are suspended until a negotiation of those changes leads to another set of requests. These two situations do not create serious consistency problems because the enforced states belong to the space of possible states of the current description. In fact, a project can terminate successfully, and its modules are suspended during the revision of their specifications by the senior designer.

As a concluding remark, we can say that if we observe an organization even for a short period of time, it is possible to witness numerous kinds of changes, going from small adjustments to major changes that make the processes more suitable to the dynamic needs of the evolving organization. Even if we consider only the few examples provided above, it is possible to note that some modifications have a strong impact on the way processes are defined and on how people work, while others are more circumscribed and their effect can be limited to a single execution of a process. It is clear that different modifications require that the user performing them possesses different competencies and a different authority within the organization.

It is not possible to define general rules, because this depends on the policies applied by the organization as well as by the specific process or task under concern (e.g., organizing a meeting vs. managing a nuclear plant). Ariadne provides a framework where policies can be defined at what is dynamically considered as the right level of granularity. Moreover, the level of control that is necessary, above all in terms of authorized changes, is strictly related to the skill of the user under concern and her role within the organization. So, for example, newcomers might not be allowed to modify the way they act in a cooperative effort, because they may not be aware of the consequences that this can have on the overall process, while this restriction can be relaxed when the user gains more experience.

In combining the knowledge and the policies collected in the specific (component of a) C^2M, in the role that is responsible for the modifications and the actor that is playing it in a contingent situation, the system can provide a high degree of flexibility in the description of the different constraints that influence the expected behavior of the members of a group and their degree of freedom in acting within the organization. Moreover, the system can use all these pieces of knowledge to tailor its interaction to the specific user in question. For example, it is possible to specify that a certain role can modify a specific component only if authorized by a supervisor whenever the actor playing it has no specific skill, the authorization can be weakened to just an acknowledgment as the experience of the user increases to leave place to a total freedom for the more experienced ones. The system can act differently in the different situation by activating automatically a devoted mechanism, a remainder or simply non-acting when this is not necessary. Ariadne therefore provides its user with the possibility of defining different policies and relaxing them on the basis of different external constraints (like, for example, the profile of a specific user).

7.5 ABACO: An Agent Based Implementation of Ariadne

Ariadne allows the construction of a C^2M by means of the elements of the notation described in the previous section. What has to be described now is the operational semantics associated to each of these elements. This goal is achieved by defining an agent based model of Ariadne, so as to obtain both the formal definition of its semantics and the overall structure of a software architecture, namely ABACO, where Ariadne can be implemented.

In ABACO agents are characterized following a behavioral criterion, as described by Genesereth and Ketchpel (1994): software agents are defined as

"components that communicate with their peers by exchanging messages in an expressive agent communication language."

Stated in another way:

"An entity is a software agent if and only if it communicates correctly in an agent communication language ... This means that the entity must be able to read and write these messages and that the entity must abide by the behavioral constraints implicit in the meanings of those messages."

This criterion does not consider other aspects (for example, social ability, proactiveness, autonomy) and we don't mean to underestimate the importance of the agent internal architecture. In our perspective, the behavioral criterion was an essential starting point for defining the macro architecture of the system. Different actual implementations of ABACO can exploit different internal structures, possibly using heterogeneous agents specialized in relation to the services that they provide, but preserving the basic communicative behavior that will be described for each type of agent. In the following, we will present the architecture of ABACO and its agent communication language.

7.5.1 The Multi-Layer Structure of ABACO

In very general terms, each component of Ariadne, from the basic elements up to the composite C^2Ms obtained from the composition of more elemental C^2Ms, is realized as an agent belonging to a specific type. Each type is characterized by its capability of communicating with the other agents that dynamically constitute the environment.

Following the idea of realizing each element of Ariadne as an agent, ABACO exhibits a multi-layer architecture since C^2Ms are compound entities that are built on top of basic elements. ABACO is organized in three layers (see Fig. 7.6).

Since the categories of articulation work (CAW) are the building blocks of C^2Ms made available by Ariadne, the agents realizing these categories populate the *first layer* of the architecture.[3] Each CAW agent manages a set of information that varies from one category to another, according to the attributes that characterize the category in the underlying model of articulation work sketched in Sect. 7.2.2. These agents can provide the managed information to other agents whenever it is needed and are characterized by a communicative behavior that makes them able to interact with other agents and with the Organizational Context where they are defined and adapted. Specifically, each CAW agent is characterized by the possibility of making the environment *aware* of its internal conditions (as explained in Sect. 7.2.4). The structure of the CAWs represents a common ontology to which all the agents of ABACO subscribe.

The *second layer* is related to single C^2Ms. From the behavior point of view, a C^2M is the parallel composition of the behaviors of the related CAWs, active artefact and protocol on the basis of their communication capabilities. As explained in Sect. 7.2.4, the artefact assumes an essential and active role in mediating the articulation work among the cooperating entities involved in the C^2M by notifying them of appropriate information in presence of particular conditions and by actively participating in the articulation work effort thanks to coordination capabilities. From the architectural point of view, an artefact is an agent specialized in the management of

---

[3] For the sake of simplicity, agents will be denoted, when this does not create ambiguity, by the name of the corresponding concept.

the related information and is able to communicate with its environment in order either to notify appropriate information in presence of defined conditions (awareness) or to collect from agents and convey to agents information which is compulsory to coordinate their work (coordination). Conventions and procedures are represented in Ariadne through the notion of protocol. A protocol is a compound entity obtained from the composition of CAWs as in a cooperative arrangement conventions and procedures can be expressed in terms of relations among tasks, roles, actors, actions, interactions and resources. From the architectural point of view, protocols correspond to agents that, among other, control the activation of other CAW agents, as specified by the underlying formal relation.

Finally, the *third layer* is populated by the agents obtained from the composition of already existing C^2Ms. The implementation of the composition of C^2Ms is based on the definition of an Interface agent specialized in managing external communication. The Interface agent plays the role of both facilitator and monitor of the embedded C^2M in order to handle the additional communication needs derived from the composition of different C^2Ms (Genesereth and Ketchpel 1994). The interface, for example, establishes which internal information can be mutually accessed by and communicated to other mechanisms and controls the access to the artefact from the external world (i.e., agents that do not belong to the mechanism of which the artefact is part). Moreover, the interface monitors the behavior of the C^2M to handle the additional communication needs derived from co-existence of different C^2Ms. Finally, the interface is the place where mechanisms can be made tolerant to the modifications of their world. In fact, interfaces can be conceived of as agents specialized not only in the management of the communication but also in the "translation" or redirection of the incoming/outcoming information in a format that can be properly interpreted. If the translation is not possible, then the interfaces will notify it and support the activation of the suitable negotiation/recovery protocols.

Notice that the Interface agent can be employed in order to establish the type of interoperability between a C^2M and the field of work whose activities the C^2M is articulating.

7.5.2 The Interoperability Language

According to their definition, agents share the same communication language. An essential step in the development of ABACO was, therefore, the definition of the language that the agents use to communicate, that we call Interoperability Language (IL). The basic primitives of the language were determined considering the types of communication each agent has to realize in order to interoperate with other agents. Three modes characterize the interactions among agents:[4]

In *subscription mode* an agent makes the behavior of another agent part of its own behavior. For example, a resource can be accessed in the subscription mode

---

[4] In an initial stage these modes were determined comparing various field studies in order to determine how C^2Ms interact. The three modes were then usefully exploited for describing the communication among ABACO agents.

to activate the policies governing its usage. Another interesting example is when a protocol subscribes to other C^2M in order to support a negotiation or to activate a process that is coordinated by another C^2M, like when a protocol make reference to a C^2M supporting conversations among roles (Winograd and Flores 1986). This C^2M can be constituted by interactions combined by causal relations and by an active artefact describing the status and history of the conversation. Through the reference to these types of C^2Ms, the communication capability of Ariadne's components (and by consequence, of the Interoperability Language) is therefore very expressive and flexible in terms of patterns of interactions (Labrou and Finin 1994).

In *inscription mode* a C^2M provides information about its current state to another C^2M (or, conversely, a C^2M obtains information about the current state of another C^2M). The inscription can be done in two ways: the reaction by the target C^2M can be either *compulsory* or *voluntary*. In the case of compulsory inscription, the target C^2M is expected to react accordingly and, if it does not do so, then the compulsory inscription mode has to incorporate time-outs and solicitation in order to reduce the risk of (partial) blocking of the involved C^2M. In the case of voluntary inscription, the reaction of the target C^2M is voluntary in that it is provided with morsels of information that are supplementary to what is imperative. That is, the voluntary inscription mode has to incorporate capabilities to allow the target C^2M to voluntarily filter the provided information (Malone et al. 1987a, Gasparotti and Simone 1990, Fuchs et al. 1995). The compulsory inscription mode typically expresses the reading from and writing to the artefact by the protocol in order to acquire and make visible imperative information. On the other hand, the voluntary inscription mode is typically used by the artefact to convey awareness of its internal changes to the other components of the mechanism.

In *prescription mode* a C^2M overwrites the definition of the target C^2M's behavior. This interaction mode allows Ariadne to honor the recursive nature of articulation work. In fact, in the prescription mode a given C^2M can change the definition of another C^2M, that is, the definition of its protocol, or its specification, for example, by enforcing a special state during its execution.

It is worth mentioning that the defined modes of interactions are used both at the level of the mechanism and its components (categories of articulation work, artefact, protocols) to express their interactions as well as in the formalization of the primitives of the notation (Divitini et al. 1996). Then, the IL has been uniformly used in the architecture not only for expressing the communication made explicit by the designer of C^2Ms (for example, to describe the communication between two C^2Ms) but also to "implement" the implicit (that is, system-defined) communication among all the elements of the notation (for example, when a CAW makes reference to another CAW in its attributes). In this way, the Interoperability Language is the basic means for realizing the compositionality of Ariadne. That is, the interoperation of coordination mechanisms and of their components is described in a uniform way and, most importantly, is determined by the semantic level of articulation work. This basic property led us to avoid using a standard Agent Communication Language (e.g. KQML Genesereth and Ketchpel 1994, Labrou and Finin 1994) and to postpone the possible mapping of IL into a standard when ABACO will be implemented in all its aspects.

ABACO has been designed so that its elements can be composed in a flexible way in order to obtain the desired expressive power to define, adapt and link C^2Ms.

The primitives that have been presented in the previous sections are all realized as services provided by the single agents. All the agents, for example, can deal with messages in a prescription mode that require for the modification of their internal structure or communicative behavior. Messages are processed by agents accordingly to locally defined knowledge. Before providing the required service, the agent verifies that it comes from an authorized source and it applies the required policies (for example, before starting a modification coming from X, the agent has to require an additional authorization to a supervisor).

A first demonstrator of the ideas presented above has been realized in order to test the Interoperability Language. Another demonstrator is currently under development in the Java environment. Here, the main effort is devoted to provide the agents of ABACO with reflective capabilities. In fact, the agents of ABACO act in a highly dynamic environment: (the components of) a C^2M can be changed at any moment in order to deal with local contingencies or permanent changes in organization; at the same time, new C^2Ms can be introduced in order to deal with different aspects of cooperative activities. In the present architecture, modifications and the subsequent propagation of changes are mainly under user control, with a little help from the system. Without entering into specific details, we claim that the relevant point here is that ABACO has to be equipped with reflective features (Maes 1988, Yonezawa 1990) in order to provide a stronger support to the management of the modifications as well as to the automatic propagation of changes implied by the adopted strategy.

7.6 Conclusions

We presented an approach to the construction of flexible coordination mechanisms supporting the articulation work of actors involved in cooperative activities. Flexibility is achieved by combining linguistic, functional and architectural features. Moreover, flexibility is presented as one of the basic requirements that make the workflow technology both a support to coordination and an enabler of the creative management and learning of the knowledge on work processes.

Different improvements of the approach are currently under consideration. First, the way in which communication is described (and implemented in ABACO) allows a direct integration of functionalities supporting the contexts in which communication occurs (Divitini and Simone 1994). More work will be devoted to User Interface agents (UI). This agent, not mentioned here, is devoted to the interaction of the system with the user, taking into account that they are working in cooperative settings and in multiple contexts. UI agents can naturally incorporate some standard services such as filtering (Sheth and Maes 1993) and intelligent assistance (Greif 1994) based on appropriate User Models (Kobsa and Wahlster 1989) and on user

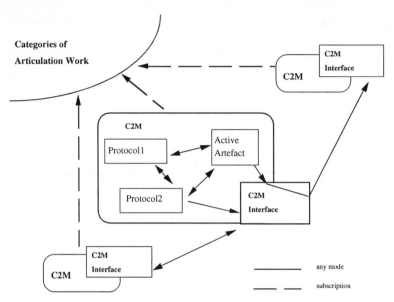

Fig. 7.6. The structure of ABACO

preferences. Moreover, providing a well established model of articulation work, the proposed framework can be the basis for the definition of the notion of Group Models and Profiles.

Second, ABACO is conceived as the first step towards an agent based software infrastructure intended to support the prototyping of CSCW applications based on the concept of Computational Coordination Mechanisms. In the presented work we have defined the architecture of the system, i.e., its component-agents and their relationships. Moreover, the main services that must be provided by each agent have been identified. The use of a more complex internal architecture could support, for example, a richer proactive behavior of the agents. More research in this direction is required.

Finally, more work is required in order to study the possibility of linking a mechanism to service agents or to legacy software. A C^2M system must be able to interoperate with existing applications; moreover, specific C^2M systems can be built whenever the use of an application in a cooperative environment requires coordination of the actors involved. The agent based approach seems to facilitate the solution of these problems. In fact, interoperability with legacy applications is a well recognized problem in the area of agent based programming and some solutions have already been proposed by Genesereth and Ketchpel (1994).

Part V

Knowledge Repositories and Libraries

8. From Natural Language Documents to Sharable Product Knowledge: A Knowledge Engineering Approach

Dietmar Rösner, Brigitte Grote, Knut Hartman, and Björn Höfling
Otto-von-Guericke-Universität Magdeburg, Germany

A great part of the product knowledge in manufacturing enterprises is only available in the form of natural language documents. The know-how recorded in these documents is an essential resource for successful competition in the market. From the viewpoint of knowledge management, however, documents have a severe limitation: They do not capture the wealth of knowledge contained in these documents, since the entire knowledge is not spelled out on the linguistic surface. In order to overcome this limitation, the notion of a document as a particular kind of realization of (or view on) the underlying knowledge is introduced. This chapter discusses the major steps in realizing this approach to documents: Knowledge acquisition, knowledge representation, and techniques to automatically generate multilingual documents from knowledge bases. Further, we describe how the required product knowledge can be represented in a sharable and reusable way.

8.1 Introduction

Currently, a great part of the product knowledge in manufacturing enterprises is only available in the form of natural language documents. Documents play a major role in the entire product life cycle, that is in design, manufacturing, quality assurance, marketing, maintenance and repair. The know-how that manifests itself in the form of such documents, for instance, product specifications, instruction manuals and trouble-shooting guides, is an essential resource for successful competition in the marketplace and should therefore be preserved and utilised as efficiently as possible.

Throughout their entire life cycle, documents are processed with computers: They are created, modified and updated with word processors, are stored in and retrieved from document data bases, are distributed over networks, and may be subject to transformations for printing or display. From the viewpoint of knowledge management, such document processing has a major limitation: It hardly captures the wealth of knowledge contained in these documents. In particular, it fails to capture the full knowledge implicitly referred to in the document. And even the knowledge that is explicitly expressed is only of limited use since it cannot be processed automatically and thus be exploited by different applications such as, for instance, automatic document generators. In order to overcome this limitation, we suggest a revised understanding of what a document is: We do not regard a document as a static entity, but take it as a particular kind of realization of (or view on) underlying knowledge. The view realized by a particular document will typically be partial, as only part of the knowledge has to be spelled out on the linguistic surface of the text. A lot can be left implicit because readers will be able to reconstruct those parts of the content that are not verbalized by drawing on their background knowledge of the subject matter and on general "world knowledge."

Automating the creation of documents from underlying knowledge sources has many advantages for both knowledge management and document processing. Documents may be generated on demand. They may be tailored to different purposes and users, thus varying in detail, style and language. They may flexibly combine not only text but other modalities like, for instance, pictures and graphics. Finally, documents generated from knowledge structures may be used as an "active" window on the underlying knowledge.

We have developed and exemplified this perspective on documents with a particular kind of natural language document—multilingual technical manuals. In the *TechDoc* project (Rösner 1994, Rösner and Stede 1994), we have analysed multilingual instructions with respect to the knowledge necessary to reconstruct these texts and have implemented a prototypical software system which demonstrates the feasibility of automatic generation of multilingual technical documents (currently in English, German and French) from such a knowledge base.

We describe the approach from a knowledge engineering perspective. For knowledge acquisition, the main source of information has been an initial manual analysis of natural language documents from our domain. Section 8.2 reviews the techniques used and the results of this analysis. The approach to knowledge representation and formalization is presented in Sect. 8.3. Section 8.4 introduces the *TechDoc* system, which has been designed and implemented as a "proof of concept" for the feasibility of automatic generation of multilingual technical documentations from a formal representation of content and thus for our perspective on documents. The presented approach has consequences for the management of corporate knowledge; these and the advantages of integrating documentations into the product life cycle are discussed in Sect. 8.5. We conclude with a discussion of the current approach in the context of related work in Sect. 8.6, and an outlook on ongoing and future work in Sect. 8.7.

8.2 Knowledge Acquisition from Natural Language Documents

In our understanding, documents are one means among others to express knowledge, and a particular document realizes a specific view on the underlying knowledge. However, one still faces two problems: First, one cannot access the entire knowledge contained in documents, because that knowledge is not completely spelled out on the linguistic surface. Instead, part of it has to be retrieved from the text by interpreting it within a broader understanding of the world ("world knowledge"). Second, neither knowledge that is expressed in the linguistic realization nor knowledge that has to be derived in the process of text understanding is available in a format ready for automatic processing. Instead, in order to spell out the entire knowledge contained in documents, and thus make it available for formal representation, we first have to identify the various kinds of knowledge that together give rise to a particular document. The task of *acquiring knowledge* from documents will be discussed in the remainder of this section. The knowledge acquisition phase results in specific demands on the knowledge bases as to what knowledge to represent and how to formalize it.

8.2.1 Approaches to Knowledge Acquisition

A number of knowledge acquisition techniques (KA) have been developed within the expert system community (Scott et al. 1991), whereas knowledge acquisition has only recently become a research topic in work on natural language generation (NLG), see for instance Reiter et al. (1997). Reiter presents four knowledge acquisition techniques, adapted from "standard" techniques in the expert system community: direct acquisition of knowledge by asking experts, creating and analysing a corpus, structured group discussions, and think-aloud sessions. The latter two mainly serve to explicate the intentions underlying certain expert decisions. At present, we are not concerned with documents that are of a persuasive nature, and therefore with the intentions motivating the production of documents. Instead, we want to obtain data on the domain knowledge encoded in documents and its realization through language. Thus, we restrict ourselves—for the time being—to the former two techniques.[1] Furthermore, we supplement the knowledge acquired this way with knowledge from additional sources.

In a nutshell, we take a twofold approach to knowledge acquisition:

- **Analysing:** We collect a range of multilingual documents from the present application domain—maintenance instructions taken from different domains such as car manuals, aircraft manuals and household appliances—and perform a thorough analysis of the documents in the corpus in terms of *content* and *structure*. A sample document from the corpus is given in Fig. 8.1.
- **Supplementing:** We supplement the resulting knowledge by knowledge acquired from experts such as mechanical engineers and technical authors. Further, we study relevant literature such as textbooks on technical documentation and mechanical engineering, guidelines and technical norms (e.g. ISO and DIN norms). Supplementing comprises two aspects:
  - enhancing the domain knowledge by simply adding more information,
  - structuring the knowledge by introducing more abstract levels of representation that combine the various fragments into a coherent whole.

Two additional points have to be mentioned with respect to the corpus analysis phase before describing its results: First, we performed a *contrastive* analysis—i.e. we studied a multilingual corpus containing German, English and French texts, and second, the analysis was conducted *manually*. The reasons for these decisions are as follows:

---

[1] We are aware, however, that one would have to employ the latter two techniques, too, if one wants to arrive at a complete picture of the knowledge contained in a document.

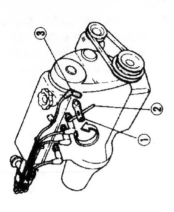
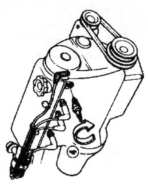
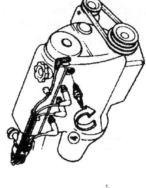

6. MAINTENANCE SERVICE

SPARK PLUGS

Recommended spark plugs:

European and Australian types: BPR6EY-11 (NGK), W20EXR-U11 (ND)

Other types: BP6EY-11 (NGK), W20EX-U11 (ND)

CAUTION: Never use spark plugs with an improper heat range; they will adversely affect engine performance and durability.

Replace plugs one at a time, so you don't get the wires mixed up.

1. Clean any dirt from around the spark plug base.
2. Disconnect the spark plug wire, then remove and discard the old plug.
3. Thread the new spark plug in by hand to prevent crossthreading.
4. After the plug seats against the cylinder head, tighten 1/2 turn with a spark plug wrench to compress the washer.

CAUTION: The spark plug must be securely tightened, but not over-tightened. A plug that's too loose can get very hot and possibly damage the engine; one that's too tight could damage the threads in the cylinder head.

①Plug Wrench   ②Plug Wrench Handle   ③Plug Cap   ④Tighten

6. PFLEGE UND WARTUNG

ZÜNDKERZEN

Empfohlene Zündkerzen:

Europäische und australische Ausführung: BPR6EY-11 (NGK), W20EXR-U11 (ND)

Andere Ausführung: BP6EY-11 (NGK), W20EX-U11 (ND)

VORSICHT: Niemals Zündkerzen mit einem falschen Wärmewert verwenden; sie beeinträchtigen Motorleistung und Haltbarkeit.

Die Zündkerzen eine nach der anderen auswechseln, damit die Zündkabel nicht durcheinandergebracht werden.

1. Die Zündkerzenbasis von jeglichem Schmutz befreien.
2. Das Zündkabel abziehen, dann die alte Zündkerze herausschrauben und wegwerfen.
3. Die neue Zündkerze von Hand einschrauben, um Gewindeüberschneiden zu vermeiden.
4. Nachdem die Zündkerze am Zylinderkopf aufsitzt, mit einem Zündkerzenschlüssel um 1/2 Umdrehung anziehen, um den Dichtungsring zusammenzupressen.

VORSICHT: Die Zündkerzen müssen fest angezogen, jedoch nicht zu fest eingeschraubt werden. Eine lose Zündkerze kann sehr heiß werden und möglicherweise den Motor beschädigen. Eine zu fest angezogene Zündkerze kann das Zylinderkopfgewinde beschädigen.

①Zündkerzenschlüssel   ②Zündkerzenschlüsselgriff   ③Zündkerzenstecker   ④Anziehen

Fig. 8.1. A multilingual text from the corpus (from the Honda Civic car manual)

- **Contrastive**: The central demand on the knowledge acquired by means of corpus analysis is that—even though the knowledge is obtained from natural language documents—it does not pertain to any specific language; in other words, it is language-independent. One way to secure this is by analysing data from various languages in parallel, because this makes it possible to abstract from the idiosyncrasies of a particular language. With this end in view, we conducted a contrastive analysis of identical sections from multilingual documents. Obviously, only non-linguistic knowledge and the more abstract linguistic levels such as text type and discourse structure are language-independent; syntactic and lexical knowledge naturally has to be language-specific at a certain level of detail.
- **Manual:** It is necessary to extract knowledge from documents that goes well beyond lexical and syntactic resources, such as content and discourse structure. However, this kind of knowledge cannot be derived from analysing text alone, but only from analysing text in the context of a broader understanding of the world. Consider, for instance, the resolution of lexical and syntactic ambiguities: These can in many cases only be resolved by employing nonlinguistic knowledge.
  At present, there exist no automated tools that could perform either of the analysis tasks in a satisfactory manner, thus we have to conduct a manual analysis, however tedious this may be at times.[2] Note, however, that this analysis only has to be performed once as part of the initial knowledge acquisition effort. The knowledge will then be readily available for use by future applications situated in a similar domain.

As noted above, the corpus analysis was performed in terms of *content* and *structure* of the documents. More specifically, this implies investigating

- content of documents: the domain knowledge underlying the document;
- macrostructure: overall structure of the document type;
- discourse structure: relations holding between parts of the text;
- linguistic realization: lexical choice and syntactic structure.

We now describe the document analysis for each of these levels in turn, and then present the results and their augmentation by means of other sources of information in case they provide substantial supplements.

8.2.2 Content of Documents

In the initial step of the corpus analysis we examined the documents with respect to what kind of domain knowledge they encode, and what kind of technical knowledge is needed to interpret the domain knowledge correctly. The content analysis aims at an informal characterization of the domain in terms of objects, properties, actions, and relations holding between them. We noted no differences in content between the

---

[2] Knowledge acquisition techniques for technical texts are a research topic in the knowledge based systems (KBS) community, so powerful tools for, at least, terminology extraction and semantic clustering should be available in near future. Initial results are described by Dagan and Church (1994) and Justeson and Katz (1995), for example.

multilingual variants of a document, as we had expected given the present domain, technical documentations, and the target languages involved.[3]

Objects, actions, and properties that are explicitly mentioned in the text provide the kernel of the domain knowledge. The sample text in Fig. 8.1 introduces a number of basic domain entities, for instance, *engine, spark plug, dipstick, tighten, remove,* etc. Objects tend to be domain specific, whereas actions are of a more general nature in that their use is not restricted to the domain of car maintenance. Conducting a contrastive analysis of a multilingual corpus helps to define the more abstract level of representation, as described above. We will return to this issue in the discussion of lexicalization.

The initial set of entities collected from the corpus has only a restricted coverage of the domain. It contains only those concepts that actually occur in the documents under consideration. Hence, there are obvious "gaps" where related concepts are missing, where an enumeration is not complete, where properties are not specified, etc. In order to arrive at a more complete picture of the domain, we took additional knowledge sources into account: experts, product models from industry, research literature, textbooks on mechanical engineering, and the like.

These steps resulted in a collection of "clusters" of domain entities, for instance, a cluster of technical objects or one of connection types, with the clusters loosely related to each other. In a further step, these have to be coordinated to form a coherent whole. Relations and concepts that act as links between fragments can be defined with the help of additional knowledge sources. We will return to this matter in Sect. 8.2.3.

8.2.3 Macrostructure

The *macrostructure* characterizes the global semantic and pragmatic structure of a particular text type. In other words, the macrostructure describes the characteristic content of a text type in terms of typical parts (*structural elements*), and the content that is usually conveyed by these parts.

We identified the macrostructure for the given text type, *maintenance instructions*, by comparing several multilingual instances of this text type with respect to recurring structures and content, and with respect to the function of the recurring parts. There appeared to be no substantial differences between the language-specific variants. The analysis provided an initial specification of the macrostructure, which we compared in a subsequent step to findings from literature on content and structure of technical documentation and to constraints imposed by DIN norms. The resulting macrostructure for maintenance instructions can be captured by the following schema:

- *name* of maintenance instruction
- *location* of objects to be repaired/maintained
- possible *replacement* parts/substances

---

[3] However, once we turn to other domains and languages (and thus cultures), which are less closely related, we might encounter differences in content due to cultural differences, too.

- *preconditions* that have to be satisfied before activity proceeds
- step-by-step description of *activity*
- further advisory information or *warnings*

The analysis further reveals constraints as to what kind of content may occur within a particular element. For instance, the activity element can contain either of the three major categories of checking a part/substance, adding a part/substance or replacing a part/substance (Rösner and Stede 1992). Either of these presents a typical content specification of the activity element. Note that the macrostructure as presented above merely describes a *potential*, since it contains optional and obligatory elements. The obligatory elements and their order of occurrence define the document type. In the example, obligatory elements are name, replacement and activity.

8.2.4 Discourse Structure

While the macrostructure defines the global content structure of a document, the discourse structure operates on a more local level (the *microstructure*): It specifies the structural and functional representation of a text and of parts of a text down to sentence level. As such, it describes how *text spans* (parts of the text) are related to each other semantically and rhetorically by means of *discourse relations* to form a coherent text.

We use *Rhetorical Structure Theory* (RST) (Mann and Thompson 1987) and its set of rhetorical relations to describe how the contents of basic semantic elements are combined to form a coherent discourse and what the specific function is that an element takes within the relation. In a nutshell, RST posits that discourse structure can be represented as a connected tree, where adjacent text spans are linked by one of approximately 20 rhetorical relations. Most relations link a *nucleus* to a *satellite*: The former is the central element, indispensable for developing the argumentation in the text, whereas the satellite has a more supportive role, presenting additional information. Consider, for instance, the *motivation* relation, which holds between a text span presenting some kind of action the writer intends the reader to perform (the nucleus), and a text span presenting information that increases the reader's desire to perform the action (the satellite). The satellite thus acts as a support for the information depicted in the nucleus. An instance of the *motivation* relation is *Thread in the new spark plug by hand to prevent crossthreading*, where *to prevent crossthreading* acts as support for instructing the reader to perform the action described in the first clause in the specified manner (*thread in ... by hand*). The corresponding analysis is given in Fig. 8.2. Note that some relations, such as *sequence* and *contrast*, do not have any satellite, but two or more nuclei.

An analysis of texts from the corpus revealed that only a subset of RST relations is employed in maintenance instructions (Rösner and Stede 1992). These are mainly of the *subject-matter* type, that is discourse relations that reflect semantic relations holding "in the world" such as causality and temporality. These relations are used to make the reader recognize that a particular semantic relation holds between related

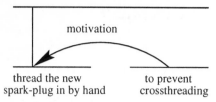

Fig. 8.2. The *motivation* relation: Analysis of sample sentence

text spans. However, the set of relations presented in the initial work on RST turned out to be insufficient: In order to cover all the phenomena found in technical manuals, a number of new discourse relations have been introduced by (Rösner and Stede 1992). These are *alternative, and, precondition, step-sequence*, and *until*. Table 8.1 presents the set of rhetorical relations most frequently encountered in the corpus. Note that only *background* and *motivation* are *not* of the subject-matter type.

Table 8.1. RST relations in manuals

alternative	motivation
and	precondition
background	sequence
contrast	step–sequence
condition	until
elaboration	volitional–result

   RST turned out to be a useful formalism in a *multilingual* setting: For almost every section we investigated, the RST trees for different language versions were identical; we observed no substantial difference between RST trees for English, German and French texts. In brief, the contrastive analysis of corresponding sections reveals discourse structure as a level of representation that captures the commonalities of English, German and French text.

   So far we have discussed *what* relations occur in the documents of the corpus. In a further step of analysis, we investigated *why* a particular relation holds at a particular point in the document. The following method was applied: We produced paraphrases, i.e. alternative linguistic realizations, for a given text span. Then, we compared the different alternatives with respect to the effect they have on the reader. Knowing about the reasons underlying the choice of a particular discourse relation is crucial when it comes to producing documents automatically from a knowledge base.

8.2.5 Linguistic Realization

In the final step we analysed the *linguistic realization* of content structures and functions in the texts of the corpus. Linguistic differences between English, German and

French versions of the texts can be classified into lexical and syntactic ones (see Grote et al. (1993) for an in-depth contrastive study).

Lexical Choice. Lexical differences hold for the realization of noun phrases: For instance, German features a proliferation of compound nouns that are expressed by entire phrases in English (*Kühlervorderseite* vs. *front of the radiator*). More interesting lexical differences relate to the use of verbs in both languages. Quite often in the corpus, a fairly general English verb coincides with more specific German or French counterparts. To illustrate this point, consider the English and German realization of the action of *dissolving a connection*. In English, it is in most cases realized by *remove* regardless of the object involved, whereas the German version displays several different realizations (Rösner and Stede 1992):

Example 8.1.

  (a)   *remove the dipstick*   *den Tauchmeßstab herausziehen*

  (b)   *remove the spark plug*   *die Zündkerze herausschrauben*

  (c)   *remove the oil filler cap*   *den Öleinfülldeckel abnehmen*

The German verbs convey additional information about the spatial characteristics of the participating objects and the nature of the connection relation. Another difference between English and German is that verbs may or may not incorporate a portion of meaning that may otherwise be expressed by an adverb, for instance, the English *re-install*, which incorporates the restitutive character of the action as opposed to the German variant *wieder anbringen* (see also Grote et al. 1993).

The results of the contrastive lexical analysis regarding *granularity* and *incorporation* have significant consequences for the design of the domain knowledge base.

Syntactic Structure. The contrastive analysis of syntactic structures was performed in the following way: When the syntactic structures between corresponding text segments were incongruent, we first took the structure of the expression found in one language and tried to gloss it in the other one, and vice versa. If both resulted in an acceptable rephrasing and we could detect no obvious reasons for the choice of one construction over the other, we took them to be mere variations (Grote et al. 1993). All cases where glossing did not lead to an acceptable sentence underwent further analysis in order to capture the reasons for choosing a particular construction over another.

The most obvious difference relates to the use of complex participles or prepositional phrases in German, where in English the same content has to be expressed by a subordinate clause. Example 8.2 illustrates the use of a prepositional phrase in German as opposed to a subordinate clause in English:

Example 8.2.
(a) *Den Kühlmittelstand im Reservetank bei normaler Betriebstemperatur des Motors kontrollieren.*
(b) *Check the coolant level in the reserve tank when the engine is at normal operating temperature.*

Finally, we find certain phenomena pertaining especially to our text type. In maintenance instructions, the reader is addressed with the imperative mood in English, whereas in the German texts we find a—more polite—infinitive construction:

Example 8.3.
(a) *Read the dipstick level.*
(b) *Den Ölstand ablesen.*

The analysis results in a specification of the range of phenomena to be covered by the linguistic knowledge bases. Obviously, the phenomena are not limited to the ones described in this section, these are only the most important ones.

Linguistic resources, such as lexicon and grammar, that are to be employed in the automatic production of multilingual technical documents thus need to have a broad coverage, be multilingual, and support flexible lexicalization.

8.3 Knowledge Representation

Once the knowledge contained in documents of a specific domain has been accumulated, the question of how to represent and formalize that knowledge arises. To manage this task, we can employ insights gained in the acquisition phase. In particular, the knowledge acquisition phase supplies:

- a collection of objects and actions of the domain together with relations holding between objects;
- a description of linguistic and syntactic phenomena to be covered;
- an informal description of the text type under consideration.

The knowledge acquisition phase contributes in another significant way to managing the representation task: Experiences from that phase help to judge the relevance of different aspects of the domain under consideration, and thus facilitate decisions on which entities to represent and which ones to omit. In combination with the requirements imposed by the application in mind, this provides a good starting point for choosing an adequate knowledge representation paradigm and an implementation system. In Sect. 8.3.1, we discuss this decision process, while Sect. 8.3.2 sketches the formalization of the knowledge within the chosen paradigm.

8.3.1 Requirements Analysis and Representation Decisions

In addition to the requirements imposed by the domain entities to be represented, we can postulate two further demands on the domain knowledge. These are motivated by the intended usage of the knowledge sources and by potential applications:

- The knowledge sources should be usable for the generation of multilingual technical documents.
- The represented knowledge should be in a state that permits sharing among different applications, and reuse for purposes other than multilingual generation.

The first requirement accounts for the fact that the use of generation techniques in the production of multilingual documents has substantial advantages over the traditional approach of creating monolingual documentations and then translating them into other languages.[4] On the other hand, generation techniques require a high initial effort in knowledge acquisition and knowledge representation. Even though this is partially justified by the benefits of that approach, the initial effort constitutes the main obstacle on the way to real applications.

These considerations suggest the need for a better cost-benefits ratio, which in turn motivates the second requirement: A significant improvement of knowledge capitalization can be achieved by sharing and reusing knowledge sources developed within a particular application. Here, *knowledge capitalization* names the surplus between the costs of producing and maintaining knowledge bases on the one hand, and the benefits from having a knowledge base at one's disposal on the other hand. Other definitions focus more on methods to maximize the benefits. For example, Simon (1996) defines knowledge capitalization as "the process which allows to reuse, in a relevant way, the knowledge of a given domain, previously stored and modelled, in order to perform new tasks."

One way to realize knowledge sharing and reuse is by means of ontologies. According to Uschold and Gruninger (1996), an *ontology* is "an explicit account or representation of (some part of) a conceptualization."; and a *conceptualization* is regarded as a "world view with respect to a given domain, which is often conceived as a set of concepts (e.g. entities, attributes, processes), their definitions and their inter-relationships."

The two demands on the domain representation discussed so far have substantial consequences for the design of the knowledge bases as such. In particular, these are:

– Reusable domain knowledge and knowledge concerning an instance of a product have to be clearly separated. This is commonly achieved by introducing abstraction barriers. We distinguish two levels of representation: an *abstract technical model*, which can be exploited for other purposes, and a *product specific model*.
– Concepts and the relationships holding between concepts of the abstract technical model have to be modelled within an ontology.
– Domain knowledge has to be language-neutral; in other words, it has to be modelled in such a way that it is not biased towards any particular natural language. This is an imperative when generating text in different languages from the same formal content representation.
– The representation has to permit an easy integration of linguistic and domain knowledge.

We identified *description logic* as a knowledge representation paradigm that makes it possible to build knowledge bases in line with the design decisions we have taken (Liebig and Rösner 1996a). This paradigm allows us to formalize abstract descriptions by supporting hierarchical concepts and relations including multiple inheritance. Concepts can be defined in such a way that they reflect important

---

[4] Section 8.5 provides a detailed discussion of the advantages of multilingual document generation.

properties of and differences between concepts, which is a characteristic feature of ontologies. In the area of natural language generation, the main inference capability of description logic, automatic classification, can support the tasks of content determination, text planning and surface realization (Reiter and Mellish 1992).

We have chosen *Loom* (LOOM 1991), a *LISP*-based descendent of the *KL-ONE* family (Brachman and Schmolze 1985), as the implementation system. The decision was motivated by the empirical analysis of six terminological representation systems presented in (Heinson et al. 1994), which identified *Loom* as the most expressive and fastest system.

Furthermore, *Loom* is a hybrid formalism that, in addition to description logics, supports other paradigms like forward and backward chaining rules and object orientation. Those are of great help when formalizing the more procedural part of technical knowledge (Liebig and Rösner 1996b). Finally, the decision was influenced by the layout of other modules of the system to be: The sentence generator we are using also employs *Loom* knowledge bases (see Sect. 8.4); staying with that representation system facilitates the cooperation between linguistic and domain knowledge.

8.3.2 Knowledge Formalization

In general, we are concerned with the formalization of two types of knowledge: abstract technical and product specific knowledge on the one hand, and linguistic knowledge on the other hand. In this section, we will restrict the discussion to the former type and its formalization within the framework of description logic. Linguistic sources such as grammar and lexis are more adequately represented using representation formalisms that are explicitly designed for linguistic purposes. Their representation will be subject of Sect. 8.4.2. An exception to this is the *Upper Model* (Bateman et al. 1994), a linguistically motivated ontology which serves as an interface between linguistic and non-linguistic knowledge, and which is formalized in the framework of description logic.

Technical and Product Model. The analysis of technical documents provides objects, actions, properties, and relations between them. In order to arrive at a formal conceptualization of these entities, we took the following steps in the design of the knowledge base:[5]

– grouping related entities (objects and relations), determining their commonalities, and describing them by means of properties;
– determining abstract descriptions which cover a wide range of phenomena;
– ensuring that conceptualizations made in a particular language are also reflected in the formal representation;
– realizing a modular description on different levels.

---

[5] Design decisions for knowledge bases are discussed in a number of articles, see for instance Brachman et al. (1991).

To illustrate these points, we present examples taken from the current domain for each of the design decisions, thereby describing the influence of these design decisions on the actual layout of the knowledge bases.

Entity grouping and the description of common properties: A number of entities in the technical domain share common properties. They are grouped together, and a more abstract superconcept is introduced that denotes the set union of these entities. Take, for instance, objects occurring in the document on changing spark plugs (given in the sample text in Fig. 8.1) and in similar texts that instruct the reader on how to change oil or how to check the coolant level. An analysis of the objects led to the introduction of several abstract concepts such as *technical-item* (spark plug, spark plug wire), *technical-instrument* (spark plug wrench, screwdriver), *measuring-instrument* (dipstick, coolant thermometer), *container* (oil tank, coolant tank), *machine* (engine), *vehicle* (car), to name a few. The common properties of these abstract concepts in turn are covered by the concept *technical-object*.

Abstract description of phenomena: There are several starting points for a more abstract description of domain specific concepts and relations. An important abstraction is captured by *part-whole* relations. In our domain they mainly hold between technical objects. A spark plug, for instance, is part of an engine, which is in turn part of a car. The part-whole relation has been studied in previous work (e.g. Winston et al. 1987, Artale et al. 1996), where several part-whole relations are distinguished and where problems regarding the transitivity of this relation are pointed out. In analogy to the inheritance of properties from superconcepts to their subconcepts, properties of the whole can be inherited by their parts and vice versa (vertical relationship). Furthermore, properties of parts can affect properties of other parts (horizontal relationship). Hence, the conceptualization has to reflect these different part-whole relations and the transitivity of the different part-whole relations. For a detailed discussion of the part-whole relation and an abstract conceptualization within the technical domain see Liebig and Rösner (1996a, 1996b).

Lexical influences on the conceptualization: The actual definition of a taxonomy for a certain area of the domain knowledge strongly interacts with results from the lexical analysis. We have introduced different lexical options for realizing one and the same concept (the *disconnect-resolvable-connection* action), which are available in English and German respectively. These different lexicalizations reflect different restrictions on the type of connection concerned and on the object involved in the action. For instance, lexicalizations may differ with respect to the level of granularity in which they reflect differences between connection types. To give an example: The analysis in Sect. 8.2.5 reveals that the German verbalization of a *disconnect-resolvable-connection* action is sensitive to the connection type: *Herausziehen* occurs when objects are connected with a *stick-in-connection*, whereas *abziehen* is chosen if objects are connected by means of a *stick-on-connection*. English does not mirror this discrimination in the choice of lexemes. In a nutshell, a representation of objects, actions and relations, which can support the appropriate verbalization of the *disconnect-resolvable-connection* action in English *and* German, has to reflect the different connection types and their distinguishing features.

Examples are thread connections (*threaded-joint*) and connections that are established by sticking some object into or onto another object (*stick-connection*).

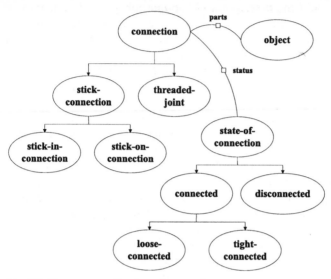

Fig. 8.3. The conceptualization of connections

Figure 8.3 shows a detail from the taxonomy for connections.[6] The taxonomy also reflects the state of a connection (*state-of-connection*), such as whether the connection holds or does not hold. As states play an important role for the conceptualization of actions, we will return to states in the next subsection.

Modular description: Since all the phenomena described so far (part-whole relation, connections) provide abstract means for formalizing many technical objects, we place them in the abstract technical model. In this view, the abstract technical model contains a collection of related ontologies. As mentioned above, a modular layout of the knowledge bases facilitates the reuse of parts of the knowledge base. This increases the benefits of the initial knowledge acquisition phase.

The conceptualization of the abstract technical model is supplemented by the analysis of additional knowledge sources. The abstract technical model is the very place where the additional knowledge that is employed by the reader when interpreting a given technical documentation is represented explicitly. Additional knowledge sources such as textbooks and encyclopedias are used to acquire the information

---

[6] We use the following notational conventions: Concepts are denoted by ellipses, whereas instances are denoted by rectangles. The *is-a* relation between concepts and the *is-instance-of* relation between an instance and a concept is indicated by arrows, while other relations between concepts are indicated by a line, labelled with the relation name. If several sister concepts represent a disjoint covering of a superconcept, such as the states *connected* and *disconnected* in Fig. 8.3, they are connected to the superconcept by branching arrows.

implicitly contained in natural language texts. Textbooks, especially those on mechanical engineering, often contain taxonomies of domain entities as well as differentiation criteria (see for instance Roth 1982), which can be exploited in setting up the abstract technical model.

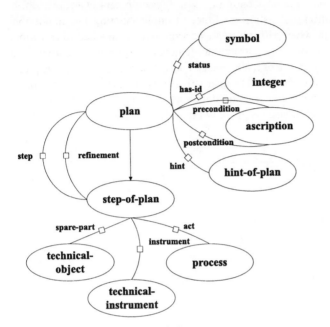

Fig. 8.4. The conceptualization of plans

Plan Structures. Instructive texts can be well formalized by means of *plans*, which represent complex actions (Fikes and Nilsson 1971). Complex actions can be decomposed into a sequence of actions. Figure 8.4 presents an abridged version of the formalization of actions and plans. For a given plan, the relation *step*, as depicted in Fig. 8.4, contains a sequence of complex or elementary actions. An action is elementary if the *act* relation is filled with an action instance, and complex if the *refinement* relation is filled by another plan instance. Each action and plan is associated with a set of conditions necessary for the action or plan to be applied, the *preconditions*, and a set of facts that hold after the action or plan has been performed, the *postconditions*. When an action is performed, the state of the objects that participate in this action may be modified. Thus, actions transform a given situation into a new one.

According to their different pre- and postconditions one can differentiate between three types of *connective-actions* in our domain: *resolve-connection-action*, *modify-connective-action* and *create-connective-action*. In Fig. 8.7 the conceptualization of connective actions is presented. Each of these actions alters the state of a connection within a given situation. States of connections are represented by the subconcepts of *state-of-connection* in Fig. 8.3. A *create-connective-action*, for instance, establishes a connection between two unconnected objects and thus alters the status of the connection from *disconnected* to *loose-connected*, whereas after the application of a *resolve-connective-action*, the connection state changes in the opposite direction.

In addition to the pre- and postconditions, warnings on potential errors and further advisory information such as information on trouble-shooting and on possible dangers that may occur when performing this action may be attached to an action. These elements correspond to the structural elements *preconditions*, *activity* and *warnings* in the macrostructure of maintenance instructions. To illustrate this point, consider the sample text in Fig. 8.1: The instructive parts of this text (how to replace spark plugs) can be modelled as a plan containing four steps and two hints. The corresponding plan representation is given in Fig. 8.5.[7]

replace-spark-plug_plan	plan
status	command
step	clean-any-dirt_step
	disconnect-spark-plug-wire_step
	remove-and-discard-old-spark-plug_step
	thread-in-new-spark-plug_step
	tighten-new-spark-plug_step
hint	tighten-but-prevent-overtighten_hint
	caution-improper-heat-range_hint

Fig. 8.5. The representation of the instructive parts in the sample text

Upper Modelling. We employ the *Upper Model* as described by Bateman et al. (1994) to bridge the gap between *non-linguistic* knowledge encoded in the product specific model and the abstract technical model, and *linguistic knowledge*. The upper model is a linguistically motivated ontology, whose classifications of entities reflect semantic distinctions in at least one of the target languages. As such, it offers a way of defining objects, actions and properties by supplying a hierarchy of general concepts, which are domain and task independent.

There are several approaches to linking domain knowledge to the upper model, in other words, to relating non-linguistic to linguistic knowledge. In the present application, we realized the linking by subordinating entities of the abstract technical model to upper model concepts. This has been mainly motivated by design deci-

---

[7] We use the following notational conventions to describe instances of the knowledge base: The heading of the table contains the name of the instance on the left side and the name of its direct superconcepts on the right side. In the body of the table for every relation the relation name is given on the left side and the current fillers on the right by side.

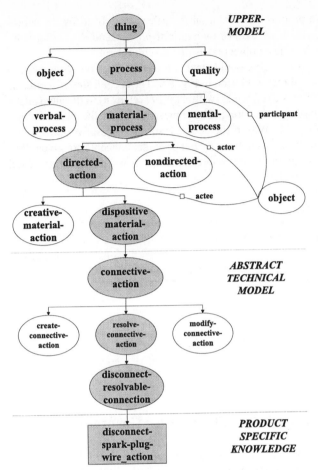

Fig. 8.6. The association of connective action with the upper model

sions of the current implementation, for another more flexible approach, which is motivated by work in lexical semantics, see Stede (1996).

To illustrate the approach, consider the taxonomy in Fig. 8.6. It exemplifies the connection between the upper model, the abstract technical model and the product specific model for particular concepts. In this example, the concept *connective-action*, as a part of the abstract technical model, is related to the upper model by subordinating it to the upper model concepts *dispositive-material-action*, *material-process*, *process* and *thing*.

As the concepts of the abstract technical model and the product specific model are subconcepts of the upper model, they inherit the relations defined for their superconcepts in the upper model. Consider the concept *disconnect-resolvable-connection* in Fig. 8.6, which is a subconcept of the concepts *process*, *material-process* and *directed-action*. The concept *process* introduces the *participant* relation to those objects that partake in a process. This relation is further specialized by the subrelations *actor* and *actee*, which are defined by *material-process* and *directed-action*. Both relations describe the role an object takes in a given process.

Recall the instructive parts of the sample text, which describe how to change the spark plugs and their formal representation in Fig. 8.5. The second step *disconnect-spark-plug-wire_step* contains a reference (within the *act* relation) to the elementary action *disconnect-spark-plug-wire_action*. The representation of the plan step and the action is given in Fig. 8.7. Within the action instance *disconnect-spark-plug-wire_action*, fillers for the relations defined by upper model concepts are given. Figure 8.6 shows how this action instance is related to concepts within the upper model and the abstract technical model.

disconnect-spark-plug-wire_step	step-of-plan
act disconnect-spark-plug-wire_action	

disconnect-spark-plug-wire_action	disconnect-resolvable-connection
actor reader_instance	
actee spark-plug-wire_instance	

Fig. 8.7. The representation of a single step within the plan

8.4 Expressing the Knowledge: The *TechDoc* Generator

We have already stressed the importance of documents within the product life cycle, and in particular noted the importance of automating access to the knowledge contained in these documents. A prerequisite for that is the formal representation of the knowledge of a particular domain, especially the knowledge that is expressed—be it explicitly or implicitly—in documents situated in the domain under consideration. An initial formalization of technical knowledge, more specifically knowledge expressed in car manuals, has been attempted in Sect. 8.3. The next step is to validate the resulting knowledge bases with respect to a particular practical application. The application we have opted for supports our view of documents as a particular view on knowledge: the automatic production of documents from a common underlying knowledge base. The quality of the documents will give valuable feedback about the quality of the underlying knowledge bases.

To meet this goal, we have developed the *TechDoc* system, a multilingual text generation system that automatically produces a particular type of document—multilingual technical manuals in English, German and French—from a common knowledge representation. The generated documents reflect a particular view on the knowledge: Given some parameters such as the reader's level of expertise, language and text type, the *TechDoc* generator creates different documents from the same knowledge pool. In this way, the *TechDoc* system can be regarded as a proof of concept, as it demonstrates the feasibility of our understanding of the interaction between knowledge bases and natural language documents.

In the remainder of this section, we describe the *TechDoc* prototype and the state of implementation in detail, and then present a sample run of the generation process as it has been implemented so far.

8.4.1 System Architecture

The overall architecture of the *TechDoc* text generation system is given in Fig. 8.8, for a detailed description see Rösner and Stede (1994) and Rösner (1994). The system components fall into three major groups:

- **knowledge sources**:
  - knowledge bases of different types and abstraction levels,
  - linguistic resources like multilingual grammars and lexica,
- **processing modules** that transform one level of representation (data structures) into another,
- **interfaces** that support the user-system interaction.

Not all processing modules are worked out in detail and hence are not fully integrated. Some aspects need further investigation and verification, and are subject to current research. We will go into some of these issues in Sect. 8.4.3.

The *TechDoc* system is based on knowledge bases encoding product specific knowledge and more abstract technical knowledge, schematic text structure and task representation. These knowledge sources are implemented in *Loom*. *TechDoc* takes as input an instance of a plan, i.e. a formal representation of a specific task. Starting from this representation, a language-independent discourse structure is generated. This step includes selecting what to express, deciding on the textual representation of selected content structures and imposing a partial ordering on them. The basic elements at this level of representation are (complex) RST relations. In a subsequent step, the discourse structure is broken down into clause sequences. This transformation must determine:

- clause boundaries,
- syntactic structure of single clauses,
- theme of clauses,
- appropriate referential expressions (pronouns, definite or indefinite descriptions) within clauses, and
- linguistic realizations (e.g. function word or phrases) that signal rhetorical relations.

Rösner and Stede (1992) propose a pattern-based algorithm that incorporates linguistic and semantic constraints and preferences to transform a plan structure into a discourse representation. A more complex treatment of text planning is currently investigated within the research group.

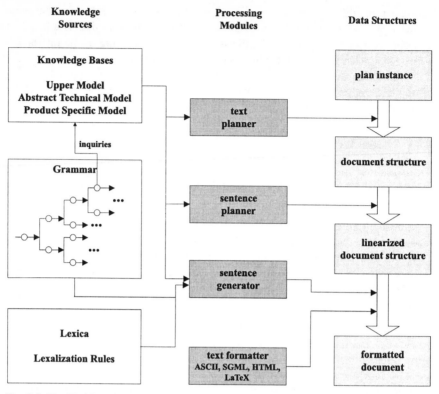

Fig. 8.8. The *TechDoc* System Architecture

The resulting sentence plans, specified in the sentence planning language (SPL) (Kasper 1989), are successively handed over to the sentence generation module. As a front-end generator, we employ the *Penman* sentence generator (Mann 1983), which has been enhanced by German and French grammars and separate morphology modules. *Penman* takes an SPL expression as input term from which it generates sentences in either English, German or French. In a final step, the document structure is exploited for an automatic formatting of the output text. The formatting module take the output medium (screen or printed) into account, and realizes generated text in the selected format (e.g. ASCII, SGML, HTML, LaTeX).

The approach to treat documents as specific views on the underlying knowledge bases is particularly well demonstrated by the hypertext versions of the generated text. Elements in the text are linked to the underlying knowledge base instances that gave rise to their existence. The user can use the text as a query interface to the knowledge sources, for instance, s/he can prompt for additional information about a technical object or action by simply clicking on the respective noun phrase or verbal structure. In this sense, documents are "active", and can change the view on the knowledge base in response to user interaction.

8.4.2 Linguistic Resources

The sentence generator requires linguistic resources—grammar, lexica—and the upper model as the interface between non-linguistic and linguistic knowledge to produce well-formed output. The linguistic resources have to meet the requirements identified in Sect. 8.2.5. In the following, we give a short account of the linguistic resources as employed by the *Penman* sentence generator.

Syntactic Knowledge. Syntactic and some lexical knowledge is encoded in a *systemic-functional grammar* (Halliday 1985, Matthiessen and Bateman 1991). Such a grammar is organized around *systems* and *choosers*. Each system represents a minimal semantic difference, and a chooser represents the criteria for choosing between the alternatives (or *features*) a system offers. Choosers are organized as decision trees, which post inquiries to knowledge bases and other external information sources at each decision point. Thus, choices in the system network (grammar) are ultimately constrained by the context in which an utterance is produced. While traversing the grammar, a set of features is accumulated, which gives rise to a specific linguistic realization. *Penman* builds natural language sentences from sentence plans as a side-effect of traversing the system network of a systemic-functional grammar.

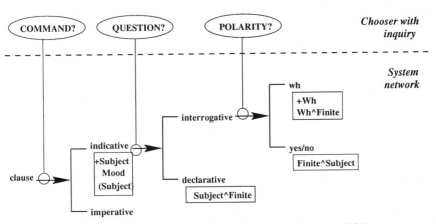

Fig. 8.9. The system network realizing *mood* (Matthiessen and Bateman 1991).

Figure 8.9 shows part of the system network and the corresponding choosers. The network can be interpreted as follows: It describes some of the options available in the realization of mood, i.e. whether a clause is realized as declarative, interrogative or imperative. These are options in the network (*declarative, interrogative, imperative*). A choice among these features has to be made for every clause, therefore the feature *clause* acts as entry condition to the network. Each feature has associated *realization statements*, which posit constraints on the resulting linguistic realization; for instance, by selecting the branch *indicative*, a subject is introduced to the clause *(+Subject)*. Realization statements are given in boxes below the feature they are associated with. "+" triggers the introduction of an element, and "∧" indicates the order of elements. As already mentioned, choices among alternative features are made by choosers that query the knowledge bases. For instance, the choice between *imperative* and *indicative* is performed by a chooser that inquires whether the utterance is intended as a command or not. In case the answer is "command", the imperative feature is chosen and the *mood* can be realized, in case the answer is "no command", *indicative* is selected and further choices have to be made.

Lexical Knowledge. Lexical knowledge can be of two kinds: On the one hand, we observe a one-to-one correspondence between concepts and lexemes. In this case, we simply introduce a lexical rule stating this correspondence. In our domain, for instance, the concept *dipstick* is always mapped on the German lexeme *Tauchmeßstab* and the English *dipstick*. We also encounter cases where German and English differ with respect to granularity, and hence, one and the same concept is realized differently in different contexts. We deal with this phenomenon by introducing *lexicalization rules* that invoke filler restrictions for the roles of the concept to be lexicalized.

Figure 8.10 presents decision trees that produce adequate German and English lexemes for the action of disconnecting a dissolvable connection. A detailed discussion of these lexicalization rules follows in the next section, where we present a sample run of the *TechDoc* generator.

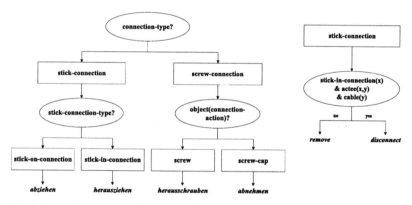

Fig. 8.10. Lexical rules for German and English disconnection concepts

8.4.3 Example

This section illustrates the automatic production of documents by means of a detailed example, the spark plug text from Fig. 8.1. For reasons of comprehensibility and space, we will restrict the discussion to a subpart of the text, the second half of the text starting with the enumeration. These paragraphs realize the structural elements *activity* and *warnings*.

The element *activity* comprises a step-by-step description of an activity eventually to be performed by the user, whereas the element *warnings* realizes further advisory information or warnings. Both elements can easily be represented as partial plan structures, in this case by the plan instance *replace-spark-plug_plan*; the corresponding representation on the knowledge level has already been introduced in Fig. 8.5. Here, the activity element is expressed by the *step* relation, the warning element matches the content of the *hint* relation. The text generation system takes plan instances as input; see Fig. 8.8 for an outline of the generation process.

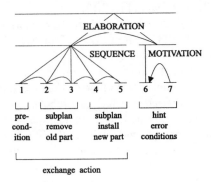

Fig. 8.11. The discourse structure built from the plan structure in Fig. 8.5

In a first step, the plan structure is transformed into a discourse structure, with the plan elements acting as leafs in the discourse tree. Figure 8.11 shows the discourse structure that has been built automatically from the *replace-spark-plug_plan*. In order to facilitate the coreference between plan and discourse elements, we list the plan elements again and assign numbers to them:

1   clean-any-dirt_step

2   disconnect-spark-plug-wire_step

3   remove-and-discard-old-spark-plug_step

4   thread-in-new-spark-plug_step

5   tighten-new-spark-plug_step

6   tighten-but-prevent-overtighten_hint

7   caution-improper-heat-range_hint

These numbers are used in the discourse structure in Fig. 8.11 to refer to a plan element. Plan steps 1 to 5 enter into a *sequence* relation. Hints 6 and 7 are governed by a *motivation* relation. Both subtrees are combined by an *elaboration* relation. We noted earlier that the plan structure as presented in Fig. 8.5 has not been fully expanded: The plan steps can be further refined by subplans and actions, containing information on their pre- and postconditions, giving rise to a more fine-grained discourse structure. At present, the transformation of plan structures to discourse structures is performed in a straightforward manner without accounting for all the interdependencies between the different tasks of the transformation step as listed in Sect. 8.4.1.

The discourse representation, that is, plan elements from the plan structure (which are the leaf nodes in the tree) and the discourse relations holding between them, are then passed to the sentence planner, which is responsible for linearising the tree and building SPLs. A sample SPL, constructed from the *disconnect-spark-plug-wire_action* instance given in Fig. 8.7), is shown in Fig. 8.12.

An SPL term has the form *(Variable / Type Attribute*)*, where *Type* refers to a concept in the knowledge base. The sample SPL term in Fig. 8.12 invokes the concepts *disconnect-resolvable-connection*, *person*, and *spark-plug-wire*. The instance *reader_instance* denotes the addressee of the utterance. Attributes describe the functional roles of specifiers, modifiers or complements of the head element. In the example, the head *disconnect-resolvable-connection*, which is a subconcept of *process* as shown in Fig. 8.6, has the attributes *actor* and *actee*. In addition to the propositional knowledge encoded by domain concepts and relations, the SPL from Fig. 8.12 contains information on the speech act (*:speechact command*). The filler of the speech act role has been derived from the filler *command* of the *status* relation within the sample plan given in Fig. 8.5. In case the status is instantiated with *description*, the sentence plan for *disconnect-spark-plug-wire_action* would contain the line *:speechact assertion*.

```
(drc / disconnect-resolvable-connection
    :actor (reader_instance / person)
    :actee (spark-plug-wire_instance / spark-plug-wire)
    :speechact command)
```

Fig. 8.12. An SPL expression built from the instance in Fig. 8.7

In the sentence planning module, SPLs are built for all leaf elements of the discourse structure. These are then successively passed to the sentence generator for syntactic and lexical realization.

The SPL in Fig. 8.12 triggers the generation of *Disconnect the spark plug wire* and *Die Zündkerze abziehen*. The corresponding assertional variant is *The reader disconnects the spark-plug-wire* and *Der Leser zieht die Zündkerze ab*. These different realizations are due to different instantiations of the *speechact* role. The filler *command* will eventually give rise to the imperative mood, as described in the discussion of the *mood* system from Fig. 8.9. In case the speech act is instantiated with *assertion*, the features *indicative* and *declarative* from the *mood* network are selected by the relevant choosers, thus yielding a declarative sentence.

Let us now turn to the lexicalization: We have already mentioned that German and English differ regarding the verbalization of processes. Hence, we introduce a set of lexicalization rules. These rules transform the language-independent SPL expressions into well-formed verbalizations in different languages.

Consider the SPL given in Fig. 8.12, which contains the *disconnect-resolvable-connection* action. The lexical realization of this action in German depends on the connection type referred to. Using the information on connection types given in Fig. 8.3 in the previous section, the lexical realization depends on whether a *screw-connection* or a *stick-connection* should be resolved. For actions of the type *stick-connection* further decisions depend on whether the connected parts stick *in* or *on* another, and for actions of the type *screw-connection* on the object of the disconnecting action. When the object is a subconcept of the concept *screw*, one would use the term *herausschrauben (screw off)*, but when it is a subconcept of the concept *cap* (e.g. *oil-filler-cap*), one would prefer the term *abnehmen (take off)*. In English, the *disconnect-resolvable-connection* action in the sample SPL would be realized by *disconnect* due to the lexicalization rule given in Fig. 8.10, which states that in case the object is a *cable* or its subconcept, *disconnect* is the proper realization, while in all other cases the system would opt for *remove*.

Spark plugs
1. Clean any dirt off the spark plug base.
2. Disconnect the spark plug wire, remove the old plug, and discard it.
3. Thread in the new spark plug by hand, in order to prevent a cross-threading.
4. After the plug seats against the cylinder head, tighten the plug securely with a spark plug wrench, in order to compress the washer.

CAUTION: The spark plugs must be tightened securely, but they shouldn't be over-tightened. A plug that is too loose can be very hot, and it can possibly damage the engine, but a too tight plug could damage the threads in the cylinder head.

Zündkerzen
1. Jeglichen Schmutz von der Zündkerzenbasis entfernen.
2. Das Zündkabel abziehen, dann die alte Zündkerze herausschrauben und sie wegwerfen.
3. Die neue Zündkerze von Hand einschrauben, um Gewindeüberschneiden zu vermeiden.
4. Nachdem die Zündkerze dem Zylinderkopf aufsitzt, die Zündkerze fest mit einem Zündkerzenschlüssel anziehen, um den Dichtungsring zusammenzupressen.

ACHTUNG: Die Zündkerzen müssen fest angezogen werden, aber sie sollten nicht überdreht werden. Eine Zündkerze, die zu lose ist, kann sehr heiß sein, und sie kann den Motor möglicherweise beschädigen, aber eine zu feste Zündkerze kann die Gewinde in dem Zylinderkopf beschädigen.

Fig. 8.13. A snapshop of a multilingual text generated by the *TechDoc* system

Figure 8.13 shows the system output for the *replace-spark-plug_plan* after it has been processed by the formatting module. The text reflects the current state of implementation of the prototype. Note that the texts still contain minor syntactic errors and some awkward lexicalization choices, but these can be removed by extending the grammar coverage and fine-tuning the lexical rules. More importantly, the texts already convey the content to be realized in a satisfactory manner. In addition, they account for syntactic and lexical peculiarities of English and German.

For instance, in the German version, directives are realized using an infinitive construction, whereas English uses the imperative. These differences do not pose any problems to multilingual generation, since all processes that are involved in mapping the abstract content representation to the linguistic surface are tailored towards the languages to be realized.

8.5 Knowledge Management

The first three stages of the knowledge engineering process have been described in the previous sections: the acquisition of knowledge, the representation and formalization of that knowledge, and finally its application. The latter plays a crucial role in the entire knowledge engineering process as it serves as a test bed for design decisions made in earlier phases. Feedback from this phase may yield changes in the knowledge bases, thus necessitating knowledge management facilities. The capitalization of knowledge makes further demands on the knowledge management task. As noted above, acquisition and representation of the knowledge required for a particular application and in a particular domain are time-consuming and cost-intensive. Hence the capitalization of knowledge is of major importance in order to make the acquisition and representation effort worthwhile. In general, there are two possibilities to improve capitalization: by reducing the cost of creation and maintenance, and by increasing the benefits of a knowledge base. In this section, we will discuss how the initial costs for creation can be reduced, how maintenance can be optimized, and how capitalization can be increased by changing the way in which knowledge is managed in an enterprise.

8.5.1 Benefits

The approach of representing knowledge in an explicit and sharable way instead of describing it by means of natural language texts (documents) has a lot in common with the broader area of *corporate memory*. In Chapter 2, p. 18, van Heijst et al. define a corporate memory as "an explicit, disembodied, persistent representation of the knowledge and information in an organization". A major advantage of a corporate memory is that by storing corporate know-how explicitly and making it available to the whole company, an enterprise's competitiveness in the marketplace can be improved (Kühn and Höfling 1994). This is, above all, due to the reduced risk of loss of information (experts may leave), better information flow (fast and easy access) and a reduction in the time and demands placed on human experts.

We argued above that at present, natural language documents constitute one of the major resources for the knowledge accumulated during product development and the product life cycle. We then demonstrated in an exemplary way how it is possible to arrive at an explicit representation of the knowledge contained in documents. The resulting knowledge bases could potentially be treated as a corporate memory of technical know-how in the car domain—of course, they would still have to be enriched.

An important observation regarding corporate know-how is that it is not static but changes over time. This could lead to problems regarding consistency and completeness of technical documentations. A crucial benefit of taking documents as a particular view on a common underlying knowledge base, and of producing documents from that knowledge base, is that changes in the corporate memory immediately find their expression in natural language documents. In a nutshell, changes and updates need only be performed at one place, within the common representation; they will then be propagated to all new document versions produced from that knowledge base. Former versions will still be available. Obviously, this will improve the effectiveness of the information flow inside (and outside) a company considerably, since documents can be produced on demand, always reflecting the current state of the know-how. Further, documentation is constantly available in different languages for enterprises operating internationally and can be tailored to different users, levels of detail and situations.

A major benefit from using knowledge bases rather than documents for preserving a company's know-how is that this knowledge is *sharable*, i.e. the knowledge bases can be exploited by further applications in addition to the generation of multilingual technical documents. This holds for the abstract technical model; representing that model in a sharable and reusable way facilitates the realization of other types of applications. For instance, one could employ the knowledge for the qualitative simulation of instruction steps in order to check for completeness and applicability of a plan. Further, we are experimenting with the automatic derivation of hints and warnings. For example, if an action has an undesired side-effect, one might want to communicate potential dangers to the reader. Both applications are described in more detail by Rösner (1994) and Liebig and Rösner (1996b).

8.5.2 Costs and Possible Optimization

The benefits of having access to corporate know-how on the domain are partially balanced by the costs of acquiring such knowledge. An initial approach to knowledge acquisition by analysing natural language document has been described in Sect. 8.2. At first glance, this seems to be a tedious, costly and time-consuming task, which is hardly outweighed by the benefits of the resulting knowledge bases. However, we can only judge the acquisition effort correctly when taking a long-term perspective on this matter. There is no doubt that knowledge acquisition does not pay-off if the knowledge bases are only used for one particular application and for a short period of time, and if knowledge sources constantly undergo significant changes.

When taking a closer look at the nature of the different knowledge sources under consideration, we notice the following: Most of the *linguistic knowledge*, like grammars and lexica, will remain stable over time. The macrostructure of a certain text type will not change either, it just might have to be adapted to changes in DIN (or ISO) norms. Similar document types can be defined as variants of the initial text types; additional analysis only has to be performed if new text types are considered.

Thus, where the initial acquisition phase is executed carefully, this large effort only has to be performed once, and pays off in later use and reduced maintenance costs.

Concerning the *nonlinguistic resources* we noted the following: Since the *abstract technical model* describes general domain knowledge, it will only change as much as the understanding of the technical foundations as such changes. In other words, only if the company's know-how on technical matters undergoes substantial transitions will the abstract technical model have to be modified. Hence, the maintenance effort for this knowledge can be neglected, even in the most innovative companies. In contrast, the *product specific knowledge base* is subject to frequent changes. To reduce maintenance efforts and to assure consistency, the maintenance of the product specific knowledge should at best be carried out by product engineers as part of their activities during the product life cycle. Once the underlying product knowledge is modelled in a formal way, changes to the product can be described formally by the product designer within this formal representation. As all the different realizations and multilingual variants are generated from this formal representation, the resulting documents necessarily reflect these changes. Thus, documentation will be tightly integrated into the overall engineering process.

Current practise in industrial companies, however, often looks somewhat different: In early stages of the product life cycle, design decisions are frequently not formalized, and product (knowledge) modelling begins only at a later design phase in combination with the definition of the geometric model. As a consequence, the output from this phase—in the worst case only technical drawings—does not reflect the motivations underlying certain design decisions (e.g. functional requirements). But these decisions and reasons are relevant for later stages like production planning. We believe that modelling this knowledge right from the start of the design phase and generating the documentations automatically would considerably improve the cooperation between different departments and engineers of a company.

In brief, the costs of building and maintaining knowledge bases mainly stem from the product specific knowledge base, since it is subject to frequent change, whereas all other knowledge bases stay constant over long periods of time. However, even the costs of maintaining product specific information can be significantly reduced by integrating this process into the product life cycle and the operating environment of product engineers.

8.5.3 A Practical Solution: The Authoring Tool

We noted that the primary maintenance effort concerns the product specific knowledge. This calls for an optimization of the management of this resource. One way to achieve this is by integrating the maintenance task into the product life cycle, and by ascribing this task to product engineers and designers. Since it cannot be expected that they are familiar with techniques for knowledge representation, this task has to be supported by special tools for the extension and modification of product knowledge. In an ideal case, these tools are integrated into software systems which are already in use (like engineering data managements (EDM) systems or CAD-software). In addition, the final creation of documentation should be supported by an authoring tool (which could be used, for instance, by the technical editors), where knowledge specifying the content of a particular document can be selected and combined into an abstract representation of that document.

In a follow-up project to *TechDoc*, a prototypical *document workbench* has been realized which provides interactive support in managing knowledge bases and creating documents (Grote et al. 1997). The three main components of this workbench are an authoring tool for the interactive planning and structuring of a document, a document generator which takes this specification as input and generates formatted multilingual documents, and a module to administer knowledge bases and support the integration of existing resources.

The interactive creation of a document using the document workbench is performed in the following way: The starting point is an abstract skeletal plan, which represents the macrostructure of the desired text type. Optional elements have to be selected by the author, while the system provides the obligatory elements. These are then successively specified and refined by the author, drawing on various knowledge sources. By selecting the desired content from the knowledge bases the author creates an instance of a *plan*, which is fed to the multilingual generation system (*TechDoc*) for realization.

8.6 Discussion

Most of the work relevant to the current approach falls into one of the following three categories:

- theories and tools for (multilingual) natural language generation,
- work on instructional texts, especially those in technical documentation,
- sharable and reusable knowledge sources.

Some of the results of other projects have been directly integrated into this work either as components (e.g. the *Penman* grammars for surface generation) or as part of the theoretical framework (e.g. RST or description logic).

Multilingual text generation. Early work on natural language generation from conceptual structures has already demonstrated the feasibility and attractiveness of multilingual delivery of knowledge structures (Goldman 1974). Nevertheless, multilingual generation has only recently received broader attention in the natural language generation community. This may be partly due to the fact that in a generation system with a single target language (i.e. English in many cases), issues of language independence of semantic representations do not play such a decisive role.

There are a number of applications other than technical documentation in which the use of multilingual generation as an alternative to (human or machine) translation of the respective texts is both attractive and feasible, e.g. generation of weather reports (in English and French) from meteorological data or generation of statistical reports from a body of statistical data (see e.g. Bourbeau et al. 1990). These successful applications have in common that the domains of discourse are rather limited and therefore there is no need for elaborate modelling. Further, the "raw material" for generation can be obtained by evaluating the data. In short, the aspect of domain modelling is an issue which has so far received only little attention in the area of multilingual generation; an issue, however, which is central to the generation approach pursued in the *TechDoc* project.

Generation of instructional text. Other projects in the generation of instructional text are more elaborate in some specialised topics. But to our knowledge, none of them aims at such an integrated and holistic treatment of document generation as we have proposed, covering aspects of generation with the same effort as those of knowledge acquisition, knowledge representation and knowledge sharing and reuse.

The projects *WIP* (Wahlster et al. 1993) and *PPP* (André et al. 1996), for example, which aim at the automatic generation of multimodal technical documentations, have developed sophisticated techniques for coordinating text and graphics. Even though there exists a multilingual version of the system, they have payed only little attention to issues of generality in domain modelling and to reusing or extending the knowledge bases.

Drafter (Paris and Vander Linden 1996) is another project in automatic generation of multilingual instruction texts that employs support for authoring. Their emphasis has been on the role of the technical author in the production of technical documentation and on providing tools for drafting document structures. Only recently have they given more attention to issues and principles of domain modelling.

Multi-purpose generation of personalised patient instruction and information is the aim of the *HealthDoc* (DiMarco et al. 1995) project. They try to avoid domain modelling and start generation as a selection process from a so-called "master document" already geared towards English as a target language. It is difficult to interpret this structure as formal knowledge representation and to imagine that it could serve as a basis for multilingual generation.

Knowledge representation. The need for reuse and exchange of knowledge bases has led to a number of research projects and standardisation efforts. An example of the latter is work on *KIF* (Genesereth and Fikes 1992), a knowledge interchange format that serves as interlingua for the translation between different knowledge representation formalisms, and thus supports the incorporation of existing knowledge bases into other knowledge sources.

Ontologies (Uschold and Gruninger 1996) are an attempt to ease the construction of knowledge based systems by providing reusable knowledge sources about recurring topics. Some ontologies are now available in the ontology library (Gruber 1993). We are investigating how to make better use of these resources and how sources taken from this library may be harmonised with the chosen abstract technical model.

The current approach to knowledge acquisition through the analysis of multilingual documents guided by abstraction principles may very well be interpreted as a methodology (among others) for the principled construction of ontologies. However, one needs to employ (semi-)automated tools for that task in in order to reduce the costs of building knowledge bases. There have recently been efforts on knowledge acquisition by constructing semantic knowledge bases (ontologies) semi-automatically, primarily within the PANGLOSS project on knowledge-based machine translation (Knight and Luk 1994); and, in the area of knowledge based systems, on terminology extraction (Dagan and Church 1994, Justeson and Katz 1995). Efforts within the natural language generation community on knowledge acquisition are described by Reiter et al. (1997) and Paris and Vander Linden (1996).

8.7 Summary and Future Work

This chapter presented a novel approach to knowledge management by

- introducing the notion of documents as views on particular knowledge structures in a particular context;
- describing techniques for the acquisition of knowledge contained in documents;
- illustrating how to create knowledge bases which can be used for automated document generation and which are reusable for other applications (e.g. qualitative simulation of actions proposed in a plan);
- presenting suggestions on how to integrate such an approach into the engineering process and discussing potential consequences for the whole product life cycle.

The development of this work has continually been accompanied by and has profited from a lot of discussions with experts from companies of various size (SMEs as well as internationally operating concerns) and from different industrial sectors. There has been much support and acceptance for the general approach but some critical questions raised demand further investigation and evaluation of the approach "in the field."

- What is the relation between cost and benefit, i.e. how much effort has to be initially invested into knowledge acquisition before the potential advantages of such a corporate memory are at least balanced?
- Will engineers accept the approach and use the authoring tools offered?
- Is convergence and cross-fertilization with other approaches to modelling of product data and product knowledge (e.g. STEP) possible?

In addition to such evaluation issues, future work must focus on investigating into ways to make the knowledge acquisition phase more efficient and less time-consuming, for instance by employing semi-automated tools for the analysis of large text corpora.

Furthermore, future work has to focus on the integration of the current approach with existing engineering data management systems. These systems contain product knowledge such as geometrical data and configuration of components, but lack, for example, knowledge on instructions for use. Hence, there is a need to investigate into a tight integration of both approaches.

A major concern will be if and how the approach will be transferable to other text types and their underlying knowledge structures. Concerning technical documentation, this will include further analysis of, for instance, explanatory manual texts (i.e. explaining the normal functioning and usage of technical objects rather than their repair and maintenance) and guides for trouble-shooting, and their relation to function models and failure models respectively. Explanatory texts for use in intelligent tutoring systems (ITS) and for interactive advisory systems seem to be other promising candidates for further elaboration.

9. Corporate Memories for Knowledge Management in Industrial Practice: Prospects and Challenges

Otto Kühn and Andreas Abecker
DFKI Kaiserslautern, Germany

A core concept in discussions about technological support for knowledge management is the Corporate Memory. A Corporate or Organizational Memory can be characterized as a comprehensive computer system which captures a company's accumulated know-how and other knowledge assets and makes them available to enhance the efficiency and effectiveness of knowledge-intensive work processes. The successful development of such a system requires a careful analysis of established work practices and available information-technology (IT) infrastructure. This is essential for providing a cost-effective solution which will be accepted by the users and can be evolved in the future. This chapter compares and summarizes our experiences from three case studies on Corporate Memories for supporting various aspects in the product life-cycles of three European corporations. Based on the conducted analyses and prototypical implementations, we sketch a general framework for the development methodology, architecture, and technical realization of a Corporate Memory.

9.1 Introduction

The global marketplace of the future will be characterized—with respect to the *products*—by shorter development cycles and harder fights on the quality battlefield, and—with respect to *organizational structures*—by lean organizations, Total Quality Management, and the advent of the Virtual Enterprise. In this situation, knowledge has been recognized as a company's most important asset for successful competition. Management strategies like *Organizational Learning* (see also Chapter 2) and *Corporate Knowledge Management* (KM) (Drucker 1993, Senge et al. 1994, Wiig 1993a) find growing interest.

Ann Macintosh (1997) from the AI Applications Institute (AIAI, Edinburgh, U. K.) motivates the need for knowledge asset management as follows:

> "Enterprises are realizing how important it is to 'know what they know' and be able to make maximum use of the knowledge. This is their corporate knowledge asset. These knowledge assets reside in many different places such as: databases, knowledge bases, filing cabinets and peoples' heads and are distributed right across the enterprise. All too often one part of an enterprise repeats work of another part simply because it is impossible to

keep track of, and make use of, knowledge in other parts. Enterprises need to know: what their corporate knowledge assets are; and how to manage and make use of these assets to get maximum return."

Knowledge management has become a hot topic both in management and computer sciences, and numerous suggestions have been made concerning various aspects of the problem. We will give a brief review of the ongoing discussion and the current state of the art in the next section. We will then focus on the question: *"What kind of computer system is best suited to support knowledge management in industrial practice?"* Such a computer system we will call "Corporate or Organizational Memory".

In order to elucidate the requirements for a Corporate Memory and to investigate possible solutions, we will present three case studies which were conducted in cooperation with major European companies. We will then summarize the lessons learned from these case studies and suggest a generic reference architecture for a Corporate Memory together with some directions for a development methodology. We will finish by presenting some core problems in the realization of a Corporate Memory which require further research.

9.2 Knowledge Management and Corporate Memories

9.2.1 Current Knowledge Management Deficits

Ann Macintosh's analysis of the current deficits in knowledge management, which was quoted above, perfectly agrees with those of other authors as well as with our own experiences from industrial practice. The most serious impediments to more productivity in knowledge-based work processes can be summarized as follows:

– *Highly-paid workers spend much of their time looking for needed information:* This ubiquitous fact is in stark contrast with the considerable efforts which have been made in enhancing the productivity of lower-paid production workers by placing every tool and part they need within the reach of their hands. Even though it may be doubted that work processes which require knowledge and creativity can be rationalized to the same extent, it is more than obvious that a huge potential for improvement exists.
– *Essential know-how is available only in the heads of a few employees:* This lack of documentation is becoming ever more serious with changing work habits (e.g. frequent job changes, shorter and more flexible work hours, tele-working), which reduce the availability of individual know-how and impede communication between employees.
– *Valuable information is buried in piles of documents and data:* Even when relevant knowledge is explictly documented, its identification is becoming more and more difficult due to the continuously growing flood of mostly irrelevant information.

- *Costly errors are repeated due to disregard of previous experiences:* This is mostly a direct consequence of the forementioned deficits. It is mentioned here explicitly, since it highlights the costs of insufficient knowledge management and offers a tangible goal for improvements.
- *Delays and suboptimal product quality result from insufficient flow of information:* This is how lack of knowledge management shows at the bottom line, since the rapid development of new products with high-quality and low costs is becoming more and more essential for a company's successful competition in the global marketplace.

9.2.2 Computer Support for Knowledge Management

Most surveys of knowledge management (KM) concepts and their operationalization coming from the management sciences treat only roughly the aspects of computer support; the topic is usually discussed by giving an unstructured list of useful computer services, such as e-mail, groupware, or hypertext systems (see e.g. Wiig 1996).

On the other hand, a series of recent and upcoming scientific events concerning the use of Information and Communication Technology (ICT) for KM support (Dieng and Vanwelkenhuysen 1996, Wolf and Reimer 1996, Dieng et al. 1997, Abecker et al. 1997) shows that computer scientists have a growing interest in the topic. Whereas they discuss in detail specific technical topics of computer support for KM, they tend to ignore the specific requirements and constraints for successful KM support in industrial practice which can only be met by a combination of several ICT technologies. Nevertheless, one can identify two main streams of work:

1. The *process-centered view* mainly understands KM as a social communication process which can be improved by various aspects of *groupware support*.
2. The *product-centered view* focuses on knowledge documents, their creation, storage, and reuse in computer-based *corporate memories*.

Groupware Support for Communication and Cooperation. Figure 9.1 gives an overview of techniques typically mentioned in the KM discussion. Interestingly, the core idea of "Improving knowledge management by applying innovative techniques for communication and cooperation" seems to be predominant in management-oriented papers.

In our opinion, these techniques are important *enabling* technologies; they form a substantial part of the necessary technical infrastructure for KM, but they are definitely not sufficient. Intranet technology or workflow management systems may still have an innovative touch for managers, but they have to be intelligently used and synergetically combined to overcome the current deficits mentioned in the previous section.

Using e-mail or video-conferencing for consulting a knowledgeable colleague depends on a yellow-page system or a personal-skills profile for finding her; building better workflows based on previously performed projects relies on a thorough

Communication

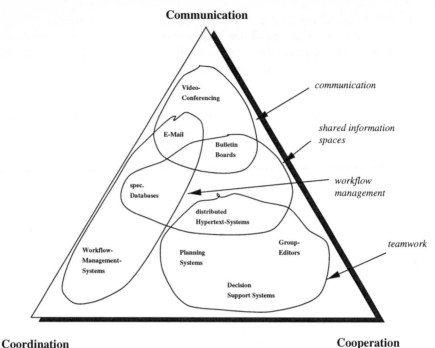

Coordination   **Cooperation**

Fig. 9.1. Dimensions of groupware support (Stammwitz 1996)

analysis of stored performance data; distributed authoring of hypertext documents makes only full use of its technical possibilities if the collaborative argumentation space built up during the group-decisions processes can be exploited in other, similar projects and the document contents can comfortably be exploited, without "getting lost in hyperspace". All these examples show that the full benefits of an improved communication and cooperation by innovative technologies will only become effective, if they are based on a flexible and comprehensive information depository in the form of a corporate memory.

Knowledge Capitalization with Corporate Memories. This view of KM is being pursued mostly by computer scientists and psychologists who have been working in Artificial Intelligence. In analogy to human memory, which allows us to build on previous experiences and avoid a repetition of errors, a Corporate Memory is to capture information from various sources in an organization and make it available for different tasks at hand.

The vision of a such a computer system, which has also been called *Organizational Memory Information System (OMIS)* (Stein and Zwass 1995), has so far been realized only in a very rudimentary way, but nevertheless, many interesting suggestions can be found in the literature:

1. Lessons-learned archives and best-practice databases typically rely on conventional Information Retrieval/Document Management techniques but introduce

business process models and application domain ontologies as additional meta-data categories for describing and indexing knowledge documents (van der Spek and de Hoog 1994, van Heijst et al. 1996, Hofer-Alfeis and Klabunde 1996).

2. (Distributed) case-bases capture problem-solving expertise for specific app-lication problems, sometimes combined with sophisticated knowledge-based retrieval mechanisms or coupled hypertext information systems (Kamp 1996, Kamp et al. 1996, Aamodt and Nygard 1995, Prasad and Plaza 1996).

3. Expert systems and formal knowledge structures represent explications of for-merly tacit corporate knowledge (Lukose 1997, Wiig 1990).

4. Formal representations of argumentation-structures record group-decision pro-cesses and embed the design documents created during theses processes (cf. Issue-Based Information Systems Reddy (1993), Buckingham Shum (1997b); see also Chapter 4, p. 60).

The heterogeneity of this enumeration shows that it is not easy to distill the main characteristics of OMIS technology which should be subject to further research and transfer into operational prototypes. One main goal of OMISs is to *capitalize on ex-isting knowledge*, i.e., make intangible knowledge assets tangible in order to manage them in a similar way as other resources a company deals with (see other definitions in Chapter 8, p. 161). For this purpose, we see two central mechanisms:

– The first mechanism is to explicate tacit knowledge and to capture it in some kind of (more or less formal) knowledge representation.
  The most typical examples are expert systems (Wiig 1990); lessons learned archives can also be seen in this category, but on the basis of an informal knowl-edge representation.

– The second mechanism starts with the knowledge sources which are already ex-plicit in the company, e.g. in paper or electronic form, but are insufficiently used. A better exploitation of these resources can often be achieved by adding formal knowledge which describes and organizes them, eases finding them, and ensures their utilization whenever useful.
  A good example for the second mechanism is reported by Kamp (1994) who uses a case-based diagnosis approach for retrieving appropriate technical documen-tation in a helpdesk application. Another example is described by Tschaitschian et al. (1997) as "information tuning": the organization of software-requirement specification texts along several formal models (of the software product, the ap-plication domain, or the development process) allows production of requirements documents of much better quality because the formal models make possible views on the thousands of specification text fragments; such views select for several tasks exactly those information units which are relevant.

9.2.3 Towards the Realization of a Corporate Memory

As pointed out in the previous section, the vision of a computer-based Corporate Memory is on the one hand rather comprehensive and abstract, whereas on the other hand several specific solutions, which however only deal with isolated aspects of the whole problem, have been proposed. There still remain many open questions which require a careful analysis and evaluation.

In order to gain a better understanding of what OMIS technology can afford, we will therefore first give a rather detailed report of three case studies on OMIS support for product development which were conducted in cooperation with major European companies.

9.3 Three Case Studies

9.3.1 Study 1: Crankshaft Design

Motivation. The development department of a German company which produces motor-powered tools and vehicles inquired about the feasibility of a computer system for enhancing product development and product maintenance, i.e. the continuous improvement of products already on the market with respect to higher quality and lower production costs. The crankshaft, as one of the core components of their products, which affects and is affected by many other design decisions, was suggested as the target domain for a system prototype.

Requirements analysis. Interviews were conducted with two engineers: a designated crankshaft expert and a team leader. Product development was done in teams composed of specialists for the various components of the product (e.g. crankshaft, casing). The crankshaft expert, as the only designated specialist for this domain, was more or less engaged in all development projects at various stages from initial product conceptualization to serial production. For product maintenance, he had to answer numerous queries from manufacturing, quality assurance, and marketing departments concerning suggested modifications and the feasibility of cost reductions. The crankshaft expert suffered from heavy work overload which prevented him from keeping track of recent technical innovations which might be exploited by his company. The indispensability of the crankshaft expert became most obvious, when during his leave incorrect advice was given to a query from manufacturing which could be corrected just in time before causing a considerable loss of time and money.

As the interviews showed, the main problem in crankshaft design consists of finding an optimal solution within the quality-cost continuum. This requires the proper consideration of many incidental circumstances, such as availability of manufacturing facilities, previously encountered quality problems, etc. Such expertise can only be acquired in many years of on-the-job experience. Since this expertise was only available in the head of the over-worked crankshaft expert, we decided that the primary goal of the to-be-developed design support system should be to capture as much as possible of this expertise and make it available for answering the different types of queries which the expert is confronted with in his job.

Contrary to more general engineering knowledge, expertise for finding an optimal design under some given circumstances is subject to rapid evolution. For instance, it was found that the crankshaft expert changed a previously adopted design guideline in order to take advantage of a new supplier for blank parts who due to a currency devaluation had become more competitive. An essential system requirement was thus to support a continuous modification and update of the captured knowledge. This knowledge evolution should be accomplished by the system users with a minimal disruption of normal work processes.

System conceptualization. The system prototype which was developed based on these criteria was named KONUS, which is a German acronym for both construction support and (knowledge) conservation support. An overview of the KONUS system is shown in Fig. 9.2. A more detailed description can be found in Kühn and Höfling (1994) and Kühn et al. (1994).

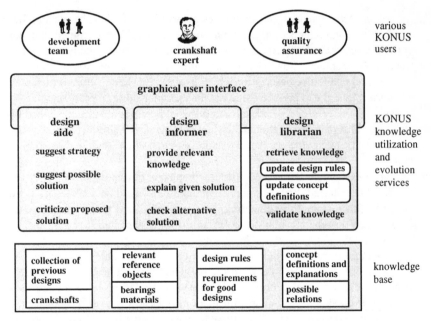

Fig. 9.2. Overview of the KONUS corporate memory for crankshaft design

The various users, such as the crankshaft expert, other engineers in the development team, and members of the quality assurance department interact with the KONUS system via a graphical user interface which integrates the different knowledge utilization and knowledge evolution services. These services can be grouped into three categories which were named according to Green (1992):

The *design aide* provides direct support for the construction and modification of crankshafts, so that this activity can now also be performed by engineers who are not crankshaft specialists. Although unable to design a crankshaft automatically, the design aide suggests a strategy, points out viable solution alternatives, and provides critique if design guidelines are violated.

The *design informer* provides answers to different types of questions about previous designs which frequently occur in everyday practice. Most important are "Why?" and "Why not?" questions which explain previously made design decisions and check the feasibility of design alternatives which are frequently proposed by the manufacturing or marketing departments.

The *design librarian* supports the management and evolution of the design knowledge by providing functionalities for knowledge

retrieval, update, and validation. For knowledge update, a rule and a concept editor are provided which have been described by Kühn et al. (1994).

The captured expertise about crankshaft design is stored in a **knowledge base** in which four different types of knowledge are distinguished.

The collection of previous designs comprises descriptions of crankshafts and other crank-drive components (e.g. the connecting rod) which are designed together with the crankshaft. Each component is described by attribute-value pairs. Contrary to the technical drawings, the attribute-value representation provides an abstract and qualitative description which lists those design features which play a central role in the experts' reasoning when solving a design problem.

The relevant reference objects such as materials and bearings are also described by attribute-value pairs. Even though they are not designed but selected, their properties must be taken into account when designing the crankshaft and its components.

The design rules contain the essence of the company's design expertise. They indicate what criteria (attribute-value combinations) should be satisfied by good designs with respect to engineering, cost-efficiency, and manufacturing concerns. Each design rule may be given an informal explanation which further elaborates why that rule should be followed.

The concept definitions and explanations constitute a kind of ontology of all terms and structures which may occur in the previously mentioned types of knowledge. Besides a formal definition of concepts and relations, it also comprises informal explanations as well as information about how the various objects are to be displayed to the users. A detailed discussion of the KONUS ontology can be found in Kühn (1994).

System realization. With the crankshaft expert as the principal source of information, knowledge acquisition was performed in a sequence of increasingly structured interviews. The expert was asked to tell what he would like his colleagues to know about crankshaft design so that they might be able to answer for themselves many of the questions they now posed to him. In addition the expert was asked to explain some exemplary cases based on available CAD drawings.

The ontology, consisting of about 150 concepts, and the 126 design rules were extracted from the interview transcripts and presented to the expert for validation in a semi-formal notation. Concept explanations and rule justifications were taken directly from the interview transcripts and were attached as text strings to the formal knowledge units. This approach, which may be seen as a combination of a formal knowledge-base with hypertext, proved very effective in conveying background information to the users without having to formalize and later re-translate this information into a user-adequate form.

The core of the KONUS prototype was implemented in LISP for which knowledge representation and processing formalisms had previously been developed (Boley et al. 1995). User interaction occurred via a graphical user interface written in TCL/TK which communicated with the LISP process on a Unix machine.

Even though the utility of a Corporate Memory as exemplified by the KONUS prototype was not disputed either by prospective users or by the department management, the company could not be convinced to invest into the development of a fully usable system. On the one hand, it was hard to estimate how much effort would have to be invested for solving technical problems such as integration with currently used CAD systems and databases. On the other hand, the department was just in the process of reorganizing its outdated IT infrastructure and wanted to postpone investments into innovative AI technologies until the improvement potential of traditional database and CAD systems had been further explored.

9.3.2 Study 2: Quality Assurance for Vehicle Components

Motivation. The head of the testing department of a German company which supplies components to the automobile and aircraft industry was impressed by a demonstration of KONUS, as it promised a solution to many problems he faced in his department. In particular, he sought computerized support to avoid costly errors, which were frequently committed due to disregard of previous experience, and to reduce the time that his engineers were spending looking for relevant information.

Requirements analysis. Interviews were conducted with 6 of the 20 members of the testing department. Quality assurance was done in parallel with product development and included roughly the following sequence of activities:

1. determine which tests have to be performed based on customer requirements, product features, legal prescriptions, etc.;
2. work out detailed testing instructions specifying test parameters, data to be collected, etc.;
3. calculate the testing costs depending on the number of patterns needed, work hours required for test set-up, execution and data analysis, etc.;
4. execute the tests according to the specifications and document the obtained results;
5. write test reports.

All of these activities were already performed with the help of computers (using word processors, spreadsheets, data analysis tools, etc.) and a lot of information about each project was already available in electronic form. The various data

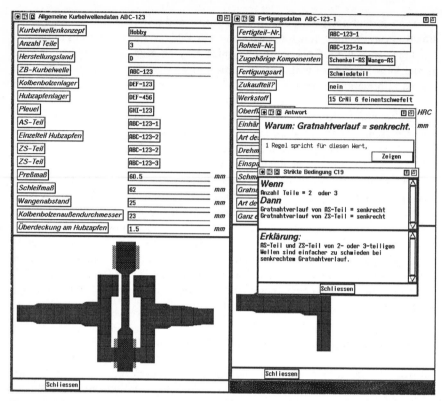

Fig. 9.3. Snapshot of the KONUS user interface

files were poorly organized, however, so that the relevant information was hard to find and was frequently overlooked. Furthermore, the most crucial information for building on previous experiences (e.g. reasons for test failures, customer complaints about employed test parameters, etc.) was not available on the computer network and its transmission depended mostly on verbal communication between the employees.

The following requirements were thus considered crucial for developing a Corporate Memory for quality assurance tests:

1. integrate all project data and documents in a systematic way so that relevant information can be accessed easily;

2. during the execution of a project capture all information which may be relevant for subsequent steps (e.g. test repetitions) in the same project or for similar projects in the future;

3. support all activities in a project by providing the specific data needed and relevant experiences from other projects in a comprehensive but concise way;

4. provide tools for capturing and continuously updating the general knowledge that may be helpful in future projects (e.g. standards required by the customer, legal regulations, technical and cost restrictions for tests);
5. provide interfaces to the other computer tools which are currently used to perform the various tasks.

System conceptualization. The global architecture of the projected system (called *RITA*) is quite similar to the KONUS architecture: The core of the system consists of an information depository containing all relevant information about the target domain. Project specific information is distinguished from general information. Information may be represented in the form of knowledge items (e.g. concept definitions, rules, constraints), data records, or documents (texts or drawings).

The information in RITA is entered and accessed via components which are tailored to the five above mentioned tasks. These components are to be interfaced with the other computer tools (e.g. word processor, CAD system) so that relevant information can be interchanged while the users perform their work processes in the accustomed way. Besides components supporting the five tasks in a testing project, the RITA architecture includes a knowledge acquisition and evolution component which is functionally similar to the design librarian in KONUS. Furthermore, a component for project control by the management was added which provides detailed information about the current state and encountered problems for individual projects, as well as summary statistics.

System realization. Since the RITA system requires a good deal of database and system interface programming, VisualWorks Smalltalk was proposed as an implementation platform that provides all relevant building blocks and system interfaces for fast and efficient system development.

The effort required for a basic realization of RITA was estimated at about 4 person years. This investment in innovative information technology was deemed as rather high by the company management, in particular, since a return of investment could not be expected within one or two years. The RITA project was thus given low priority and was indefinitely postponed.

9.3.3 Study 3: Bid Preparation for Oil Production Systems

Motivation. An international engineering company was expanding its business in the domain of oil production system (PS) which heretofore had played only a marginal role. Besides hiring new experts, who are scarce and heavily contested among competitors, the company strove for a better capitalization on available know-how by means of better IT support. Financial benefits were expected primarily from shorter bid-preparation times and an improved quality of submitted bids, which would help the company to expand its share of a rapidly growing market.

Requirements analysis. Due to the large scope of the project, an elaborate requirements analysis was performed comprising some 30 hours of interviews with engineers, management, secretaries, and personnel from the IT department.

Work processes dealt with the preparation of bids and the execution of projects after winning a bid. The former was analyzed in more detail, since bid preparation was the primary target for computer support. The sequence of activities in bid preparation can be characterized as follows:

1. After receiving a request to submit a bid from a prospective customer, the requirements for the projected facility are collected in as much detail as possible. Relevant data are the chemical composition of the crude oil, location of the field, expected yield, prescribed security standards, etc. Most of these data can be extracted from documents supplied by the customer, which however are often enough incomplete, vague, or contradictory so that a further clarification is required.
2. A conceptual design of the facility is developed and verified with the help of a process simulator.
3. Based on the components specified in the design, equipment costs and mobilization costs are computed or estimated. For precise cost estimates, which are essential for winning a bid and not losing money, a lot of experience is needed. Many factors have to be taken into account such as worker productivity in different countries, quality and reliability of components bought from different suppliers, etc.
4. The bid document to be sent to the customer is compiled by integrating the information determined in the preceding steps together with general information about the company, standards and legal procedures to be applied, etc. The consistency and completeness of the bid document together with its overall quality is essential for winning a bid.

Concerning the current level of IT support and desired improvements, the opinions of management and staff differed considerably. Management judged that basic IT support for managing and archiving data and documents was well established and that intelligent tools for the collection of customer requirements (called *"automated questionnaire"*) and for the configuration of production facilities (called *"design assistant"*) were needed.

Staff members, however, agreed that current data and document management was a total mess. Due to the recent growth of the department nobody knew where to find relevant information and whom to ask. Instead of an automated questionnaire and a design assistant they desired a workflow management and document archiving system with an emphasis on support for cost estimation and compilation of bid documents. The latter was judged particularly important, since embarassing errors had occurred in bid documents which were created from old documents by a cut and paste process.

System conceptualization. In our system conceptualization, we tried to take into account all the voiced user requirements and to provide support for all work processes in bid preparation with a possible later extension to the execution of won projects. The scope of the Corporate Memory (called *PS-Advisor*) was delimited by the tasks for which shared product data and relevant know-how was already available.

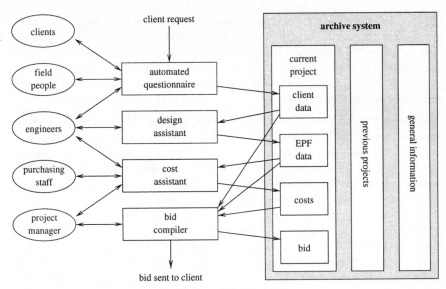

Fig. 9.4. Architecture and information flow of the PS-Advisor system

An overview of the architecture for the PS-Advisor system is shown in Fig. 9.4. The information depository (called *archive system*) contains information about individual projects as well as general information. The figure also shows how information for a current project is successively added and retrieved by four tools, each of which is tailored to support one of the four main tasks in the bid preparation process.

Each of these tools was to be used by several user groups in different situations. For the automated questionnaire, for instance, three possible usage scenarios were considered:

1. a client accesses the questionnaire via WWW,
2. field people complete the questionnaire together with a client on a portable computer,
3. an engineer extracts client requirements from supplied documents.

The support given by the automated questionnaire was of course to be tailored to the background knowledge and the information needs of the different users. Giving all of them access to the same information was however considered essential for encouraging mutual learning and collaboration.

The main function of the design assistant was to support the reuse of both available equipment and of previous design experiences. Relevant design parameters were to be acquired directly from a hydrocarbon simulator, which was used by the engineers to test the viability of various design alternatives.

The cost assistant was to select relevant information from previous cases based on equipment descriptions (obtained from the design assistant) as well as supplier and region data (obtained from a corporate database). In addition, it was to employ rules for cost calculations and estimations acquired from human experts.

The bid compiler was to employ rather conventional technology (e.g. text-processing macros) in order to facilitate the creation of bid documents and verify their consistency. Even though conceptually simple, it was considered crucial for the entire PS-Advisor system, since it made accumulated information from the bidding process not merely accessible but directly usable and thus facilitated the completion of a rather boring routine task.

System realization. The PS-Advisor system was planned to be realized in cooperation with a large software company mostly by customizing and enhancing software packages available on the market. An innovative approach was to be employed for the automated questionnaire, which was to be realized with HTML and Java and be made available via the World Wide Web. Effort estimations for a basic realization of all systems components amounted to some 10 person years.

When the proposal for the PS-Advisor sytem was presented to the chief executive of the business unit, he was convinced of its usefulness and that a return of investment was to be expected within a few years. From past experiences, however, he considered it "philosophically wrong" to finance the development of any software just for his own department. He suggested discussing the project together with other business units, many of which also sought better IT support for bid preparation, and the IT department. A final decision about a realization of the PS-Advisor system has not yet been reached. The IT department is currently busy with the introduction of new data and workflow management software on a company-wide scale, into which the PS-Advisor system or a more general bid-support system may be integrated in the future.

9.4 Lessons Learned from the Case Studies

9.4.1 Crucial Corporate Memory Requirements

From the numerous interviews conducted with prospective users and the discussions with IT personnel and management, the following requirements were identified as crucial for the success of an OMIS project in industrial practice:

Collection and systematic organization of information from various sources. Knowledge needed in work processes is currently scattered among various sources, such as paper documents, electronic documents, databases, e-mails, CAD drawings, and the heads and private notes of employees. The primary requirement for an OM is to prevent the loss and enhance the accessibility of all kinds of corporate knowledge by providing a centralized and well-structured information depository.

Integration into existing work environment. In order to be accepted by the users, an OM has to tap into the flow of information that is already happening in an organization (Conklin 1996). At a technical level, this means that the OM has to be directly interfaced with the tools that are currently used to do the work (e.g. word-processors, spreadsheets, CAD systems, simulators). For example, in the KONUS project, a tight integration with a widespread CAD system would be necessary. As another example: the knowledge-based integration of several application systems was an important part of the PS-Advisor system design.

Minimization of up-front knowledge engineering. Even though the benefits of having an OM are generally recognized, organizations are reluctant to invest time and money in a novel technology the benefits of which are still far off. Furthermore, prospective users have little or no time to spend for requirements and knowledge acquisition. An OM thus has to exploit readily available information (mostly databases and electronic or paper documents), must provide benefits soon, and be adaptable to newly arising requirements.

Active presentation of relevant information. In industrial practice, costly errors are often repeated due to an insufficient flow of information. This cannot be avoided by a passive information system, since workers are often too busy to look for information or don't even know that pertinent information exists. An OM therefore should actively remind workers of helpful information and be a competent partner for cooperative problem solving.

Exploiting user feedback for maintenance and evolution. For the same reasons as up-front knowledge engineering, maintenance efforts for an OM have to be kept at a minimum. At the same time, an OM has to deal with incomplete, potentially incorrect, and frequently changing information. Keeping an OM up-to-date and gradually improving its knowledge can only be achieved by collecting feedback from its users, who must be enabled to point out deficiencies and suggest improvements without causing a major disruption of the usual flow of work.

9.4.2 Corporate Memory versus Expert System

On the one hand, the three case studies have shown that there exists a considerable industrial interest and application potential for Corporate Memories. On the other hand, none of the three projects went beyond the prototype stadium, which makes it obvious that companies shun the risks and costs of investing in novel technologies that have not yet found widespread application. This reservation is partly due to the unsatisfying results obtained from expert system technology with which all of the three companies had experimented in the past. It is therefore important to look closer at the differences (and commonalities) between a Corporate Memory and an Expert System.

The main objective of expert systems has been the automatic solution of a particular task, e.g. the generation of a lathe production plan. Why this is extremely difficult for a complex, real-world task is elucidated by Fig. 9.5. For an expert solution of any such task three kinds of knowledge are required: common-sense knowledge, domain knowledge, and task expertise. Capturing only the latter was attempted in first-generation expert systems, but was found to be insufficient for providing good-enough solutions under varying circumstances. Adding deeper knowledge was a primary concern of second generation expert systems, but the resulting knowledge acquisition, representation, and processing tasks were found to be enormous so that

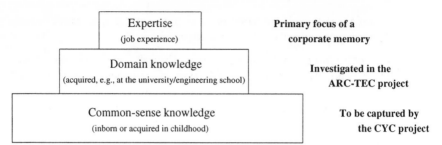

Fig. 9.5. The knowledge pyramid

practical and cost considerations usually prohibited the development of such ambitious systems.

A Corporate Memory therefore adopts a more moderate goal which has been motivated by the industrial success of database and hypertext systems (e.g. workflow and product-data management systems, Internet and Intranets). Such systems store and supply relevant corporate information but leave its interpretation and evaluation in a particular task context mostly to the user. On the other hand, a Corporate Memory enhances these technologies by knowledge processing in order to improve the quality of task support which can be provided to the user.

This approach is exemplified by the OMIS prototype developed in the first case study. The design process is monitored by a design assistant which provides critique and suggests solution alternatives, without the users having to be aware that a better alternative might exist. Thanks to knowledge processing, the design informer can directly answer practically important "Why?" and "Why not?" questions. In a mere database and hypertext system, users would have to look up relevant information for answering such questions themselves, having to sift through large amount of potentially relevant information, which however does not apply in the particular case.

9.4.3 Core Functionalities of an Organizational Memory

Let us summarize and move towards a vision of the next generation OMIS: A Corporate Memory/OMIS is an enterprise-internal application-independent information and assistant system. It stores large amounts of data, information, and knowledge from different sources of an enterprise. These are represented in various forms, such as databases, documents, and formal knowledge-bases. The OMIS will be permanently extended to keep it up-to-date and can be accessed enterprise-wide through an appropriate network infrastructure (see Fig. 9.6).

The ultimate goal of an OMIS is to provide the necessary knowledge whenever it is needed. To assure this, the OMIS realizes an *active knowledge dissemination approach* which does not rely on users' queries but automatically provides knowledge useful for solving the task at hand. To prevent information overload, this approach has to be coupled with a highly selective assessment of relevance. The resulting system shall act as an intelligent assistant to the user.

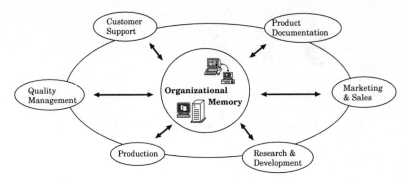

Fig. 9.6. Enterprise-wide knowledge management in an OMIS

As the design assistant of the KONUS system exemplifies, monitoring the execution of a task and providing critique when a suboptimal solution approach is detected is one technique which can be used for this end. User modeling techniques such as those used in information filtering systems, may be applied to enable not only a task-specific but also a user-specific dissemination of information.

Finally, an OMIS not only has to disseminate information but it also has to be always ready to accept new information from its users. Techniques for an integrated knowledge utilization and evolution (Kühn et al. 1994), which collect usage statistics and encourage user feedback at various levels of detail can be exploited for this purpose.

9.4.4 Corporate Memory Architecture

Figure 9.7 suggests the general architecture for a Corporate Memory which was derived by abstracting from the three case studies. Naturally, at the core of the system stands the *Information Depository*. The information contained can be structured with regard to two dimensions. Figure 9.7 also gives some examples for the several kinds of information we found in our case studies.

According to the complexity and the representation format of information, we can distinguish data, knowledge, and documents. In an enterprise, *data* and *documents* usually are already stored in databases, paper-based or electronical document archives, or hypertext information systems. The *knowledge*—characterized by complex formal representations that can be processed with complex inferences (such as deduction, induction, abduction), and not only with retrieval mechanisms—has to be captured by AI techniques to be developed together with the Corporate Memory system.

According to the level of abstraction, its role in the problem solving process, and the temporal stability of information, we can distinguish three information layers: *Case-Specific Information* describes process and control information used/generated during concrete executions of the operational task under consideration. *General Information* abstracts from specific task instances and describes how to use and to

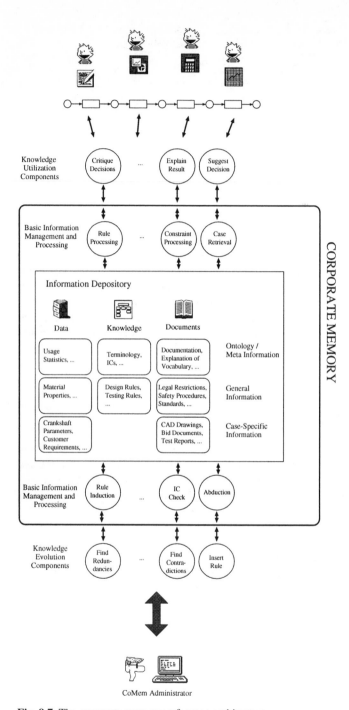

Fig. 9.7. The corporate memory reference architecture

interpret the concrete case data. Such information can be employed to generate suggestions, critique, or explanations. Another form of general information can be data or documents of general importance relevant for several task executions and not depending on a concrete situation. The most abstract kind of information is managed in the *Ontological*, or the *Meta Information* layer. Generalizing the idea of a database schema, it represents the basic assumptions underlying the system development and representation. The ontology mainly describes the conceptual framework for the other system parts and is thus essential for controlling the knowledge-base evolution (Kühn 1994). A simple example is the automatic generation of structure-based rule and concept editors (Kühn et al. 1994) from ontological information that make syntactically incorrect or semantically meaningless inputs impossible.

The central information depository is accessed by a number of *Basic Information Management and Processing Services*. Principally, this generalizes the database management system in a conventional IT solution. However, because of the more heterogeneous information storage mechanisms and the more complex possible inferences, we can have a lot of different components here. Now, we can have combined *Knowledge Utilization and Evolution Components* employing the basic mechanisms for solving subtasks occurring in the work processes to be supported. The workflow, a result of requirements analysis, describes the respective subtasks, performed by the end-user(s), typically using already existing (standard) software, with specific information demands and support needs. Knowledge evolution should be a continuous activity performed by a Corporate Memory Administrator in close cooperation with the users who can make improvement/update suggestions tightly integrated into their work processes (Kühn et al. 1994).

9.4.5 How to Develop a Corporate Memory

As in every software project, the first step in developing a corporate memory has to be a careful requirements analysis in which the following questions should be asked:

1. What are the *tasks* to be supported?
2. What is the *information needed* to perform these tasks?
3. What is the *current task environment* ?
4. Which type of *support* is *desired by the users* ?
5. What are the *costs and benefits* for providing different kinds of support?
6. What are the *changes to be expected* in the future?

While quite obvious, we repeat that each knowledge-based system development is first of all a software project, such that all observations valid for conventional software project management also hold true for the design and implementation of a Corporate Memory. Nevertheless, we want to draw attention to some topics that are of particular importance here:

Human Factors. A main reason for failure of early expert system projects was that the developers ignored the real needs, abilities, and goals of the intended system users (Malsch et al. 1993). Since our system is not intended to replace an expert, but to support him or her, the thorough analysis of human factors in the operational task under consideration becomes even more important (Kühn et al. 1994). The question how to motivate users for storing valuable personal expertise into the OMIS requires careful analysis in each concrete application.

Cost-Benefit Analysis. Knowledge-based techniques are not yet off-the-shelf products, rather they are hand-made, especially tailored to an application, which causes relatively high and not-easy-to-estimate development costs. Moreover, the benefit achievable by better IT support is very hard to quantify. Thus, we propose to minimize the risks of a Corporate Memory project by focusing it in a twofold way. First, a project introducing Corporate Memory technology in an enterprise should concentrate on a product or process central to the operational outcome, already suffering from the lack of support or exposed to a high risk of (costly) errors caused by insufficient information. This was a main characteristic of the crankshaft design example, described in Sect. 9.3.1. Second, we should not overload the initial system with too many services, which may be desirable but do not promise a quick return on investment.

Knowledge Evolution. Corporate Memory maintenance is an important topic for several reasons. First, electronic support is especially valuable in areas being subject to rapid change in the enterprise itself and in its economic/political environment, because under such conditions it is extremely difficult to provide up-to-date, consistent information at any time. Second, for practical reasons, a Corporate Memory may often be put into action with an initial knowledge seed which is to be extended, improved, and refined during its use; so, we must care about how to keep the (heterogeneous) stored information consistent during this evolution process. Third, capturing knowledge in an electronic form that was previously distributed over the personal expertise of several experts and partially stored in separate, non-interacting systems, opens new possibilities for *Knowledge Discovery* and *Data Mining.* Here, the knowledge can both be subject to analyses in order to detect, e.g., inconsistent decisions or new decision alternatives, or it can be used as background knowledge for analysing and interpreting the data and documents (see Sect. 9.4.4). We understand *Knowledge Evolution* as a life-long quality-improving maintenance activity for knowledge bases, technically achieved by the combination of validation and exploration activities. Hinkelmann and Kühn (1995) discuss this topic in some more detail. This was also the subject of our basic research in the VEGA project (Abecker et al. 1995).

Technical Realization. The knowledge-processing part of our case studies, as the most innovative part from the IT point of view, was surprisingly easy to manage. With state-of-the-art knowledge-based system technology, tailored to technical domains, one can already be notably useful in real-world applications. However, the real world provides enough other difficult problems. One has not only to incorporate and integrate existing data and information bases (which was relatively harmless in the described projects, but is still an active research area in the *Enterprise Integration* and *Knowledge Sharing and Reuse* communities) and to realize tightly coupled data and knowledge processing. One also has to closely interweave knowledge-based support with the already existing work processes typically performed using available standard software. For example, it should be possible to have a knowledge-based validation of the data actually processed within an Excel spreadsheet. To tackle this problem, we found the concept of client-server architectures as especially useful (which is already suggested by the logical system architecture as depicted in Fig. 9.7). Another contribution to Corporate Memories is to have commonly agreed upon standards for communication, product and process data, as well as knowledge and meta-knowledge interchange.

9.5 Future Work

As already pointed out in Sect. 9.4.2, we regard an OMIS not only as an information system, but rather as an intelligent assistant to the user. It accompanies the execution of tasks, makes suggestions to the users, or provides relevant information that enables the employees to do their work better and more effectively. Besides this knowledge supply, the OMIS makes it easy for the user to extend or refine it whenever he or she becomes aware of new knowledge.

In Sect. 9.3, we described several application projects as pragmatic approaches to implement handcrafted solutions that realize parts of our OMIS vision. All projects failed to jump into daily operational work. The main reasons were the costs of customer-tailored solutions with unpredictable return on investment, insufficient experience with OMIS applications, and poor integration into the conventional IT landscape. This leads to the demand for further substantial application-oriented basic research with the ultimate goal to provide software modules necessary for building OMIS as off-the-shelf solutions.

In order to identify the main research goals to be attacked, let us first sketch once again the kinds of knowledge to be managed in an OMIS and the way how active user support can be achieved by synergetically exploiting formal and non-formal knowledge.

Kinds of Knowledge and Their Roles in an OMIS. Our view of how a next generation OMIS could work is shown in Fig. 9.8. The OMIS makes available individual knowledge across the organization, thus enabling organizational learning and supporting problem solving and decision making. This can be done by handling *formal* knowledge items, e.g. business rules or design guidelines which typically represent "condensed" knowledge. An overwhelming part of individual knowledge, however, will not be available in this form. Instead, *semi-structured* representations (e.g. keyword-oriented memos, notes, e-mails) are widespread and suitable to capture the employees' experiences and lessons learned. They need not be processed automatically, but provided to colleagues when needed.

Paper-based or electronic *documents*, e.g. letters, manuals, technical documentation, are another important carrier of knowledge in an organization. The OMIS

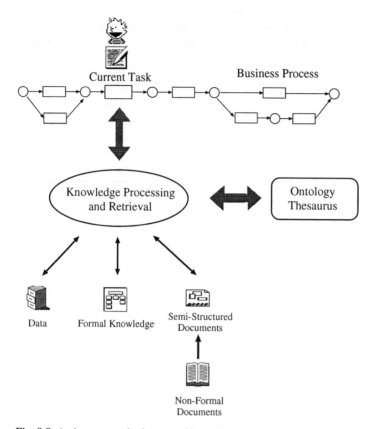

Fig. 9.8. Active support by integrated knowledge processing and retrieval

should ease the capitalization on this company legacy knowledge by context-dependent, active presentation within the human work process. By providing appropriate descriptions this material can be treated similarly to the semi-structured items. Finally, the large amounts of *data* stored in databases or data warehouses can be regarded as some kind of formal knowledge. The resulting system intelligently assists the user on the basis of formal, semi-structured and non-formal knowledge. The role of the formal knowledge is two-fold:

On the one hand, it enables support of a user's decision making or automatically solving certain tasks (like a conventional knowledge-based system). However, if the limits of the formal knowledge are reached, the OMIS still offers support by presenting relevant non-formal knowledge: to explain formal inferences or to provide information instead of or in addition to formally derived answers.

On the other hand, the formal knowledge and the inferences enable a precise and effective retrieval. The goal of the inferences is to exactly determine the information needs and to map the particularities of the current domain and the task at hand to the information access structures. This mapping is supported by ontological and/or thesaurus background knowledge in order to be robust against changing vocabulary, and it is triggered by information-need specifications attached to the workflow model.

Research Questions. For realizing our visionary OMIS architecture, the following research questions must be attacked:

1. *Integrate Data Models, Thesauri, and Ontologies.* A basis for the combined exploitation of data, documents, and formal knowledge is a unified meta data model. First steps in this direction are already done in the KACTUS project (Ostermayer et al. 1996). Another interesting point in this area (regarding the requirement of a minimum of up-front knowledge engineering) is to develop techniques for automatic thesaurus generation from existing document corpora. These techniques can profit from available ontological knowledge. The combined ontology/thesaurus can be used to improve retrieval, filtering, and routing of documents.

2. *Combine Inference and Information Retrieval.* Conjoint exploitation of formal and non-formal knowledge representations is a consequent extension of the logic-based view on Information Retrieval and the conceptual indexing approach (van Rijsbergen 1989, van Bakel et al. 1996). For tackling this research goal, expressive document representation formalisms and feasible inference methods must be investigated (Rölleke and Fuhr 1996, Meghini and Straccia 1996, Abecker et al. 1998). Inference is used as a powerful and declarative retrieval mechanism which is able to take into account several kinds of background knowledge (e.g. retrieval heuristics or thesaurus knowledge).

3. *Bring Together Business Processes and Knowledge Management.* Business process models can be content of the OMIS knowledge base as well as meta-information for annotating other knowledge elements at the meta level. The formal representation and seamless integration of business process models into other knowledge-based processes in the enterprise is an important prerequisite. First steps are done in the knowledge acquisition community (Decker et al. 1996) and in the field of Enterprise Ontologies (Fox et al. 1995, Uschold et al. 1995). The ultimate goal is to detect an information need within an ongoing process execution and to determine knowledge relevant in the particular task execution context. A first, pragmatic step in this direction is described by Hinkelmann and Kieninger (1997) where the authors propose to exploit task-context information for Information Filtering.

9.6 Summary

A Corporate Memory integrates product data with product legacy knowledge in order to bring previously accumulated experiences to bear on new tasks. Thereby, a repetition of errors can be avoided, know-how can be enhanced systematically, and knowledge-intensive work processes can be made more efficient and effective. In contrast to expert systems (and, to a lesser degree, also to intelligent assistant systems), the primary target of a corporate memory is not the support of one particular task but the better exploitation of the essential corporate resource: "knowledge".

We reported on three industrial case studies, all aiming at providing better IT support for crucial operational tasks by a Corporate Memory. A Corporate Memory uses state-of-the-art knowledge-processing technology, tightly coupled with the existing applications as well as data and document management systems in order to achieve a better exploitation of knowledge as a corporate resource.

A main insight of our studies was that developing a Corporate Memory essentially amounts to developing a complex software system and must thus be guided by conventional software engineering principles. The following issues are of particular importance: current organization of work processes and information interchange, human factors in cooperative problem solving and know-how sharing, cost-benefit considerations for desired system features and functionalities, and technical integration into the available IT infrastructure.

We sketched a general architecture for a Corporate Memory which has been evolved over several years based on experiences from various case studies. It is used as a general schema or template for approaching other Corporate Memory projects in the domain of helpdesks and customer support on which we are currently working. Based on feedback from practice, the conceptual framework for Corporate Memories will be further developed towards a technology with generic modular system components and an established project methodology.

Acknowledgements

Parts of the work reported here were performed in the projects ARC-TEC, IMCOD, VEGA, and KnowMore funded by the German Ministry for Education and Research (BMBF). The vision of the next generation OMIS heavily profited from discussions in the KnowMore project team: Bernd Bachmann, Ansgar Bernardi, Andreas Dengel, Knut Hinkelmann, and Michael Sintek.

References

AAMODT, A., NYGARD, M. (1995): Different Roles and Mutual Dependencies of Data, Information, and Knowledge – An AI Perspective on their Integration. Data & Knowledge Engineering 16:3, 191–222

ABECKER, A., BOLEY, H., HINKELMANN, K., WACHE, H., SCHMALHOFER, F. (1995): An Environment for Exploring and Validating Declarative Knowledge. DFKI Technical Memo TM-95-03. DFKI. Also in: Proc. Workshop on Logic Programming Environments at ILPS'95, Portland, OR, Dec. 1995

ABECKER, A., DECKER, S., HINKELMANN, K., REIMER, U., eds. (1997): Workshop on Knowledge-Based Systems for Knowledge Management in Enterprises at the 21st German Conf. on AI. Freiburg, Germany. http://www.dfki.uni-kl.de/km/ws-ki-97.html

ABECKER, A., SINTEK, M., WIRTZ, H. (1998): From Hypermedia Information Retrieval to Knowledge Management in Enterprises. Proc. 1st Int. Forum on Multimedia & Image Processing (IFMIP'98), Anchorage, AK

AGOSTINI, A., DE MICHELIS, G., GRASSO, M., PRINZ, W., SYRI, A. (1996): Contexts, Work Processes, and Workspaces. Computer Supported Cooperative Work – An International Journal 5:2-3, 223–250

Alta Vista: http://altavista.digital.com/

Amazon.com: http://www.amazon.com/

ANDRÉ, E., MÜLLER, J., RIST, T. (1996): The PPP Persona: A Multipurpose Animated Presentation Agent. Advanced Visual Interfaces. ACM Press, pp. 245–247

ARGYRIS, C., SCHON, C. A. (1978): Organizational Learning: A Theory of Action Perspective. Reading, MA: Addison-Wesley

ARTALE, A., FRANCONI, E., GUARINO, N., PAZZI, L. (1996): Part-Whole Relations in Object-Centered Systems: An Overview. Data & Knowledge Engineering 20:3, 347–383

BackWeb: http://www.backweb.com/

BALABANOVIC, M., SHOHAN, Y. (1997): Fab: Content-Based, Collaborative Recommendation. Communications of the ACM 40:3, 66–72. http://fab.stanford.edu/

BANNON, L. J., KUUTTI, K. (1996): Shifting Perspectives on Organizational Memory: From Storage to Active Remembering. Proc. Annual Hawaii Int. Conf. on System Sciences (HICCS'96). Los Alamitos, CA: IEEE Computer Society Press

BATEMAN, J. A., MAGNINI, B., RINALDI, F. (1994): The Generalized Italian, German, English Upper Model. Proc. ECAI'94 Workshop on Comparison of Implemented Ontologies, Amsterdam, The Netherlands

BELL, D., BOBROW, D., RAIMAN, O., SHIRLEY, M. (1996): Dynamic Documents and Situated Process: Building on Local Knowledge in Field Service. Proc. 1st Int. Working Conf. on Enterprise Information and Processes: Rethinking Documents, Boston, MA

BELLOTTI, V., BUCKINGHAM SHUM, S., MACLEAN, A., HAMMOND, N. (1995): Multidisciplinary Modelling in HCI Design in Theory and in Practice. In: Katz, I. R., Mack, R., Marks, L., Rosson, M. B., Nielsen, J. (eds.): Proc. ACM CHI'95 Conf. on Human Factors in Computing Systems, Denver, CO. New York: ACM Press, pp. 146–153

BENFORD, S. D., BOWERS, J. M., FEHLÉN, L. E., GREENHALGH, C. M., SNOWDON, D. N. (1995): User Embodiement in Collaborative Virtual Environments. Proc. ACM CHI'95 Conf. on Human Factors in Computing Systems, Denver, CO. New York: ACM Press

BENTLEY, R., DOURISH, P. (1995): Medium versus Mechanism: Supporting Collaboration through Customization. In: Marmolin, H., Sundblad, Y., Schmidt, K. (eds.): Proc. 4th Europ. Conf. on Computer-Supported Cooperative Work, Stockholm, Sweden. Dordrecht: Kluwer, pp. 133–148

BENTLEY, R., APPLET, W., BUSBACH, U., HINRICHS, E., SIKKEL, S., TREVOR, J., WOETZEL, G. (1997): Basic Support for Cooperative Work in The World Wide Web. Int. Journal of Human-Computer Studies: Special Issue on Innovative Applications of the World Wide Web

BERLIN, L. M., JEFFRIES, R., O'DAY, V. L., PAEPCKE, A., WHARTON, C. (1993): Where Did You Put It? Issues in the Design and Use of a Group Memory. Proc. of ACM/IFIP INTERCHI'93: Conf. on Human Factors in Computing Systems. pp. 23–30

BERNARDINELLO, L., DE CINDIO, F. (1992): A Survey of Basic Net Models and Modular Net Classes. Advances in Petri Nets. Lecture Notes in Computer Science **609**. Berlin: Springer-Verlag, pp. 304–351

BERNARDINELLO, L., POMELLO, L., SIMONE, C. (1996): A Class of Morphisms for the Refinement of EN Systems. Technical Report 181/96. DSI-Milano, Italy

BIEBER, M., VITALI, F., ASHMAN, H., BALASUBRAMANIAN, V., OINAS-KUKKONEN, H. (1997): Fourth Generation Hypermedia: Some Missing Links for the World Wide Web. Web Usability: Special Issue of Int. Journal of Human–Computer Studies. Buckingham Shum, S. and McKnight, C. (eds.) **47**:1, 31–65

BOLEY, H., HANSCHKE, P., HINKELMANN, K., MEYER, M. (1995): CoLab: A Hybrid Knowledge Representation and Compilation Laboratory. Annals of Operations Research **55**, 11–79

BORGHOFF, U. M., SCHLICHTER, J. H. (1996): On Combining the Knowledge of Heterogeneous Information Repositories. J. Universal Computer Science **2**:7, 515–532. Electronic version: http://www.iicm.edu/jucs

BORGHOFF, U. M., CHEVALIER, P.-Y., WILLAMOWSKI, J. (1996): Adaptive Refinement of Search Patterns for Distributed Information Gathering. In: Verbraeck, A. (ed.): Proc. Int. Conf. EuroMedia/WEBTEC '96, London, UK. San Diego, CA: The Society for Computer Simulation, pp. 5–12

BOURBEAU, L., CARCAGNO, D., GOLDBERG, E., KITTREDGE, R., POLGUÈRE, A. (1990): Bilingual Generation of Weather Forecasts in an Operations Environment. In: Kargren, H. (ed.): Proc. 13th Int. Conf. on Computational Linguistics, Helsinki, Finland. pp. 318–320

BOWERS, J., BUTTON, G., SHARROCK, W. (1995): Workflow from Within and Without: Technology and Cooperative Work on the Print Industry Shopfloor. Proc. 4th Europ. Conf. on Computer-Supported Cooperative Work. Dordrecht: Kluwer, pp. 51–66

BOWERS, J. (1991): The Politics of Formalism. In: Lea, M. (ed.): Contexts of Computer-Mediated Communication. Harvester Wheatsheaf, pp. 232–261

BOWKER, G. (1998): Lest We Remember: Organizational Forgetting and the Production of Knowledge. Accounting, Management and Information Technologies. http://alexia.lis.uiuc.edu/~bowker/paper.html

BRACHMAN, R. J., SCHMOLZE, J. (1985): An Overview of the Kl-ONE Knowledge Representation System. Cognitive Science **9**:2, 171–216

BRACHMAN, R., McGUINNESS, D., PATEL SCHNEIDER, P., RESNICK, L., BORGIDA, A. (1991): Living with CLASSIC: When and How to Use a KL-ONE-Like Language. In: Sowa, J. (ed.): Principles of Semantic Networks. San Mateo, CA: Morgan Kaufmann

BRAUER, W., REISIG, W., ROZENBERG, G., eds. (1987): Petri Nets: Central Models and Their Properties. Lecture Notes in Computer Science **254**. Berlin: Springer-Verlag

BROOKES, C. (1996): Gaining Competitive Advantage through Knowledge Management. White Paper. graveVINE Technologies Ltd.

BROOKING, A., MOTTA, E. (1996): A Taxonomy of Intellectual Capital and a Methodology for Auditing It. 17th Annual National Business Conf., McMaster Univ. Ontario, Canada. http://kmi.open.ac.uk/~simonb/org–knowledge/ic–paper.html

BROWN, J. S., DUGUID, P. (1996): The Social Life of Documents. First Monday **1**. http://www.firstmonday.dk/issues/issue1/documents/

BUCKINGHAM SHUM, S., HAMMOND, N. (1994): Argumentation-Based Design Rationale: What Use at What Cost? Int. Journal of Human–Computer Studies **40**:4, 603–652

BUCKINGHAM SHUM, S., McKNIGHT, C. (1997): World Wide Web Usability. Special Issue of Int. Journal of Human–Computer Studies **47**:1, 1–222

BUCKINGHAM SHUM, S., MACLEAN, A., BELLOTTI, V., HAMMOND, N. (1997): Graphical Argumentation and Design Cognition. Human-Computer Interaction **12**:3, 267–300

BUCKINGHAM SHUM, S. (1993): QOC Design Rationale Retrieval: A Cognitive Task Analysis and Design Implications. Xerox Research Centre Europe, Cambridge, UK. EPC–93–105

BUCKINGHAM SHUM, S. (1996): Analyzing the Usability of a Design Rationale Notation. In: Moran, T. P., Carroll, J. M. (eds.): Design Rationale: Concepts, Techniques, and Use. Hillsdale, NJ: Lawrence Erlbaum Associates, pp. 185–215

BUCKINGHAM SHUM, S. (1996): Design Argumentation as Design Rationale. The Encyclopedia of Computer Science and Technology **35**:20, 95–128

BUCKINGHAM SHUM, S. (1997): Balancing Formality with Informality: User–Centred Requirements for Knowledge Management Technologies. In: Dieng et al. (1997)

BUCKINGHAM SHUM, S. (1997): Negotiating Multidisciplinary Integration: From Collaborative Argumentation to Organisational Memory. In: Dieng et al. (1997)

BURGESS YAKEMOVIC, K. C., CONKLIN, J. (1990): Report on a Development Project Use of an Issue–Based Information System. Proc. 3rd Int. Conf. on Computer-Supported Cooperative Work, Los Angeles, CA. New York: SIGCHI/SIGOIS ACM, pp. 105–118

Calliope: http://www.xerox.fr/ats/digilib/calliope/

CARROLL, J. M, MORAN, T. P. (1991): Special Issue on Design Rationale. Human–Computer Interaction Journal **6**:3&4

CONKLIN, J., BEGEMAN, M. L. (1988): gIBIS: A Hypertext Tool for Exploratory Policy Discussion. ACM Transactions on Office Information Systems **6**:4, 303–331

CONKLIN, J., BURGESS YAKEMOVIC, K. C. (1991): A Process–Oriented Approach to Design Rationale. Human–Computer Interaction **6**:3&4, 357–391. Reprinted in: T. P. Moran and J. M. Carroll (eds.) Design Rationale: Concepts, Techniques, and Use, pp. 393–427. Hillsdale, NJ: Lawrence Erlbaum Associates, 1996

CONKLIN, J., YOURDON, E. (1993): Groupware for the New Organization. American Programmer, pp. 3–8

CONKLIN, J. (1989): Design Rationale and Maintainability. Proc. 22nd Annual Hawaii Int. Conf. on System Sciences (HICCS'89). Los Alamitos, CA: IEEE Computer Society Press, pp. 533–539

CONKLIN, J. (1996): Designing Organizational Memory: Preserving Intellectual Assets in a Knowledge Economy. Washington, DC: Group Decision Support Systems. http://www.gdss.com/DOM.htm

DAGAN, I., CHURCH, K. (1994): Termight: Identifying and Translating Technical Terminology. Proc. European Chapter of the Association for Computational Linguistics (EACL'94). pp. 34–40

DAVENPORT, T. (1996): Some Principles of Knowledge Management. Graduate School of Business, Univ. of Texas at Austin. http://knowman.bus.utexas.edu/pubs/kmprin.htm

DAVIS, R., SHROBE, H., SZOLOVITS, P. (1993): What Is A Knowledge Representation? AI Magazine **14**:1, 17–33. http://medg.lcs.mit.edu/ftp/psz/k–rep.html

DE CINDIO, F., DE MICHELIS, G., POMELLO, L., SIMONE, C. (1982): Superposed Automata Nets. Application and Theory of Petri Nets. IFB **52**. Berlin: Springer-Verlag

DE HOOG, R., BENUS, B., METSELAAR, C., VOGLER, M., MENEZES, W. (1994): Organisation Model: Model Definition Document. Technical Report. Univ. Amsterdam and Cap Programmator. Deliverable DM6.2c of ESPRIT Project P5248 (KADS-II)

DE MICHELIS, G., PARESCHI, R., eds. (1996): Proc. PAKM'96, Workshop on Adaptive Workflow, Basel, Switzerland

DECKER, S., ERDMANN, M., STUDER, R. (1996): A Unifying View on Business Process Modelling and Knowledge Engineering. In: Dieng and Vanwelkenhuysen (1996)

DICHTER, E. (1966): How Word-of-mouth Advertising Works. Harvard Business Review **44**, 148–152

DIENG, R., VANWELKENHUYSEN, J., eds. (1996): Proc. 10th Knowledge Acquisition for Knowledge-Based Systems Workshop KAW'96, Special Track on Corporate Memory and Enterprise Modeling. http://ksi.cpsc.ucalgary.ca:80/KAW/KAW96/KAW96Abstracts.html

DIENG, R., GAINES, B. R. ET AL., eds. (1997): AAAI Spring Symposium on Artificial Intelligence in Knowledge Management. Stanford, CA. http:// ksi.cpsc.ucalgary.ca/ AIKM97/ AIKMDrafts.html

DIMARCO, C., HIRST, G., WANNER, L., WILKINSON, J. (1995): HealthDoc: Customizing Patient Information and Health Education by Medical Condition and Personal Characteristics. Workshop on Artificial Intelligence in Patient Education, Glasgow

DIVITINI, M., SIMONE, C. (1994): A Prototype for Providing Users with the Contexts of Cooperation. Proc. ECCE7, GMD, Bonn, Germany. pp. 253–270

DIVITINI, M., SIMONE, C. (1996): Ariadne: A Framework to Construct Flexible Workflow Systems. In: Wolf and Reimer (1996)

DIVITINI, M., SIMONE, C., SCHMIDT, K. (1996): ABACO: Coordination Mechanisms in a Multi-agent Perspective. Proc. 2nd Int. Conf. on the Design of Cooperative Systems, INRIA, France. pp. 103–122

DOURISH, P., HOLMES, J., MACLEAN, A., MARQVARDSEN, P., ZBYSLAW, A. (1996): Freeflow: Mediating between Representation and Action in Workflow Systems. In: Ackerman, M. S. (ed.): Proc. 7th Int. Conf. on Computer-Supported Cooperative Work, Boston, MA. New York: SIGCHI/SIGOIS ACM, pp. 190–198

DRUCKER, P. F. (1993): The Post-Capitalist Society. Butterworth-Heinemann

Each-to-each: http://www.each.com/

EHRIG, H., NAGL, M., ROZENBERG, G., eds. (1983): Proc. 2nd Int. Workshop on Graph-Grammars and Their Application to Computer Science. Lecture Notes in Computer Science **153**. Berlin: Springer-Verlag

EISENSTADT, M., BUCKINGHAM SHUM, S., FREEMAN, A. (1996): KMi Stadium: Web-based Audio/Visual Interaction as Reusable Organisational Expertise. Workshop on Knowledge Media for Improving Organisational Expertise, 1st Int. Conf. on Practical Aspects of Knowledge Management, Basel, Switzerland. http://kmi.open.ac.uk/kmi–abstracts/kmi–tr–31–abstract.html

ELDRIDGE, M., LAMMING, M., FLYNN, M. (1992): Does a Video Diary Help Recall? Proc. HCI'92 Conf. on People and Computers VII

ELLIS, C. A., NUTT, G. J. (1980): Office Information Systems and Computer Science. ACM Computing Surveys **12**:1, 27–60

ELLIS, C. A., WAINER, J. (1994): Goal-Based Models of Collaboration. Collaborative Computing **1**:1, 61–86

ELLIS, C. A., KEDDARA, K., G., ROZENBERG (1995): Dynamic Change within Workflow Systems. Proc. ACM SIGOIS/IEEECS TC-OA Conf. on Organizational Computing Systems (COOCS '93). New York: ACM Press, pp. 10–21

EUZENAT, J. (1996): Corporate Memory Through Cooperative Creation of Knowledge Bases and Hyperdocuments. In: Gaines, B. R. (ed.): Proc. 10th Banff Workshop on Knowledge Acquisition for Knowledge-Based Systems. Banff, Canada: SDRG Publications. ftp://ksi.cpsc.ucalgary.ca/KAW/KAW96/22euzenat.ps.Z

FELDMAN, M. S., MARCH, J. G. (1981): Information in Organizations as Signal and Symbol. Administrative Science Quarterly **26**, 171–186

FIKES, R. E., NILSSON, N. J. (1971): STRIPS: A New Approach to the Application of Theorem Proving to Problem Solving. Artificial Intelligence **2**, 198–208

FISCHER, G., LEMKE, A. C., MCCALL, R., MORCH, A. I. (1991): Making Argumentation Serve Design. Human–Computer Interaction **6**:3&4, 393–419. Reprinted in: T. P. Moran and J. M. Carroll (eds.) Design Rationale: Concepts, Techniques, and Use, pp. 267–293. Hillsdale, NJ: Lawrence Erlbaum Associates, 1996

FISCHER, G., LINSTAEDT, S., OSTWALD, J., STOLZE, M., SUMNER, T., ZIMMERMAN, B. (1995): From Domain Modeling to Collaborative Domain Construction. Proc. 1st ACM Conf. on Design of Interactive Systems (DIS'95), Michigan. New York: ACM Press

FITZPATRICK, G., KAPLAN, S., MANSFIELD, T. (1996): Physical Spaces, Virtual Places and Social Worlds: A Study of the Work in the Virtual. In: Ackerman, M. S. (ed.): Proc. 7th Int. Conf. on Computer-Supported Cooperative Work, Boston, MA. New York: SIGCHI/SIG-OIS ACM, pp. 334–343

FOX, M. S., BARBUCEANU, M., GRUNINGER, M. (1995): An Organisational Ontology for Enterprise Modelling – Preliminay Concepts for Linking Structure and Behaviour. Proc. 4th Workshop on Enabling Technologies – Infrastructures for Collaborative Enterprises, West Virginia Univ. pp. 1–15

FRASER, J. (1994): Managing Change through Enterprise Models. Proc. Expert Systems '94, the 14th Annual Conf. of the British Computer Society Specialist Group on Expert Systems, Cambridge, UK

FREI, H.-P., HARMAN, D., SCHÄUBLE, P., WILKINSON, R., eds. (1996): Proc. 19th Annual Int. ACM SIGIR Conf. on Research and Development in Information Retrieval, Zürich, Switzerland. New York: ACM Press

FRENZEN, J., NAKAMOTO, K. (1993): Structure, Cooperation, and the Flow of Market Information. Journal of Consumer Research **20**:3, 360–375

FUCHS, L., PANKOKE-BABBATZ, U., PRINZ, W. (1995): Supporting Cooperative Awareness with Local Event Mechanisms: The Groupdesk System. Proc. 4th Europ. Conf. on Computer-Supported Cooperative Work. Dordrecht: Kluwer, pp. 247–262

GARCIA, A. C. B., HOWARD, H. C. (1992): Acquiring Design Knowledge Through Design Decision Justification. Artificial Intelligence for Engineering Design, Analysis and Manufacturing 6:1, 59–71

GASPAROTTI, P., SIMONE, C. (1990): A User Defined Environment for Handling Conversations. Proc. IFIP WG8.4 Conf. on Multi-User Interfaces and Applications. pp. 271–289

GDSS (1996): QuestMap. Washington, DC: Group Decision Support Systems. http://www.gdss.com/OM.htm

GENESERETH, M. E., FIKES, R. E. (1992): Knowledge Interchange Format, Version 3.0 Reference Manual. Technical Report Logic-92-1. Computer Science Department, Stanford Univ., Stanford, CA

GENESERETH, M. R., KETCHPEL, S. P. (1994): Software Agents. Communications of the ACM 37:7, 48–54

GLANCE, N. S., HUBERMAN, B. A. (1994): Dynamics of Social Dilemmas. Scientific American 270:3, 76–81

GLANCE, N., PAGANI, D., PARESCHI, R. (1996): Generalized Process Structure Grammars (GPSG) for Flexible Representations of Work. In: Ackerman, M. S. (ed.): Proc. 7th Int. Conf. on Computer-Supported Cooperative Work, Boston, MA. New York: SIGCHI/SIGOIS ACM, pp. 180–189

GOLDBERG, D., NICHOLS, D., OKI, B. M., TERRY, D. (1992): Using Collaborative Filtering to Weave an Information Tapestry. Communications of the ACM 35:12, 61–70

GOLDMAN, N. M. (1974): Computer Generation of Natural-Language from a Deep Conceptual Base. Dissertation. Department of Computer Science, Yale Univ.

GRÄTHER, W., PRINZ, W., KOLVENBACH, S. (1997): Enhancing Workflows by Web-Technology. In: Hayne, S., Prinz, W. (eds.): Proc. Int. ACM SIGGROUP Conf. on Supporting Group Work (GROUP'97), Phoenix, AZ. New York: ACM Press, pp. 271–280

GREEN, M. (1992): Conceptions and Misconceptions of Knowledge Aided Design. In: Green, M. (ed.): Knowledge Aided Design. Knowledge-Based Systems. New York: Academic Press

GREIF, I. (1994): Desktop Agents in Group-Enabled Products. Communications of the ACM 37:7, 100–105

GROTE, B., RÖSNER, D., STEDE, M. (1993): From Knowledge to Language—Three Papers on Multilingual Text Generation. Technical Report. Forschungsinstitut für angewandte Wissensverarbeitung (FAW) (Research Institute for Applied Knowledge Processing) Ulm, Germany

GROTE, B., MOLL, M., ROSE, T. (1997): Ein Arbeitsplatz zur teilautomatisierten Erstellung mehrsprachiger technischer Dokumentation (Dokumentationsarbeitsplatz). Technical Report. Abschlußdokumentation. Forschungsinstitut für angewandte Wissensverarbeitung (FAW) (Research Institute for Applied Knowledge Processing) Ulm, Germany

GRUBER, T. R. (1993): A Translation Approach to Portable Ontology Specifications. Knowledge Acquisition 5:2, 199–220

GRUDIN, J. (1988): Why CSCW Applications fail: Problems in the Design and Evaluation of Organizational Interfaces. Proc. 2nd Int. Conf. on Computer-Supported Cooperative Work, Portland, OR. New York: SIGCHI/SIGOIS ACM, pp. 85–93

GRUDIN, J. (1994): Groupware and Social Dynamics: Eight Challenges for Developers. Communications of the ACM 37:1, 92–105

GRUDIN, J. (1996): Evaluating Opportunities for Design Capture. In: Moran, T. P., Carroll, J. M. (eds.): Design Rationale: Concepts, Techniques, and Use. Hillsdale, NJ: Lawrence Erlbaum Associates, pp. 453–470

GRUNINGER, M., FOX, M. S. (1994): The Design and Evaluation of Ontologies for Enterprise Engineering. Proc. ECAI Workshop on Comparison of Implemented Ontologies, Amsterdam, The Netherlands

Gustos: http://www.gustos.com/index.htm

HALLIDAY, M. A. K. (1985): An Introduction to Functional Grammar. London: Edward Arnold

HARDIN, G. (1968): The Tragedy of the Commons. Science **162**, 1243–1248

HEINSON, J., KUDENKO, D., NEBEL, B., PROFITLICH, H.-J. (1994): An Empirical Analysis of Terminological Representation Systems. Artificial Intelligence **2**:68, 367–397

HILL, W. C., HOLLAN, J. D. (1994): History-enriched Digital Objects: Prototypes and Policy Issues. The Information Society **10**:2, 139–45

HILL, W. C., STEAD, L., ROSENSTEIN, M., FURNAS, G. (1995): Recommending and Evaluating Choices in a Virtual Community of Use. Proc. ACM CHI'95 Conf. on Human Factors in Computing Systems, Denver, CO. New York: ACM Press, pp. 194–201

HINKELMANN, K., KIENINGER, T. (1997): Task-Oriented Web-Search Refinement and Information Filtering. DFKI

HINKELMANN, K., KÜHN, O. (1995): Revising and Updating a Corporate Memory. Proc. European Symp. on Validation and Verification of Knowledge-based Systems (EUROVAV'95)

HOFER-ALFEIS, J., KLABUNDE, S. (1996): Approaches to Managing the Lessons Learned Cycle. In: Wolf and Reimer (1996)

HUBERMAN, B. A., KAMINSKY, M. (1996): Beehive: A System for Cooperative Filtering and Sharing of Information. Technical Report. Xerox PARC

Individual: http://www.individual.com/

JARCZYK, A., LOFFLER, P., SHIPMAN, F. (1992): Design Rationale for Software Engineering: A Survey. Proc. 25th Annual Hawaii Int. Conf. on System Sciences (HICCS'92). Los Alamitos, CA: IEEE Computer Society Press

JOHNSON, P. (1992): Supporting Exploratory CSCW with the EGRET Framework. In: Turner, J., Kraut, R. E. (eds.): Proc. 4th Int. Conf. on Computer-Supported Cooperative Work, Toronto, Canada. New York: SIGCHI/SIGOIS ACM, pp. 298–305

JORDAN, B., GOLDMAN, R., SACHS, P. (1995): Tools for the Workplace. Communications of the ACM **38**:9, 42

JUSTESON, J. S., KATZ, S. M. (1995): Technical Terminology: Some Linguistic Properties and an Algorithm for Identification in Text. Natural Language Engineering **1**, 9–27

KAMP, G., PIRK, P., BURKHARD, H.-D. (1996): Falldaten: Case-based Reasoning for the Diagnosis of Technical Devices. Technical Report LKI-M-96/02. Labor für Künstliche Intelligenz, Univ. Hamburg. Also in: Proc. 20th Annual German Conf. on Artificial Intelligence, Lecture Notes in Artificial Intelligence **1137**. Berlin: Springer-Verlag

KAMP, G. (1994): Integrating Semantic Structure and Technical Documentation in Case-Based Service Support Systems. Technical Report LKI-M-94/04. Labor für Künstliche Intelligenz, Univ. Hamburg. Also in: Topics in Case-Based Reasoning – Selected Papers from EWCBR'93, Lecture Notes in Computer Science **837**. Berlin: Springer-Verlag

KAMP, G. (1996): Using Description Logics for Knowledge Intensive Case-Based Reasoning. Technical Report LKI-M-96/03. Labor für Künstliche Intelligenz, Univ. Hamburg.

Also in: Proc. 4th European Workshop on Case-Based Reasoning – EWCBR'96, Lausanne, Switzerland, Lecture Notes in Computer Science **1168**. Berlin: Springer-Verlag

KAPLAN, S. M., TOLONE, W. J., BOGIA, D. P., BIGNOLI, C. (1992): Flexible, Active Support for Collaborative Work with Conversation Builder. In: Turner, J., Kraut, R. E. (eds.): Proc. 4th Int. Conf. on Computer-Supported Cooperative Work, Toronto, Canada. New York: SIGCHI/SIGOIS ACM, pp. 378–385

KARBE, B., RAMSPERGER, N., WEISS, P. (1990): Support of Cooperative Work by Electronic Circulation Folders. In: Lochovsky, F. H., Allen, R. B. (eds.): Proc. Conf. of Office Information Systems, Cambridge, MA. New York: ACM Press, pp. 109–117

KASPER, R. T. (1989): A Flexible Interface for Linking Applications to PENMAN's Sentence Generator. Proc. DARPA Workshop on Speech and Natural Language, Marina del Rey, CA

KAUTZ, H., SELMAN, B., SHAH, M. (1997): The Hidden Web. AI Magazine **18**:2, 27–36

KAUTZ, H., SELMAN, B., SHAH, M. (1997): Referral Web: Combining Social Networks and Collaborative Filtering. Communications of the ACM **40**:3, 63–65

KIDD, A. (1994): The Marks are on the Knowledge Worker. In: B. Adelson, S. Dumais, Olson, J. (eds.): Proc. ACM CHI'94 Conf. on Human Factors in Computing Systems, Boston, MA. ACM Press: New York, pp. 186–191

KLÖCKNER, K., MAMBREY, P., SOHLENKAMP, M., PRINZ, W., FUCHS, L., KOLVENBACH, S., PANKOKE-BABATZ, U., SYRI, A. (1995): POLITeam: Bridging the Gap between Bonn and Berlin for and with the Users. In: Marmolin, H., Sundblad, Y., Schmidt, K. (eds.): Proc. 4th Europ. Conf. on Computer-Supported Cooperative Work, Stockholm, Sweden. Dordrecht: Kluwer, pp. 17–32

KNIGHT, K., LUK, S. (1994): Building a Large Knowledge Base for Machine Translation. Proc. American Association of Artificial Intelligence Conf. (AAAI'94), Seattle, WA

KNIPSCHEER, C. P. M., ANTONUCCI, TONI C., eds. (1990): Social Network Research: Substantive Issues and Methodological Questions. Amsterdam, The Netherlands: Swets and Zeitlinger

KOBSA, A., WAHLSTER, W., eds. (1989): User Models in Dialog Systems. Berlin: Springer-Verlag

KONSTAN, J. A., MILLER, B. N., MALTZ, D., HERLOCKER, J. L., GORDON, L. R., RIEDL, JOHN (1997): GroupLens: Applying Collaborative Filtering to Usenet News. Communications of the ACM **40**:3, 77–87. http://www.cs.umn.edu/Research/GroupLens

KREIFELTS, T., LICHT, U., SEUFFERT, P., WOETZEL, G. (1984): DOMINO: A System for the Specification and Automation of Cooperative Office Processes. In: Myhrhaug, B., Wilson, D.R. (eds.): Proc. Advances in Microprocessing and Microprogramming (EUROMICRO'84), Copenhagen. Amsterdam: North-Holland, pp. 33–41

KREIFELTS, T., HINRICHS, E., KLEIN, K. H., SEUFFERT, P., WOETZEL, G. (1991): Experiences with the DOMINO Office Procedure System. In: Bannon, L., Robinson, M., Schmidt, K. (eds.): Proc. 2nd Europ. Conf. on Computer-Supported Cooperative Work, Amsterdam, The Netherlands. Dordrecht: Kluwer, pp. 117–130

KREIFELTS, T., VICTOR, F., WOETZEL, G., WOITASS, M. (1991): Supporting the Design of Office Procedures in the DOMINO System. Studies in Computer Supported Cooperative Work. Theory, Practice and Design. Amsterdam: North-Holland, pp. 131–144

KREIFELTS, T., HINRICHS, H., WOETZEL, G. (1993): Sharing To-Do Lists with a Distributed Task Manager. Proc. 3rd Europ. Conf. on Computer-Supported Cooperative Work. Dordrecht: Kluwer, pp. 31–46

KREMER, R. (1996): Toward a Multi-User, Programmable Web Concept Mapping "Shell" to Handle Multiple Formalisms. In: Gaines, B. R. (ed.): Proc. 10th Banff Workshop on Knowledge Acquisition for Knowledge-Based Systems. Banff, Canada: SDRG Publications. ftp://ksi.cpsc.ucalgary.ca/KAW/KAW96/77kremer.ps.Z

KÜHN, O., HÖFLING, B. (1994): Conserving Corporate Knowledge for Crankshaft Design. Proc. 7th Int. Conf. on Industrial and Engineering Applications of Artificial Intelligence and Expert Systems (IEA-AIE'94), Austin, TX

KÜHN, O., BECKER, V., LOHSE, G., NEUMANN, P. (1994): Integrated Knowledge Utilization and Evolution for the Conservation of Corporate Know-How. Proc. Int. Symp. on the Management of Industrial and Corporate Knowledge (ISMICK'94)

KÜHN, O. (1994): An Ontology for the Conservation of Corporate Knowledge about Crankshaft Design. Proc. ECAI'94 Workshop on Comparison of Implemented Ontologies

KYNG, M. (1994): Experience with Participative Application Development. In: Brunnstein, K., Raubold, E. (eds.): Proc. IFIP 13th World Congress. Elsevier (North-Holland), pp. 107–119

LABROU, Y., FININ, T. (1994): A Semantics Approach for KQML: A General Purpose Communication Language for Software Agents. Proc. 3rd Int. Conf. on Information and Knowledge Management (CIKM'94). Available as http://www.cs.umbc.edu/kqml/papers/kqml-semantics.ps

LALIBERTE, D. (1995): HyperNews. National Center for Supercomputing Applications, Univ. of Illinois at Urbana–Champaign. http:// union.ncsa.uiuc.edu/ HyperNews/ get/ hypernews.html

LEE, J., LAI, K. (1991): What's in Design Rationale? Human-Computer Interaction 6:3&4, 251–280. Reprinted in: T. P. Moran and J. M. Carroll (eds.) Design Rationale: Concepts, Techniques, and Use, pp. 21–51. Hillsdale, NJ: Lawrence Erlbaum Associates, 1996

LEE, J. (1990): SIBYL: A Tool for Managing Group Design Rationale. Proc. 3rd Int. Conf. on Computer-Supported Cooperative Work, Los Angeles, CA. New York: SIGCHI/SIGOIS ACM, pp. 79–92

LEE, J. (1991): Extending the Potts and Bruns Model for Recording Design Rationale. Proc. 13th Int. Conf. on Software Engineering, Austin, TX. New York: ACM, pp. 114–125

LIEBIG, T., RÖSNER, D. (1996): Description Logic as Core Machinery for the Automatic Generation of Multilingual Technical Documents. Proc. Int. Workshop on Description Logics, Boston, MA. AAAI Press

LIEBIG, T., RÖSNER, D. (1996): Modelling of Reuseable Product Knowledge in Terminological Logics – a Case Study. In: Wolf and Reimer (1996), Basel, Switzerland

LinkWorks User Manual, Digital. http://www.digital.com/info/linkworks

LOOM (1991): The LOOM Knowledge Representation System. Technical Report. Documentation Package. USC/Information Sciences Institute, Marina Del Rey, CA

LOTUS (1996): ScreenCam. Lotus Development Corporation. http://www.lotus.com/screencam/

LUKOSE, D. (1997): Knowledge Management Using MODEL-ECS. In: Dieng et al. (1997)

Lycos: http://www.lycos.com/

MACINTOSH, A. (1997): Knowledge Asset Management. AIring 20, 4–6

MACLEAN, A., YOUNG, R. M., MORAN, T. (1989): Design Rationale: The Argument Behind the Artifact. Proc. ACM CHI'89 Conf. on Human Factors in Computing Systems. New York: ACM Press, pp. 247–252

MACLEAN, A., CARTER, K., LÖVSTARND, L., MORAN, T. (1990): User-tailorable Systems: Pressing the Issue with Buttons. Proc. ACM CHI'90 Conf. on Human Factors in Computing Systems. New York: ACM Press

MACLEAN, A., YOUNG, R. M., BELLOTTI, V., MORAN, T. (1991): Questions, Options, and Criteria: Elements of Design Space Analysis. Human–Computer Interaction **6**:3 & 4, 201–250. Reprinted in: T. P. Moran and J. M. Carroll (eds.) Design Rationale: Concepts, Techniques, and Use, pp. 53–105. Hillsdale, NJ: Lawrence Erlbaum Associates, 1996

MACLEAN, A., BUCKINGHAM SHUM, S., BELLOTTI, V. (1992): Design Rationale Tutorial. Tutorials at HCI'92–94: British Computer Society HCI Conf., UK

MAES, P. (1988): Computational Reflection. Knowledge Engineering Review pp. 11–19

MALONE, T. W., GRANT, K. R., LAI, K.-Y., RAO, R., ROSENBLITT, D. (1987): Semistructured Messages are Surprisingly Useful for Computer-Supported Coordination. ACM Transactions on Office Information Systems **5**:2, 115–131

MALONE, T. W., GRANT, K. R., TURBAK, F. A., BROBST, S. A., COHEN, M. D. (1987): Intelligent Information Sharing Systems. Communications of the ACM **30**:5, 390–402

MALONE, T. W., LAI, K. Y., FRY, C. (1992): Experiments with Oval: A Radically Tailorable Tool for Cooperative Work. In: Turner, J., Kraut, R. E. (eds.): Proc. 4th Int. Conf. on Computer-Supported Cooperative Work, Toronto, Canada. New York: SIGCHI/SIGOIS ACM, pp. 289–297

MALONE, T. W., CROWSTON, K., J., LEE, PENTLAND, B. (1993): Tools for Inventing Organizations: Toward a Handbook of Organizational Processes. Proc. 2nd IEEE Workshop on Enabling Technologies Infrastructure for Collaborative Enterprises, Morgantown

MALSCH, T., BACHMANN, R., JONAS, M., MILL, U., ZIEGLER, S. (1993): Expertensysteme in der Abseitsfalle? – Fallstudien aus der industriellen Praxis. Berlin: Edition Sigma, Reiner Bohn Verlag

MALTZ, D., EHRLICH, K. (1995): Pointing the Way: Active Collaborative Filtering. Proc. Conf. on Computer-Human Interaction. New York: ACM Press, pp. 202–209

MANN, W. C., THOMPSON, S. A. (1987): Rhetorical Structure Theory: A Theory of Text Organization. In: Polanyi, L. (ed.): The Structure of Discourse. Norwood, NJ: Ablex

MANN, W. C. (1983): An Overview of the PENMAN Text Generation System. Proc. National Conf. on Artificial Intelligence. AAAI Press, pp. 261–265

Marimba: http://www.marimba.com/

MARK, G., PRINZ, W. (1997): What Happened to our Document in the Shared Workspace? The Need for Groupware Conventions. In: Howard, S., Hammond, J., Lindgaard, G. (eds.): Proc. Human-Computer Interaction (INTERACT'97). London: Chapman & Hall, pp. 412–420

MARSHALL, C. C., III, F. M. SHIPMAN, MCCALL, R. J. (1994): Putting Digital Libraries to Work: Issues from Experience with Community Memories. Proc. Conf. on Digital Libraries

MATTHIESSEN, C., BATEMAN, J. A. (1991): Text Generation and Systemic-Functional Linguistics: Experiences from English and Japanese. London, New York: Frances Pinter Publishers and St. Martin's Press

MEGHINI, C., STRACCIA, U. (1996): A Relevance Terminological Logic for Information Retrieval. In: Frei et al. (1996)

MILNER, R. (1980): A Calculus of Communicating Systems. Lecture Notes in Computer Science **92**. Berlin: Springer-Verlag

MORAN, T. P., CARROLL, J. M. (1996): Design Rationale: Concepts, Techniques, and Use. Hillsdale, NJ: Lawrence Erlbaum Associates

MORAN, T. P., PALEN, L., HARRISON, S., CHIU, P., KIMBER, D., MINNEMAN, S., VAN MELLE, W., ZELLWEGER, P. (1997): "I'll Get That Off the Audio": A Case Study of Salvaging Multimedia Meeting Records. Proc. ACM CHI'97 Conf. on Human Factors in Computing Systems, Atlanta, GA. New York: ACM Press.
http://www.acm.org/sigchi/chi97/proceedings/paper/tpm.htm

MORITA, M., SHINODA, Y. (1994): Information Filtering Based on User Behavior Analysis and Best Match Text Retrieval. Proc. 17th Annual Int. SIGIR Conf. on Research and Development. pp. 272–281

MULTICOSM (1996): Microcosm / Webcosm. http://www.webcosm.com/

MYNATT, E. D., ADLER, A., ITO, M., O'DAY, V. L. (1997): Design For Network Communities. Proc. Conf. on Computer-Human Interaction, Atlanta, GA. New York: ACM Press, pp. 210–217

Netscape: http://www.netscape.com/

NEWMAN, S., MARSHALL, C. (1991): Pushing Toulmin Too Far: Learning from an Argument Representation Scheme. Xerox Palo Alto Research Center. SSL 92–45

NICHOLS, D. M., TWIDALE, M. B., PAICE, C. D. (1997): Recommendation and Usage in the Digital Library. Technical Report CSEG/2/97. Computing Department, Lancaster Univ., UK

NONAKA, I., TAKEUCHI, H. (1995): The Knowledge Creating Company: How Japanese Companies Create the Dynamics of Innovation. New York: Oxford Univ. Press

ORR, J. (1986): Narratives at Work: Story Telling as Cooperative Diagnostic Activity. Proc. Conf. on Computer-Supported Cooperative Work (CSCW '86), Austin, TX. ACM Press, pp. 62–72

OSTERMAYER, R., MEIS, E., BERNARAS, A., LARESGOITI, I. (1996): Guidelines on Domain Ontology Building. Technical Report Esprit Project 8145, Deliverable DO1c.2. KACTUS Consortium

PANKOKE-BABATZ, U., MARK, G., KLÖCKNER, K. (1997): Design in the POLITeam Project: Evaluating User Needs through Real Work Practice. Proc. ACM Conf. on Design of Interactive Systems (DIS'97), Amsterdam, The Netherlands

PARIS, C., VANDER LINDEN, K. (1996): DRAFTER: An Interactive Support Tool for Writing Multilingual Instructions. IEEE Computer 29:7, 49–56

PIROLLI, P., CARD, S. (1995): Information Foraging in Information Access Environments. Proc. ACM CHI'95 Conf. on Human Factors in Computing Systems. New York: ACM Press, pp. 51–58

PITKOW, J., PIROLLI, P. (1997): Life, Death, and Lawfulness on the Electronic Frontier. Proc. ACM CHI'97 Conf. on Human Factors in Computing Systems. New York: ACM Press, pp. 383–390

PointCast: http://www.pointcast.com/

POMELLO, L., ROZENBERG, G., SIMONE, C. (1992): A Survey of Equivalence Notions for Petri Net based Systems. Advances in Petri Nets. Lecture Notes in Computer Science 609. Berlin: Springer-Verlag, pp. 410–472

POTTS, C., BRUNS, G. (1988): Recording the Reasons for Design Decisions. Proc. 10th IEEE Int. Conf. on Software Engineering. Los Alamitos, CA: IEEE Computer Society Press, pp. 418–427

POTTS, C., TAKAHASHI, K., ANTON, A. (1994): Inquiry-Based Requirements Analysis. IEEE Software pp. 21–32

PRAHALAD, C. K., HAMEL, G. (1990): The Core Competence of the Organization. Harvard Business Review pp. 79–91

218   References

PRASAD, M. V. NAGENDRA, PLAZA, E. (1996): Corporate Memories as Distributed Case Libraries. In: Dieng and Vanwelkenhuysen (1996)

PRINZ, W., KOLVENBACH, S. (1996): Support for Workflows in a Ministerial Environment. In: Ackermann, M. S. (ed.): Proc. 7th Int. Conf. on Computer-Supported Cooperative Work, Boston, MA. New York: SIGCHI/SIGOIS ACM, pp. 199–208

RAMESH, B. (1993): Supporting Systems Development by Capturing Deliberations During Requirements Engineering. IEEE Transactions on Software Engineering SE–18:6, 498–510

REDDY, Y. (1993): Computer Support for Concurrent Engineering. Computer 26:1, 12–16

REIMANN, P., SPADA, H., eds. (1996): Learning in Humans and Machines: Towards an Interdisciplinary Learning Science. London: Elsevier

REITER, E., MELLISH, C. (1992): Using Classification to Generate Text. Proc. 30th Annual Meeting of the Association for Computational Linguistics (ACL'92)

REITER, E., CAWSEY, A., OSMAN, L., ROFF, Y. (1997): Knowledge Acquisition for Content Selection. Proc. 6th European Workshop on Natural Language Generation. Duisburg, Germany: Gerhard-Mercator Univ.

RESNICK, P., IACOVOU, N., SUCHAK, M., BERGSTROM, P., RIEDL, J. (1994): GroupLens: An Open Architecture for Collaborative Filtering of Netnews. Proc. Conf. on Computer-Supported Cooperative Work, Chapel Hill, NC. New York: ACM Press, pp. 175–186

RITTEL, H. W. J., WEBBER, M. M. (1973): Dilemmas in a General Theory of Planning. Policy Sciences 4, 155–169

RITTEL, H. W. J. (1972): Second Generation Design Methods. Reprinted in: Developments in Design Methodology, N. Cross (ed.), 1984, pp. 317–327, J. Wiley & Sons: Chichester 1, 5–10

RIVEST, R., SHAMIR, A., ADLEMAN, A. (1978): A Method for Obtaining Digital Signatures and Public-Key Cryptosystems. Communications of the ACM 21:2, 120–126

RÖLLEKE, T., FUHR, N. (1996): Retrieval of Complex Objects Using a Four-Valued Logic. In: Frei et al. (1996)

RÖSNER, D., STEDE, M. (1992): Customizing RST for the Automatic Production of Technical Manuals. In: Dale, R., Hovy, E. H., Rösner, D., Stock, O. (eds.): Aspects of Automated Natural Language Generation – Proc. 6th Int. Workshop on Natural Language Generation. Berlin: Springer-Verlag, pp. 199–214

RÖSNER, D., STEDE, M. (1994): Generating Multilingual Documents from a Knowledge Base: The TECHDOC Project. Proc. 15th Int. Conf. on Computational Linguistics (COLING'94), Kyoto, Japan. pp. 339–346

RÖSNER, D. (1994): Automatische Generierung von mehrsprachigen Instruktionstexten aus einer Wissensbasis. Habilitationsschrift. Fakultät für Informatik, Univ. Stuttgart, Germany

ROTH, K. (1982): Konstruieren mit Konstruktionskatalogen. Berlin: Springer-Verlag

RUCKER, J., POLANCO, M. J. (1997): Siteseer: Personalized Navigation for the Web. Communications of the ACM 40:3, 73–75

SCHAEL, T., ZELLER, B. (1993): Workflow Management System for Financial Services. In: Kaplan, S. (ed.): Proc. ACM SIGOIS/IEEECS TC-OA Conf. on Organizational Computing Systems (COOCS '93), Milpitas, CA. New York: ACM, pp. 142–153

SCHMIDT, K., SIMONE, C. (1996): Coordination Mechanisms: Towards a Conceptual Foundation for CSCW Systems Design. Computer Supported Cooperative Work – An International Journal 5:2/3, 155–200

SCHMIDT, K. (1997): Of Maps and Scripts: The Status of Formal Constructs in Cooperative Work. Risoe Technical Report. Roskilde, Denmark

SCHNEIDER, W. (1993): SeCuDE – Overview. Technical Report GMD-Arbeitspapiere 775. GMD, Bonn

SCHRAGE, M. (1990): Shared Minds: The New Technologies of Collaboration. New York: Random House

SCOTT, A., CLAYTON, B., GIBSON, F. (1991): A Practical Guide to Knowledge Acquisition. New York: Addison-Wesley

SCOTT, W. RICHARD (1992): Organizations: Rational, Natural, and Open Systems. Englewood Cliffs, NJ: Prentice-Hall

SELVIN, A. (1997): An Issue-Based Hypertext Approach to Collaborative Process Redesign. NYNEX Science & Technology Technical Memorandum, White Plains, NY. TM 97–0007

SENGE, P., ROBERTS, C., ROSS, R., SMITH, B., KLEINER, A. (1994): The Fifth Discipline Fieldbook: Strategies and Tools For Building A Learning Organization. New York: Doubleday

SHARDANAND, U., MAES, P. (1995): Social Information Filtering: Algorithms for Automating Word of Mouth. Proc. Conf. on Computer-Human Interaction. New York: ACM Press. Also see: http://www.firefly.com

SHEPHERD, A., MAYER, N., KUCHINSKY, A. (1990): Strudel: An Extensible Electronic Conversation Toolkit. Proc. 3rd Int. Conf. on Computer-Supported Cooperative Work, Los Angeles, CA. New York: SIGCHI/SIGOIS ACM, pp. 93–104

SHETH, B., MAES, P. (1993): Evolving Agents for Personalized Information Filtering. Proc. 9th Conf. On Artificial Intelligence for Applications. Los Alamitos, CA: IEEE Computer Society Press, pp. 1–11

SIMON, G. (1996): Knowledge Acquisition and Modelling for Corporate Memory: Lessons Learned from Experience. Proc. 10th Knowledge Acquisition for Knowledge-Based Systems Workshop (KAW'96)

SIMONE, C., DIVITINI, M., SCHMIDT, K. (1995): A Notation for Malleable and Interoperable Coordination Mechanisms for CSCW Systems. In: Kaplan, S. (ed.): Proc. ACM SIG-OIS/IEEECS TC-OA Conf. on Organizational Computing Systems (COOCS '93), Milpitas, CA. New York: ACM Press, pp. 44–54

sixdegrees: http://www.sixdegrees.com/

SMOLENSKY, P., BELL, B., FOX, B., KING, R., LEWIS, C. (1987): Constraint-Based Hypertext for Argumentation. Proc. ACM Conf. Hypertext'87. New York: ACM Press, pp. 215–245

SOHLENKAMP, M., FUCHS, L., GENAU, A. (1997): Awareness and Cooperative Work: The POLITeam Approach. In: Nunamaker, J. F., Sprague, R. H. (eds.): Proc. 30th Annual Hawaii Int. Conf. on System Sciences (HICCS'97), Maui, HI. Los Alamitos, CA: IEEE Computer Society Press, pp. 549–558

STAMMWITZ, G. (1996): The CIM Center Kaiserslautern CSCW Lab. Presentation Slides, WMK'96–1. Workshop Wissensmanagement Kaiserslautern, http://www.cck.uni-kl.de/wmk/

STAMPS, D. (1997): Off the Charts. Training Magazine, pp. 77–83

STAR, S. L., GRIESEMER, J. R. (1989): Institutional Ecology, 'Translations' and Boundary objects: Amateurs and Professionals in Berkeley's Museum of Vertebrate Zoology, 1907-1939. Social Studies of Science 19, 387–420

STEDE, M. (1996): Lexical Semantics and Knowledge Representation in Multilingual Sentence Generation. Dissertation. CSRI-347. Computer Systems Research Institute, Univ. of Toronto

STEFIK, M. (1986): The Next Knowledge Medium. AI Magazine 7:1, 34–46

STEIN, E. W., ZWASS, V. (1995): Actualizing Organizational Memory with Information Technology. Information Systems Research **6**:2, 85–117

STEIN, E. W. (1995): Organizational Memory: Review of Concepts and Recommendations for Management. International Journal of Information Management **15**:2, 17–32

STUTT, A., MOTTA, E. (1995): Recording the Design Decisions of Knowledge Engineers to Facilitate Re–use of Design Models. In: Gaines, B. R., Musen, M. (eds.): Proc. 9th Banff Workshop on Knowledge Acquisition for Knowledge-Based Systems. Banff, Canada: SDRG Publications

SUCHMAN, L. (1993): Do Categories have Politics? The Language/Action Perspective Reconsidered. In: de Michelis, G., Simone, C., Schmidt, K. (eds.): Proc. 3rd Europ. Conf. on Computer-Supported Cooperative Work, Milan, Italy. Dordrecht: Kluwer, pp. 1–14

SUMNER, T., BUCKINGHAM SHUM, S. (1998): From Documents to Discourse: Shifting Conceptions of Scholarly Publishing. Proc. ACM CHI'98 Conf. on Human Factors in Computing Systems, Los Angeles, CA. New York: ACM Press

SWENSON, K. D., MAXWELL, R. J., MATSUMOTO, T., SAGHARI, T., IRWIN, K. (1994): A Business Process Environment Supporting Collaborative Planning. Collaborative Computing **1**:1, 15–34

SYRI, A. (1997): Tailoring Cooperation Support through Mediators. In: Hughes, H., Prinz, W., Rodden, T., Schmidt, K. (eds.): Proc. 5th Europ. Conf. on Computer-Supported Cooperative Work, Lancaster, UK. Dordrecht: Kluwer, pp. 157–173

TREVOR, J., RODDEN, T., BLAIR, G. (1993): COLA: a Lightweight Platform for CSCW. Proc. 3rd Europ. Conf. on Computer-Supported Cooperative Work. Dordrecht: Kluwer, pp. 15–30

TREVOR, J., KOCH, T., WOETZEL, G. (1997): MetaWeb: Bringing Synchronous Groupware to the World Wide Web. In: Hughes, H., Prinz, W., Rodden, T., Schmidt, K. (eds.): Proc. 5th Europ. Conf. on Computer-Supported Cooperative Work, Lancaster, UK. Dordrecht: Kluwer, pp. 65–80

TSCHAITSCHIAN, B., ABECKER, A., SCHMALHOFER, F. (1997): Putting Knowledge Into Action: Information Tuning With KARAT. Proc. 10th European Workshop on Knowledge Acquisition, Modeling, and Management (EKAW'97). Lecture Notes in Computer Science **1319**. Berlin: Springer-Verlag

USCHOLD, M., GRUNINGER, M. (1996): Ontologies: Principles, Methods and Applications. The Knowledge Engineering Review **11**:2, 93–136

USCHOLD, M., KING, M., MORALEE, S., ZORGIOS, Y. (1995): The Enterprise Ontology. Technical Report. Edinburgh: AIAI

VAN BAKEL, B., BOON, R. T., MARS, N. J., NIJHUIS, J., OLTMANS, E., VAN DER VET, P. E. (1996): Condorcet Annual Report. Technical Report UT-KBS-96-12. Knowledge-Based Systems Group, Univ. Twente

VAN DER SPEK, R., DE HOOG, R. (1994): Towards a Methodology for Knowledge Management. Proc. Int. Symp. on the Management of Industrial and Corporate Knowledge (ISMICK'94)

VAN DER SPEK, R., DE HOOG, R. (1995): A Framework for a Knowledge Management Methodology. In: Wiig, K. M. (ed.): Knowledge Management Methods. Arlington, TX: Schema Press, pp. 379–393

VAN DER SPEK, R., SPIJKERVET, A. (1996): Knowledge Management: Dealing Intelligently with Knowledge. Utrecht, The Netherlands: IBIT series No **1**, Kenniscentrum CIBIT

VAN HEIJST, G., FALASCONI, S., ABU-HANNA, A., SCHREIBER, A. T., STEFANELLI, M. (1995): A Case Study in Ontology Library Construction. Artificial Intelligence in Medicine **7**, 227–255

VAN HEIJST, G., VAN DER SPEK, R., KRUIZINGA, E. (1996): Organizing Corporate Memories. In: Gaines, B. R. (ed.): Proc. 10th Banff Workshop on Knowledge Acquisition for Knowledge-Based Systems. Banff, Canada: SDRG Publications. ftp://ksi.cpsc.ucalgary.ca/KAW/KAW96/25vanheijst.ps.Z

VAN RIJSBERGEN, C. J. (1989): Towards an Information Logic. Proc. 12th Annual Int. ACM SIGIR Conf. on Research and Development in Information Retrieval. New York: ACM Press

VANLEHN, K. (1985): Theory Reform Caused by an Argumentation Tool. Xerox Palo Alto Research Center. ISL–11

VANWELKENHUYSEN, J., MIZOGUCHI, R. (1994): Maintaining the Workplace Context in a Knowledge Level Analysis. In: Mizoguchi, R., Motoda, H., Boose, J., Gaines, B., Compton, P. (eds.): Proc. 3rd Japanese Knowledge Acquisition for Knowledge-Based Systems Workshop (JKAW'94), Hatoyama, Japan. pp. 33–47

VANWELKENHUYSEN, J. (1995): Embedding Non-Functional Requirements Analyses in Conceptual Knowledge Systems Designs. In: Gaines, B. R., Musen, M. (eds.): Proc. 9th Banff Knowledge Acquisition for Knowledge-Based Systems Workshop. Banff, Canada: SDRG Publications, pp. 45.1–45.15

WAHLSTER, W., ANDRÉ, E., FINKLER, W., PROFITLICH, H.-J., RIST, T. (1993): Plan–Based Integration of Natural Language and Graphics Generation. Artificial Intelligence **63**, 387–427

WIIG, K. M. (1990): Expert Systems: A Manager's Guide. Arlington, TX: Schema Press

WIIG, K. M. (1993): Knowledge Management: Foundations. Arlington, TX: Schema Press

WIIG, K. M. (1993): Knowledge Management, The Central Management Focus for Intelligent-Acting Organizations. Arlington, TX: Schema Press

WIIG, K. M. (1996): Knowledge Management is No Illusion! In: Wolf and Reimer (1996)

WINOGRAD, T., FLORES, F. (1986): Understanding Computers and Cognition: A New Foundation for Design. Norwood, NJ: Ablex

WINSTON, M. E., CHAFFIN, R., HERRMANN, D. (1987): A Taxonomy of Part-Whole Relations. Cognitive Science **11**, 417–444

WOLF, M., REIMER, U., eds. (1996): Proc. 1st Int. Conf. on Practical Aspects of Knowledge Management (PAKM'96), Basel, Switzerland

Yahoo: http://www.yahoo.com/

YONEZAWA, A., eds. (1990): ABCL: An Object-Oriented Concurrent System. Cambridge, MA: MIT Press

Contributors

ANDREAS ABECKER
DFKI, D-67608 Kaiserslautern, Germany
E-mail: Andreas.Abecker@dfki.de

DAMIÁN ARREGUI
XRCE—Xerox Research Centre Europe,
Grenoble Laboratory. 6, Chemin de
Maupertuis, F-38240 Meylan, France
E-mail: arregui@xrce.xerox.com

UWE M. BORGHOFF
XRCE—Xerox Research Centre Europe,
Grenoble Laboratory. 6, Chemin de
Maupertuis, F-38240 Meylan, France
E-mail: borghoff@xrce.xerox.com

MANFRED DARDENNE
XRCE—Xerox Research Centre Europe,
Grenoble Laboratory. 6, Chemin de
Maupertuis, F-38240 Meylan, France
E-mail: dardenne@xrce.xerox.com

MONICA DIVITINI
IDI—Norwegian University of Science and
Technology. Trondheim, Norway
E-mail: Monica.Divitini@idi.ntnu.no

ANJA EICHLER
Witten-Herdecke University, and
PARC—Xerox Palo Alto Research Center,
3333 Coyote Hill Road, Palo Alto, CA, USA
E-mail: aeichler@parc.xerox.com

NATALIE GLANCE
XRCE—Xerox Research Centre Europe,
Grenoble Laboratory. 6, Chemin de
Maupertuis, F-38240 Meylan, France
E-mail: glance@xrce.xerox.com

RON GOLDMAN
Bell Atlantic Science and Technology, and
IRL—Institute for Research and Learning,
66 Willow Place, Menlo Park, CA, USA
E-mail: ron_goldman@irl.org

BRIGITTE GROTE
Otto-von-Guericke-Universität Magdeburg,
Institut für Informations- und
Kommunikationssysteme. P.O. Box 41 20,
D-39016 Magdeburg, Germany
Email: grote@iik.cs.uni-magdeburg.de

KNUT HARTMANN
Otto-von-Guericke-Universität Magdeburg,
Institut für Informations- und
Kommunikationssysteme. P.O. Box 41 20,
D-39016 Magdeburg, Germany
Email: hartmann@iik.cs.uni-magdeburg.de

GERTJAN VAN HEIJST
Kenniscentrum CIBIT, Arthur van
Schendelstraat 570. P.O. Box 573, NL-3500
AN Utrecht, The Netherlands
E-mail: gvheijst@cibit.nl

BJÖRN HÖFLING
Otto-von-Guericke-Universität Magdeburg,
Institut für Informations- und
Kommunikationssysteme. P.O. Box 41 20,
D-39016 Magdeburg, Germany
Email: hoefling@iik.cs.uni-magdeburg.de

DAN K. HOLTSHOUSE
Xerox Corp., Business Strategy Knowledge
Initiatives. 800 Long Ridge Road, Stamford,
CT, USA
E-mail: Dan_Holtshouse@ea.xerox.com

BRIGITTE JORDAN
PARC—Xerox Palo Alto Research Center,
3333 Coyote Hill Road, Palo Alto, CA,
USA, and IRL—Institute for Research and
Learning, 66 Willow Place, Menlo Park,
CA, USA
E-mail: jordan@parc.xerox.com or
brigitte_jordan@irl.org

EELCO KRUIZINGA
Kenniscentrum CIBIT, Arthur van
Schendelstraat 570. P.O. Box 573, NL-3500
AN Utrecht, The Netherlands
E-mail: ekruizinga@cibit.nl

OTTO KÜHN
DFKI, D-67608 Kaiserslautern, Germany
E-mail: Otto.Kuehn@dfki.de

REMO PARESCHI
Xerox Professional Document Services.
Strada Padana Superiore 28,
I-20063 Cernusco S/N, Italy
E-mail: remo_pareschi.rxi@eur.xerox.com

WOLFGANG PRINZ
GMD—German National Research Center
for Information Technology. Schloß
Birlinghoven, D-53754 Sankt Augustin,
Germany
E-mail: wolfgang.prinz@gmd.de

DIETMAR RÖSNER
Otto-von-Guericke-Universität Magdeburg,
Institut für Informations- und
Kommunikationssysteme. P.O. Box 41 20,
D-39016 Magdeburg, Germany
Email: roesner@iik.cs.uni-magdeburg.de

SIMON BUCKINGHAM SHUM
Knowledge Media Institute, The Open
University. Milton Keynes, MK7 6AA, UK
E-mail: S.Buckingham.Shum@open.ac.uk

CARLA SIMONE
Dip. di Informatica, Universita' di Torino.
Corso Svizzera 185, I-10149 Torino, Italy
E-mail: simone@di.unito.it

ROB VAN DER SPEK
Kenniscentrum CIBIT, Arthur van
Schendelstraat 570. P.O. Box 573, NL-3500
AN Utrecht, The Netherlands
E-mail: rvdspek@cibit.nl

ANJA SYRI
GMD—German National Research Center
for Information Technology. Schloß
Birlinghoven, D-53754 Sankt Augustin,
Germany
E-mail: anja.syri@gmd.de

List of Figures

List of Tables

Index

Printing: Mercedesdruck, Berlin
Binding: Buchbinderei Lüderitz & Bauer, Berlin